POLITICAL PHILOSOPHY AND THE
CHALLENGE OF REVEALED RELIGION

POLITICAL PHILOSOPHY AND THE CHALLENGE OF REVEALED RELIGION

HEINRICH MEIER

Translated by Robert Berman

THE UNIVERSITY OF CHICAGO PRESS
CHICAGO AND LONDON

The University of Chicago Press, Chicago 60637
The University of Chicago Press, Ltd., London
© 2017 by The University of Chicago
All rights reserved. Published 2017.
Paperback edition 2018

27 26 25 24 23 22 21 20 19 18   2 3 4 5 6

ISBN-13: 978-0-226-27585-7 (cloth)
ISBN-13: 978-0-226-56570-5 (paper)
ISBN-13: 978-0-226-27599-4 (e-book)
DOI: 10.7208/chicago/9780226275994.001.0001

Originally published as *Politische Philosophie und die Herausforderung der Offenbarungsreligion* by Heinrich Meier, © Verlag C.H.Beck oHG, München 2013

The translation of this work was funded by the Thiel Foundation.

Library of Congress Cataloging-in-Publication Data

Names: Meier, Heinrich, 1953– author.
Title: Political philosophy and the challenge of revealed religion / Heinrich Meier ; translated by Robert Berman.
Description: Chicago ; London : The University of Chicago Press, 2017. | Translation of: Politische Philosophie und die Herausforderung der Offenbarungsreligion. | Includes index.
Identifiers: LCCN 2016006709 | ISBN 9780226275857 (cloth : alk. paper) | ISBN 9780226275994 (e-book)
Subjects: LCSH: Political science—Philosophy. | Philosophy and religion. | Strauss, Leo. Thoughts on Machiavelli. | Rousseau, Jean-Jacques, 1712–1778. Du contrat social. | Political theology. | Religion and politics.
Classification: LCC B65.M4513 2013 | DDC 320.01—dc23
LC record available at http://lccn.loc.gov/2016006709

CONTENTS

	Preface	vii
	Note on Translation	ix
	Note on Citations	ix
I.	Why Political Philosophy?	1
II.	The Renewal of Philosophy and the Challenge of Revealed Religion: On the Intention of Leo Strauss's *Thoughts on Machiavelli*	23
III.	The Right of Politics and the Knowledge of the Philosopher: On the Intention of Jean-Jacques Rousseau's *Du contrat social*	115
	Appendix: Leo Strauss, *Thoughts on Machiavelli*: The Headings	187
	Index of Names	199

PREFACE

The present book sets out to determine political philosophy as a philosophic concept and to test it face to face with the challenge posed by revealed religion. It is guided by the insight that philosophy must prove its right and its necessity in confrontation with the most powerful objection that can be raised against philosophy, and it asserts that this confrontation is the officium of political philosophy. As little as philosophy is understood here as an academic discipline or as a province in the realm of culture, just as little is political philosophy understood as a special department or as a field in the garden of philosophy. Instead, it is a distinctive turn, a change in the direction of view and inquiry, which for philosophy makes a difference in the whole. For philosophy can reach its full reflexivity solely in the reflection on its own presuppositions and in the encounter with its most demanding alternative. The first part of the book specifies the concept of political philosophy in its fourfold determination: according to its object, the political or human things; as a mode of philosophy or in view of the political defense of the philosophic life; in regard to the rational justification of the philosophic way of life; and finally, uniting these three determinations, as the locus of the philosopher's self-knowledge. The four moments are so intertwined with one another that they constitute an articulated and internally dynamic whole that is historically diverse and nevertheless maintains its inner unity. In the second and third parts, the concept is developed further through the interpretation of two masterpieces of political philosophy.

At the center is a thorough investigation of Leo Strauss's most complex and controversial book, *Thoughts on Machiavelli*. Strauss, who introduced the term "political philosophy" into philosophic discussion, links in his longest work the problem of Socrates, which designates the starting point of political philosophy, with the problem of Machiavelli, which names the beginning of modern political philosophy. Between Socrates and Machiavelli stands the theological and the political challenge of revealed religion, about which Strauss has presented with *Thoughts on Machiavelli* the most astonishing treatise.

The third part contains a new interpretation of Jean-Jacques Rousseau's *Du contrat social*. By a precise explanation of the argument and the structure of the writing, it is shown that Rousseau's most famous work cannot be adequately understood as long as it is not understood as a coherent political-philosophic response to the conception of theocracy in all of its manifestations. No other book of a philosopher in modernity achieves the clarity with which *Du contrat social* determines the right and the limits of politics.

Why Political Philosophy? has its origin in the inaugural lecture that I gave on February 16, 2000, in the Great Hall of Ludwig-Maximilians-Universität in Munich. It appeared as an independent writing in two editions in 2000 and 2001 and was translated into five languages. The German original has been out of print for quite some time. The two chapters that substantiate the programmatic outline from the year 2000 were written especially for this book. I worked out "The Renewal of Philosophy and the Challenge of Revealed Religion" in two seminars on *Thoughts on Machiavelli* that I taught at Ludwig-Maximilians-Universität in Munich in summer 2010 and in the Committee on Social Thought of the University of Chicago in spring 2011. "The Right of Politics and the Knowledge of the Philosopher" was prepared by a seminar on the *Contrat social* in Chicago in spring 2012. Parts of sections I and II I presented in public lectures at the University of Halle, the University of Zurich, and the Free University of Berlin in September, October, and December 2012. I have been preoccupied with the *Contrat social* since 1974. I devoted two of my Rousseau seminars in Munich to it, one in winter 2000/2001, the other in summer 2006, and long before this it was the subject of a seminar that I conducted jointly with Wilhelm Hennis at his invitation at Albert-Ludwigs-Universität in Freiburg im Breisgau in summer 1980. *Thoughts on Machiavelli* has accompanied me since I first read it in October 1977. It is one of the books that challenge and reward the reader day and night.

Chicago, April 8, 2013
H. M.

NOTE ON TRANSLATION

Chapter I is a revised and updated version of "Why Political Philosophy?," first published as translated by Marcus Brainard in the *Review of Metaphysics* 56, no. 2 (December 2002).

The English translations of Rousseau's French in chapter III rely in the main on *The Social Contract and Other Later Political Writings*, edited by Victor Gourevitch (Cambridge, 1997). On occasion, however, when conveying the author's own German translations of Rousseau's French, the English translation here may deviate from Gourevitch's renderings, reflecting instead those of the author.

The aim of the translation, from the first to the last word, has been to eliminate to the vanishing point the distance between English and the author's German in which he has presented his thought so that the reader experiences the language that is foreign to the author as if it were his native tongue.

NOTE ON CITATIONS

The abbreviation P. and the term "Footnote" refer, respectively, to pages and footnotes in this writing. The abbreviations p. and n. are used for references to pages and notes, respectively, in other publications.

CHAPTER ONE

Why Political Philosophy?

We all know the picture of the philosopher that Aristophanes drew in the *Clouds* for both philosophers and nonphilosophers. As he is shown to us in this most famous and thought-worthy of comedies, the philosopher, consumed by a burning thirst for knowledge, lives for inquiry alone. In choosing his objects, he allows himself neither to be led by patriotic motives or social interests nor to be determined by the distinctions between good and evil, beautiful and ugly, useful and harmful. Religious prohibitions frighten him as little as do the power of the majority or the ridicule of the uncomprehending. His attention is fixed on questions of the philosophy of nature and of language, in particular, on those of cosmology, biology, and logic. By the keenness of his mental powers, the intransigence of his scientific manner, and the superiority of his power of discourse, he casts a spell on his pupils and gains co-workers, who assist him in his zoological experiments, astronomical and meteorological observations, or geometrical measurements. His self-control and endurance enable him to withstand every deprivation that results from carrying out his scientific projects. By contrast, he lacks moderation. Piety and justice do not count among the qualities on which his reputation is based. Authority and tradition mean nothing to him. In making his innovations, he no more takes into consideration what is time-honored than in his teaching he takes account of the vital needs of the society on whose fringes he places himself along with his friends and pupils. The laboratory in which he pursues his studies is supported for the most part by voluntary donations and owes its existence, moreover, to its relative seclusion and inconspicuousness. It is like a bubble connected to its surroundings only by a modest exchange of air. However, the precautions taken by the school are so insufficient and the restrictions on entrance so slight that outsiders can be allowed in, if they so desire, without close scrutiny of their fitness and can thereby become witnesses to the most shocking statements and arguments. Such as when the philosopher reveals to a neophyte in almost as many words that the supreme God who is honored in the political community not only does not exist but also does not deserve to be honored, and therefore is not a God.[1]

The picture I have briefly sketched of the pre-Socratic philosopher in the *Clouds* stands with reason at the beginning of my attempt to answer the question concerning what political philosophy is and to what end it is needed. For pre-Socratic philosophy not only precedes the turn to political philosophy historically but at the same time is prior to it in substance.

---

1. Cf. Aristophanes, *Clouds* 367.

In view of that turn, the *Clouds* has to be accorded a key role, regardless of whether the philosopher with whose name it is most intimately linked and who embodies the pre-Socratic philosopher in Aristophanes' comedy—Socrates—himself made that turn in advanced years or whether the turn from the pre-Socratic Socrates to the Socrates of political philosophy was carried out by Plato and Xenophon. In either case, one may justly attribute great importance to the catalytic effect the play had on a process of world-historical significance.[2] Here I am thinking primarily not of Socrates' conviction by the people of Athens in the year 399, although this event did contribute decisively to the unmistakable signature of political philosophy, and although Aristophanes almost literally anticipates both of the later charges in his comedy: Socrates does not believe in the Gods in whom the polis believes but instead has introduced new divinities, and he corrupts the youth.[3] Where the historian may above all have the death of Socrates in mind, it is fitting that the philosopher give thought to the birth of political philosophy. And it is here that the poet of the *Clouds* deserves the praise proper to the midwife.

The critique to which the play subjects the pre-Socratic Socrates is not the critique of an enemy. If the comedy anticipates both of the charges brought in the trial before the people's court, then it does so with the telling difference that, on the one hand, Aristophanes includes himself among the new divinities of his Socrates, the clouds, lending them his voice and even placing himself at the head of the rest,[4] and, on the other hand, the youth whom Socrates "corrupts" in the *Clouds* is corrupted by his own father before everyone's eyes and brought to Socrates with a corrupt intention, before he ever falls under the dangerous influence of philosophic teachings. The course of the action of the comedy—beginning with the head of the school, who hovers in the airy heights and there devotes himself to his natural philosophic contemplations, and ending with the destruction of the entire *phrontisterion* or "thinkery" by a simple citizen who, driven by moral indignation, actively supported by a slave, and applauded by a God, burns down the house of Socrates and his companions—contains a clear warning. It is the warning of a friend, and Aristophanes gives it to Socrates

---

2. In this connection, see Leo Strauss, *Socrates and Aristophanes* (New York, 1966), p. 314.

3. Xenophon, *Memorabilia* 1.1.1; *Apology of Socrates to the Jury* 10; Plato, *Apology of Socrates* 24b–c; *Euthyphro* 2c–3b; Diogenes Laertius, *Lives of Eminent Philosophers* 2.40.

4. Aristophanes, *Clouds* (parabasis) 518–626.

well in advance. Whether concern for his friend or other considerations and motives were decisive for the poet need not occupy us here.[5]

For political philosophy, four points of the critique that Aristophanes in his way levels against the young Socrates[6] are of particular importance. The first thing that the pre-Socratic philosopher lacks is self-knowledge. He is wanting not only in the insight into what is good for him, or the Socratic *daimonion* that would keep him from getting involved with men and things that are not good for him. He lacks, above all, a clear awareness of the degree to which he and his friends are dependent upon the political community within whose walls they live and what consequences philosophic inquiry and teaching have or can have for the foundations of this political community, for the force of its laws and institutions, for the integrity of the family, for the political opinions and religious convictions of its citizens. Closely connected with the first point of criticism is, second, the apparent incapacity of the philosopher to argue convincingly for the philosophic way of life, and, third, the almost equally disturbing inability to defend it effectively. In all three respects—self-knowledge, the justification of one's own activity, and protection from external attack—the poet lays claim to a position of superiority for himself since he knows how to steer the opinions of the citizens with his means, since he knows how to shape the political-theological reality in which the philosopher must assert himself. The poet's superior powers of formation are in the end grounded—and we thereby arrive at the fourth point—in a superior understanding of the *politika*, as well as in a better knowledge of human nature. Unlike Socrates and his pupils, who devote themselves in the seclusion of their phrontisterion to the study of the *physiologia*, Aristophanes and the other clouds, who in his comedy address the public, speaking to both the wise and the unwise, are aware of the diversity of human natures, of intellectual abilities, and of psychic needs. The word "soul" does not once cross the lips of Aristophanes' Socrates.[7]

The four points of Aristophanes' critique lead us on a straight path to the fourfold determination of political philosophy, which we wish to treat in what follows, or to the fourfold answer to the question of why philosophy must make the turn to political philosophy. The four moments of the answer concern first the subject matter of political philosophy, second the

---

5. Cf. Plato, *Philebus* 48a–50a, and Strauss, *Socrates and Aristophanes*, pp. 5–6.
6. Cf. Plato, *Second Letter* 314c.
7. "he replaces soul by air." Strauss, *Socrates and Aristophanes*, p. 31. Here once more I refer emphatically to Strauss's late work, the most significant philosophic commentary not only on the *Clouds* but also on Aristophanes' entire œuvre.

political defense of the philosophic life, third its rational justification, and fourth political philosophy as the locus of the philosopher's self-knowledge. As we shall see, the four moments are so intertwined with one another that together they constitute an articulated and internally dynamic whole. What constitutes the rank of the critique Aristophanes presents in what in the poet's own judgment is the wisest of his comedies[8] is precisely that his critique requires one answer: It provokes a philosophic founding. This raises it above and beyond even the most penetrating confrontation in modernity with that "one turning point and vortex of so-called world history"[9] and distinguishes it from all other attempts to initiate the trial of Socrates anew that were inspired by Aristophanes' critique after more than two millennia. Nietzsche's critique of "theoretical man," which takes up Aristophanic motifs so as to turn them against the Platonic Socrates, is part of Nietzsche's own political philosophy. Intrinsically, it presupposes the philosophic founding of which we are speaking here and moves, not only historically, along the path that that founding marks out.[10] The political attack of a Sorel, by contrast, which takes aim at Socrates the citizen of Athens and is interested in the philosopher only insofar as he exerted influence as a public person, may appeal to the conservative spirit out of which Aristophanes' critique is held to have been born.[11] But it hardly approaches the force of a critique that, although or precisely because it breathes the spirit of friendship, is able to promote the most fundamental reflection and finally to compel a turn that makes a distinction in the whole.

A distinction in the whole is made by the turn to political philosophy insofar as philosophy can achieve the fulfillment of its reflexivity solely in political philosophy. The political philosophy at issue here is a special part and mode of philosophy, and we are speaking of it in constant consideration

---

8. Aristophanes, *Clouds* 522.

9. Friedrich Nietzsche, *Die Geburt der Tragödie, Kritische Gesamtausgabe*, ed. Giorgio Colli and Mazzino Montinari (*KGW*), III, 1, p. 96.

10. Cf. Nietzsche, *Jenseits von Gut und Böse*, Vorrede, aphs. 28, 30, 40, 61, 190, 191.

11. Georges Sorel, *Le procès de Socrate. Examen critique des thèses socratiques* (Paris, 1889). "L'État transformé en Église, la force publique mise à la disposition des sectes, tel était l'idéal des Socratiques. Avec une pareille organisation, tout, dans les cités, tendrait vers le *bien*, tel que le comprendraient les chefs. 'La fraternité ou la mort!' hurlaient les hallucinés de 93" (p. 9). "Comme tous les sophistes, il [sc. Socrate] travaillait à ruiner les vieilles mœurs. La nouvelle génération trouvait ridicules toutes les œuvres qui avaient été tant admirées par les anciens. Les conservateurs, aussi bien Anytus qu' Aristophane, pensaient que l'on ne pouvait former des générations héroïques que par la vieille méthode, en nourrissant la jeunesse des poèmes héroïques. Après les grands désastres de la guerre, tous les hommes sensés devaient partager cette manière de voir. Il fallait restaurer ou périr" (p. 235).

of the meaning it possesses for *philosophy tout court*. The fourfold determination of the cause that occupies us has only tangentially to do with the usage of the concept as it is commonly encountered today, where it is applied indiscriminately to political theories of any and every kind. It most certainly has nothing to do with the inflated use of the epithet "political philosophy" to describe arbitrary political opinions, programs, and convictions, as has recently become fashionable. Since the end of the ideologically established division of the world and the decline of the political utopias that had prevailed until then, the appeal to "political philosophies" has experienced a boom. But even where fundamental questions of political theory are given thought or the foundations of the res publica are discussed with great seriousness, we still do not have political philosophy. Neither the competent theoretical approach to political questions and problems nor one's seriousness in dealing with them is, taken on its own, proof of political philosophy. It is no more equivalent to a "philosophie engagée" than to a "public philosophy" or to a "Philosophie der bestehenden Ordnung." Political philosophy achieves its ownmost task neither in establishing political meaning, in uplifting and edifying the public, nor in educating citizens in morality or in offering practical guidance for political action—regardless of how great or slight political philosophy's contribution in such matters may be considered. This task, which distinguishes it from all others, the task it possesses *as philosophy* and *for the philosopher*, is what we have in view when attempting to answer the question *Why political philosophy?*

Political philosophy has as its object the political things: the foundations of the political community, the duties and rights of its members, the ends and means of their action, war and peace internally and in relation to other political communities. Although political philosophy, as far as its subject matter is concerned, makes up merely a part of philosophy, it by no means has a narrowly circumscribed segment of human life as its object. Nor do we meet in this object, say, an autonomous domain of life that exists alongside a number of autonomous domains of life or "provinces of culture" of equal rank. The central questions of political philosophy, the questions of the best political order, of the right life, of just rule, of the necessary weight of authority, knowledge, and force, can be properly raised only in conjunction with those other questions of the nature of man, of his place between beast and God, of the abilities of the human mind, the capacities of the human soul, and the needs of the human body. The object of political philosophy is thus the human things in the comprehensive sense, and the questions of political philosophy all lead back to a question that is posed to man as man: the question of what is right. If he wishes to answer it *seriously*, if he seeks to gain clarity *for himself*, he finds himself faced with conflicting claims. He is subject to the law of the political community, the commandment of God or of men, and he meets with answers that are advanced with the demand for obedience or with the will to enforcement. The question of what is right is posed to man, in other words, in the sphere of the political. In this way, both the rank of the political is indicated and its urgency for philosophy is designated.

In view of the urgency of the political, how is it to be explained that philosophers could ever disparage or neglect the confrontation with the political things? I shall limit myself here to three brief remarks toward a possible answer: Precisely those conflicting political and theological claims that induce the philosopher to question the *nomoi* with regard to what precedes or founds them, and that thereby lead him to the discovery of *physis*, induce him to follow his own nature; the insight into the conventional character of political institutions confirms him in the rightness of his way of life, which is determined by his inclinations. His thirst for knowledge and his thought are aimed at the whole; at first glance, the political things do not seem to have any exceptional significance within it; contemplation of the unchanging, reflection on the first principles, or even listening to the dispensation of Being seems, on the contrary, to be worthy of far greater esteem than is the occupation with the political or the merely human in all its frailty, irrationality, and uncertainty. And can the philosophic understanding of the political things not also be regarded as secondary, in the sense that knowledge of the most universal principles or laws of nature must come first, since only such knowledge makes it possible to leave the shadow-world of opinions behind and lift the political into the realm of knowledge and accord it its proper place therein?

To these and similar considerations, which shed light on the sense in which philosophy precedes political philosophy, we respond: The political turn of philosophy occurs not least due to the insight that the expectations of philosophy and the valuations of the philosophers must themselves be subjected to scrutiny that can be carried out only on the path of confrontation with the political things. The notions of the sublime, the noble, or the beautiful, which are bound up with philosophy, must be questioned with regard to their dependence on the political, moral, and religious opinions within the political community that the philosophers seek to transcend, no less than must the desire for devotion to truth or the will to certainty, each of which is in danger, in its own way, of fostering a new dogmatism or a self-forgetfulness of philosophy. What is dearest to philosophy must be subjected to its most critical investigation. That holds also for the pre-Socratic belief that the political could be elucidated most compellingly in light of the first principles or that the opinions, conventions, institutions of the polis could be reconstituted on the basis of a preceding knowledge of what truly is, a position that Plato calls to mind in the *Republic*'s image of the cave in order to follow it, with a critical intention, to its most extreme consequence, the postulate of the philosopher-king. This holds no less for the prospect of a *bios theoretikos* that finds its perfect self-sufficiency in the happy contemplation of the noble and most sublime things—likewise a pre-Socratic vision—for which Aristotle erected a monument in the tenth book of the *Nicomachean Ethics*.[12] This holds, in short, for an ideal of wisdom that dissociates a universal knowledge of principles from the philosopher's self-knowledge[13] or severs an allegedly pure knowledge from that knowledge which grows out of suffering[14] and is lent wings by joy.

Let us return to our argument. If the central questions of political philosophy are related to the question of what is right, and if this question is posed to the philosopher in the sphere of the political, then for political philosophy this means that it cannot evade the risk of the political. From the occupation with its object arises the necessity of political caution, just as possibilities of political influence are opened up. Put differently: Its object conditions its mode. From the beginning, political philosophy was therefore always also *political* philosophy, political action by philosophers, and was in fact forced by the prevailing circumstances to be primarily political action in the service of philosophy: the protection and defense of the philosophic life or an act of a politics of friendship that includes the interests of future philosophers. But, as we have seen, philosophy does not require protection only at the moment it publicly thematizes the question of what is right and enters into the more precise investigation of the political things. As a way of life, philosophy is in itself an answer to the question of what is right. It knows friendship and enmity. It, therefore, remains—whether it accounts to itself for such or not—fundamentally in need of political defense.

It is an error to assume that the discovery of nature could ever have been made in "political innocence." And it is no less an error—even if we have

---

12. Aristotle, *Nicomachean Ethics* X, 6–9 (esp. 1177a12–28, b19–26, 1178b7–23); cf. VI, 7 (1141a16–20, 1141b1–8) and I, 3 (1095b19, 1096a4); cf. also *Protrepticus*, ed. Ingemar Düring, (Frankfurt am Main, 1969), B 29, 50, 86.

13. The self-misunderstanding that is expressed in the view that the ideal of wisdom at issue here is to serve the philosophic life as a lodestar has been captured succinctly by Seth Benardete, "Wisdom is an idol of the cave," *Socrates' Second Sailing: On Plato's Republic* (Chicago, 1989), p. 179; cf. pp. 178 and 192.

14. Cf. Aeschylus, *Agamemnon* 178; *Prometheus* 585–86.

encountered it in recent times in philosophers—to believe that a move behind political philosophy, a step back to the pre-Socratic thought of *physis*, could be combined with the return to an "original harmony" from which political philosophy distanced itself and us, as if the critique of the *nomoi* had not been coeval with that thought.[15] Aristophanes' *Clouds* and the charge of impiety brought against Anaxagoras just a few years before its premiere, a charge that drove the Ionian philosopher of nature out of Athens, suffice to remind us that the study of the *physiologia* at times can be a highly political affair. The turn to the *politika* is made owing to the precarious situation in which philosophy naturally finds itself. It enables the political defense of philosophy before the forum of the political community and at the same time the philosophic examination of the latter's political-moral-religious law so as to influence a change for the better. How successful political philosophy has been in both respects is shown by the reputation that could be garnered for philosophy by Plato, Xenophon, and Aristotle in the Greek polis or by Cicero in Rome, the continued existence of the philosophic way of life that could be secured by Alfarabi, Avicenna, and Averroes in the Islamic world or by Maimonides in Judaism, and the protection by the state that the political philosophers of modernity, especially Machiavelli, Bacon, Hobbes, and Spinoza, were able to win for the freedom of philosophizing. Alone the fact that the majority of the writings of the philosophers just mentioned have come down to us, whereas in the case of the pre-Socratics we must be satisfied with meager fragments, speaks eloquently.

Political philosophy, which in the spirit of a politics of friendship seeks to guarantee the political presuppositions of the philosophic way of life for both the present and subsequent generations, must attend no less to philosophy's beneficial effect on the political community than to the current, immediate protection of philosophy. Over time, however, the former aim may very well come into conflict with the latter. Likewise, the historical acquisition of institutionalized guarantees against political or religious persecution can nurture a false sense of security in philosophy and deceive it—not only to its own detriment—about the tension that exists in principle between it and the political community. The philosophic politics of friendship therefore requires a reflection on the necessities of philosophy, on the one hand, and on the necessities of the well-constituted political community,

---

15. On this point see my epilogue, "Eine theologische oder eine philosophische Politik der Freundschaft?" in *Carl Schmitt, Leo Strauss und "Der Begriff des Politischen". Zu einem Dialog unter Abwesenden* (Stuttgart/Weimar, second, expanded edition, 1998; third edition, 2013), pp. 179–80.

on the other. Such a reflection will keep a philosophic politics of friendship from allowing the political defense to degenerate into a mere apologetics for philosophy or from linking philosophy to a political status quo, placing it in the service of a historical moment, a religious mission, or a national uprising, in a word: from turning it into anyone's handmaid. What is good for the philosophic life need not be good for the political community, and what is suitable for philosophy is by no means simply on that account suitable for politics. The philosophic life has its raison d'être in the fact that it is grounded in unreserved questioning and stops at no answer that owes its authentication to an authority. The vital element of society is made up, by contrast, of opinions and faith; society draws its power from the fact that its basic principles are held to be true, its norms followed without question, its taboos observed as matters of course, its institutions met with broad trust. Instead of doubt and the suspension of judgment, society requires resolute action and the courageous engagement if not the enthusiasm of its citizens for the common good, which, however, remains a particular and partial good. The well-ordered political community is built on identification, on devotion and agreement, whereas the philosophic *eros* is "completely at home" nowhere but in its "homelessness."[16] The exhortation to live dangerously is as appropriate a maxim for the autonomous thinking of the philosopher as its application to politics has to be fatal;[17] and conversely, the maxim of the mean and measure, which makes complete sense for political praxis and for society as a whole, would, if appropriated by philosophy, clip the wings of philosophic *mania* before it had even begun its ascent in theory. A similar discrepancy arises in view of the chances for insight that the exception, in contradistinction to the rule, holds ready for philosophy, whereas the dangers for politics entailed in an orientation toward the exceptional case are obvious. To say nothing of the phases of institutional dissolution or epochs of social decline. The great political philosophers, from Plato to Rousseau, have given expression to the insuperable tension that exists between philosophy and the political community by assigning the best state for the species or for society and the best and happiest state for the individual or for the philosophic life to diverse ages or to different stages in the development of humanity.[18]

---

16. Seth Benardete, *On Plato's "Symposium"—Über Platons "Symposion"* (Munich, 1994; third, revised edition, 2012), p. 77.

17. Cf. Nietzsche, *Die fröhliche Wissenschaft*, aph. 283.

18. Cf. Plato, *Politikos* 271d–273a, 274b–d; *Nomoi* 713a–e; Jean-Jacques Rousseau, *Discours sur l'origine et les fondemens de l'inégalité parmi les hommes*, critical edition, ed. Heinrich Meier (Paderborn, 1984; sixth edition, 2008), pp. 166, 192–94, 256, 264–270, 342.

Philosophy needs political philosophy not only in view of its political defense but first and foremost with regard to its rational justification. Political philosophy addresses the theologico-political claims with which the philosophic life sees itself confronted. It concentrates its attention on that way of life by which its own answer to the question of what is right might be defeated. It turns to the commandments and prohibitions that compel philosophy to assert its right with reasons—if it is not to rest on the razor's edge of a mere decision or on an act of faith. For philosophy is able to justify its right and its truth only when it includes in the philosophic investigation the opinions and objections that are raised or can be raised against philosophy by appealing to a human or superhuman authority. That philosophy in this sense has to become *political* in order to acquire a *philosophically* sound foundation is the decisive insight inherent in the Socratic turn.[19] The rational justification of the philosophic life is not to be achieved on the path of theoretical positings and deductions, nor can that justification be made dependent upon the accomplishment of systematic efforts whose conclusion and success lie in an uncertain future. Philosophy must demonstrate its rationality elenctically, in confrontation with its most powerful antagonists and with the most demanding alternative. And it must undertake this confrontation in the present. A confrontation that is *fundamental* for the philosophic life cannot be postponed any more than it can be delegated.

This is the context in which the critique of political theology gains its special interest for philosophy. For in its objection to philosophy, political theology appeals to no less an authority than the omnipotent God. Like political philosophy, political theology has the political things as its object. Both agree that the conflict over what is right, which arises in the sphere of the political, is the most important conflict and that the question *How should I live?* is the first question for man. Both distinguish themselves by being reflexive conceptions that aim at self-understanding, conceptions that demand, albeit for very different reasons, that they account for themselves: the thought and action of the philosopher, as well as of the theoretician who believes in revelation, become, therefore, the heart of political philosophy and political theology, respectively. In contrast to political philosophy, however, political theology claims to present a political theory or political doctrine that in the final analysis is based on divine revelation. Whereas political theology builds unreservedly on the answer of faith and hopes to find

---

19. Cf. Plato, *Phaedo* 96a–100b; Xenophon, *Memorabilia* I, 1.11–16; and Marcus Tullius Cicero, *Tusculanae Disputationes* V, 10.

its security in the truth of revelation, which it attempts to interpret and apply, political philosophy raises the question of what is right—to speak with the Platonic Socrates—entirely on the ground of "human wisdom,"[20] in an effort to develop it here as fundamentally and comprehensively as man can while relying on his own resources. Political theology, which understands itself on the basis of the *obedience of faith*[21] and wishes to place itself as theory in the service of the sovereign authority, considers itself to

---

20. Plato, *Apology of Socrates* 20d–e; cf. Leo Strauss, *Persecution and the Art of Writing* (Glencoe, IL, 1952), p. 107.

21. Calvin comments on the Pauline phrase in Romans 1: 5 as follows: "Unde colligimus, Dei imperio contumaciter resistere, ac pervertere totum eius ordinem, qui Euangelii praedicationem irreverenter et contemptim respuunt, cuius finis est nos in obsequium Dei cogere. Hic quoque observanda est fidei natura, quae nomine obedientiae ideo insignitur, quod Dominus per Euangelium nos vocat: nos vocanti, per fidem respondemus. Sicuti contra, omnis adversus Deum contumaciae caput, est infidelitas." *Commentarius in Epistolam Pauli ad Romanos*, ed. T. H. L. Parker (Leiden, 1981), p. 16. ("We hence learn, all who irreverently and contemptuously reject the preaching of the Gospel resist the authority of God and pervert his entire order; for the purpose of the Gospel is to constrain us to obedience to God. Notice also here the nature of faith: it is described by the name of obedience, because the Lord calls us by the Gospel in order that we respond to his call by faith. As on the other hand, the epitome of all disobedience to God is unbelief.")—Erik Peterson has presented the commandment of obedience as a positive entitlement of God, which is said to meet man in the Gospel *jure divino* and is extended "into dogma and sacrament" ("The Gospel is, after all, not good news that is directed 'to everyone'—how could it then be distinguished from the Communist Manifesto?—but rather it is a positive entitlement of God, who out of the body of Christ meets each one of us concretely, specifically meets [each of us] jure divino") in order to objectify the obedience of faith in this way in the dogma of the church. ("But only through the dogma does it also become visible that obedience belongs to revelation. For in the obedience the dogma demands, obedience to Christ is fulfilled.") That he was able thereby to rid himself of the problems that the commandment of obedience raises for historical action in general and for the historical action of the political theologian in particular is, to be sure, doubtful. The question of subjectivism and self-deception that follows the obedience of faith like a shadow and that several of the most important political theologians of Christianity sought to grasp and to domesticate for themselves in the conflict between grace and justice—this problematic is only concealed or displaced, but not resolved, by the reference to the dogma that "has subalternized all human knowledge" and by the flight to an intermediary authority. Erik Peterson, *Was ist Theologie?* (Bonn, 1925), pp. 20, 23–24, 25; cf. pp. 8, 16 (*Theologische Traktate*, ed. Barbara Nichtweiss [Würzburg, 1994], pp. 13–14, 16; cf. pp. 4–5, 11). The consequence that Peterson draws for theology from the subordination of theology to church dogma should at least be mentioned here: "There *is* no theology among the Jews and pagans; there *is* theology only in Christianity and only under the assumption that the incarnate word of God has spoken. The Jews may engage in exegesis and the pagans in mythology and metaphysics; there has been theology in the genuine sense only since the incarnate has spoken of God" pp. 18–19 [12]. As far as I can see, this pronounced, politically distinguishing concept of theology of Peterson's has not received any attention from the authors who appeal to the famous concluding thesis of his political-theological treatise, *Der Monotheismus als politisches Problem. Ein Beitrag zur Geschichte der politischen Theologie im Imperium Romanum* (Leipzig, 1935), p. 99.

be duty-bound to historical action, to political decision, and to the negation of a life that seeks to follow natural reason alone and grants primacy to knowledge. In political theology, philosophy meets a demanding alternative. It has every reason to confront a position thoroughly that not only can endanger it politically, but also places its very principle into question.[22]

The insight that a rational justification of the philosophic way of life can be achieved only in the confrontation with the most demanding alternative or on the path of a radical critique also remains determinative for those attempts at philosophic self-examination that go beyond a scrutiny in the light of the opposing theological and political positions in order to challenge philosophy before the tribunal of nature. We can grasp them as an answer to a historical course of development in which philosophy—not least as a consequence of its political turn—gained so much prestige and acted for social ends or allowed itself to be enlisted for them to such a degree that it sank to the level of a kind of higher matter of self-evidence. The historical success of philosophy's teaching and philosophy's influence on politics also had the result that philosophic doctrines and conceptions increasingly impregnated the prevailing worldviews and left deep marks on the contrary theologico-political positions. The sharpening of its self-critique is one of the strategies of which philosophy can avail itself in order to counteract its social domestication as well as its petrification in the tradition. If, in opposition to the biases of the humanistic tradition in favor of philosophy, Nietzsche wanted to "transpose man back into nature" and get down to the "eternal basic text homo natura,"[23] or if Rousseau attempted to go back from the idea of the *animal rationale*, which had long since become congealed into a general opinion, to man's first, solitary, bestial state of nature, we are faced in either case not with self-forgetful speculations of natural philosophic provenance, but with authentic pieces of their political philosophy that belong to the self-examination, self-critique, and self-understanding at issue here.

---

22. Compare Heidegger's statement "that faith in its innermost core remains as a specific possibility of existence the mortal enemy of the form of existence that belongs essentially to philosophy and that is factually quite alterable. So absolutely that philosophy does not even begin to want to fight that mortal enemy in any way!" The conclusion that Heidegger draws in 1927–28 from the "existential opposition between faith and one's freely taking one's entire existence upon oneself" sheds sudden light on the fundamentally pre-Socratic position of his philosophy. Martin Heidegger, *Phänomenologie und Theologie* (Frankfurt am Main, 1970), p. 32; *Gesamtausgabe* (*GA*) 9, p. 66.

23. Nietzsche, *Jenseits von Gut und Böse*, aph. 230; cf. aph. 259 and *Die fröhliche Wissenschaft*, aph. 109, as well as *Nachgelassene Fragmente*, in *KGW* VIII, 1, p. 130.

Rousseau, who called philosophy most radically into question within the horizon of nature, knew as hardly anyone else has known that he had to adopt an eccentric position if he wanted to arrive as a philosopher at being wholly *bei sich*.[24]

If at the beginning of our discussion of the four determinations of political philosophy we said that political philosophy is a special part and mode of *philosophy* in order to delimit it from political theories of the most diverse kinds and origins, we are now in a position to refine that statement: Political philosophy is *the part* of philosophy in which *the whole* of philosophy is in question. For the three determinations that we have discussed thus far are, as it were, united into one in the fourth determination, namely, political philosophy as the locus of the self-knowledge of the philosopher. For the sake of his self-knowledge, the philosopher must make the political things the object of his inquiry and observation. And from the knowledge of the precarious political situation in which philosophy finds itself as a matter of principle results the twofold task of the political defense and the rational justification of the philosophic life, a task that, in turn, is in both branches suitable for promoting the self-knowledge of the philosopher. The self-knowledge of the philosopher thus proves to be the comprehensive determination that binds together the other three and orders them in relation to one another. Beyond that, however, the fourth determination has its own function and significance.

This holds first of all in view of the philosophic life itself; its inner unity and concrete form are bound up with the knowledge of its distinct character, its limits, and its presuppositions. If it is true that men are naturally led to philosophizing and that philosophy, in the persistent effort to unlock the whole by questioning, merely makes its vocation that which grows out of the necessities of human life and human being-in-the-world, then it is no less true that the philosophic life rests on a discontinuity, on a conscious separation, and thus on a choice that determines this life thoroughly and that is held fast in it in the face of all resistance. The awareness of the difference thus does not remain extrinsic to this life. The experience of detachment and departure that stands at its beginning and marks a caesura can be illustrated by way of the image of the seafarer who sets out onto the open sea, not knowing whether he will ever set foot on terra firma again. This and related experiences, which distinguish philosophy from a discipline that in principle

---

24. See my "Einführender Essay über die Rhetorik und die Intention des Werkes" to the critical edition of the *Discours sur inégalité*, pp. lviii–lxviii, lxxvi–lxxvii.

can restrict the treatment of scientific problems to an enclosable sphere of life, become thematic in political philosophy, since in it the choice that is constitutive of the philosophic way of life and the authoritative objection against which it must assert itself become the central topic.[25] The insight into how much philosophy, as a distinct and conscious way of life, owes to that objection is not the least important fruit of self-knowledge that political philosophy holds ready.

The locus of self-knowledge is political philosophy, moreover, in the sense that it compels the philosopher to subject his opinions, convictions, and prejudices in things political, moral, and religious to precise scrutiny and thereby makes it possible for him to gain distance from what is dearest to him owing to his origin, on the basis of his inclinations, or in view of what are supposedly matters of self-evidence in his time. For the individual philosopher no less than for philosophy in general, it holds that what is dearest requires the most critical investigation. When as a philosopher he confronts the political things, he will not spare his "personal opinion" from unreserved examination. On the contrary, there is every reason to expect that he will attest the truth of Plato's *Republic*, according to which the ascent of philosophy begins with the political opinions that are obligatory or binding for the individual and is consummated as the insight into their nature or their limits. The experience of separation and departure, which we tried to capture in the archetypal image of the seafarer, receives its individual expression for the political philosopher in his taking leave of the nationalist hopes or the socialist dreams of his youth, in his wresting himself free of the resentments cultivated by his family or the class from which he stems, in his distancing himself from the belief that the power of the government is a God-given institution or that the history of humanity has reached its goal in liberal democracy, and other such views. What weight is to be attributed to political philosophy in light of this fourth moment becomes obvious when one considers more closely those philosophers who have not made the turn to political philosophy—who, therefore, have remained "pre-Socratics" in a precise sense. Heidegger would have to be men-

---

25. In 1933, an important theologian captured the objection raised from the standpoint of faith in revelation in the sentence: "Faith can judge the choice of the philosophic existence only as an act of the self-grounding freedom of the man who denies his subordination to God." Rudolf Bultmann, *Theologische Enzyklopädie*, ed. Eberhard Jüngel and Klaus W. Müller (Tübingen, 1984), p. 89.

tioned here.²⁶ Likewise, the diaries of Wittgenstein and Frege provide some illustrative material.²⁷

In its core, the turn to political philosophy is a turn and reference of philosophy back to itself. The political critique that confronts philosophy with its own questionableness causes a reversal of the original, first, and dearest direction of inquiry. The resistance the philosopher runs up against when he allows himself to be led by his *eros*, the objection he must confront if he follows his nature, keeps him from losing sight of himself when investigating the world. The answer that the Socratic-Platonic-Xenophontic turn gives in the form of political philosophy to Aristophanes' critique links the question of philosophy back to the question of the good; it links knowledge back to the self-knowledge of the philosopher. It is for that reason that the Platonic attempt to articulate the whole by means of the *What is?* question occurs within the horizon of the question *What good is it?* The linkage of both questions establishes the connection of philosophic inquiry and

---

26. More instructive than the much-discussed errors and illusions that accompanied the "uprising" (*Aufbruch*) in the sphere of the political, which was as sudden as it was short-lived, when Heidegger believed himself to have been called in the "historical moment" of the year 1933 to act politically and to be able to "lead the leader," are the expectations (verging increasingly on the metaphysical) placed on politics on which that action was based and the burdening of his philosophy with piety, which after the shattering of his political hopes in the present was oriented toward an event that would bring about the all-important reversal in the future. Cf. *Beiträge zur Philosophie, GA 65* (Frankfurt am Main, 1989), pp. 11–13, 28, 369–70, 399–400, 411, 412–14. The absence of political philosophy becomes visible particularly clearly where Heidegger seems to pursue a political intention and speaks of political things or avails himself of a political language. On this see *Abendgespräch in einem Kriegsgefangenenlager in Rußland zwischen einem Jüngeren und einem Älteren*, which Heidegger dates May 8, 1945 ("On the day the world celebrated its victory and did not yet recognize that it has been the vanquished of its own rebellion for centuries already"), in *Feldweg-Gespräche (1944–45)* (Frankfurt am Main, 1995, *GA 77*); consider, on the one hand, pp. 208–9, 215–16, 235–36, 242, 240 and, on the other hand, pp. 216–17, 224–25, 227, 231, 233–34, 237, 244, 240.

27. Ludwig Wittgenstein, *Geheime Tagebücher 1914–1916* (Vienna, 1991), p. 21 (9/12/1914), pp. 49–50, 70, 71, 72 (5/27/1916). *Denkbewegungen. Tagebücher 1930–1932, 1936–1937* (Innsbruck, 1997), I, pp. 39–40 (65), 43 (75), 51 (95), 54 (102), 75 (160–61), 78 (167), 80 (174), 91 (204), 96 (217–18), 99 (225–26), 101–2 (232–33). Cf. *Vermischte Bemerkungen*, in *Werkausgabe* (Frankfurt am Main, 1989), vol. 8, pp. 495–96 and 497.—Frege's "Political Diary" shows us an author who at the end of his life gives expression to hopes, opinions, and resentments *in politicis* that we could have predicted with some likelihood in a contemporary of his origin, education, and social background—so long as we were to disregard, in other words, the fact that we are dealing with a philosopher. Gottlob Frege, [*Tagebuch*], in *Deutsche Zeitschrift für Philosophie* 42, no. 6 (1994): 1067–98; see esp. pp. 1075, 1078 (4/3/1924), 1080, 1081–82, 1083 (4/13/1924), 1087 (4/22/1924), 1088–89, 1091, 1092 (4/30/1924), 1094–95, 1096–97. The final sentence of the diary reads: "A life of Jesus, as I imagine it, would have to have, I believe, the effect of establishing a religion, without its coming to the fore as an intention" (p. 1098).

philosophic life in the particular case and gives expression to the reflexivity of philosophy in the concrete object[28]—and the most important applications of the *What is?* question concern the central objects of political philosophy.[29] The linkage proves itself no less with respect to the concept of political philosophy itself, and it is thus no accident that our fourfold determination answers both questions: *What is political philosophy?* and *What good is it?* It thereby gives an account of the cause of political philosophy, for which the comprehensive determination of the self-knowledge of the philosopher is of constitutive significance. To that extent, one can characterize the fundamental structure of political philosophy as Platonic.[30]

Political philosophy, which is determined by the four moments sketched above, proves in the respective forms in which we encounter it to be an internally dynamic and changeable whole. It is internally dynamic since the four moments interlock with and affect one another. We can speak of a changeable whole since the weighting of those moments is variable within a given political philosophy, and as a result, their organization within one whole can differ considerably from that in another. The dynamics that the quadrilateral—*confrontation with the political things, political defense and rational justification of philosophy, self-knowledge or self-examination of the philosopher*—harbors within itself recedes behind the statics of the firmly established and often artfully articulated presentation of political philosophy to such an extent that it is all too easy to lose sight of it. The only way we as interpreters can attempt to do justice to the internal dynamics of political philosophy is by setting out from the level of the doctrinal presentation and inquiring back to the intention of the author in order to involve

---

28. In his commentary on Plato's *Politikos*, Seth Benardete indicates the fundamental character of this reflexivity when he writes: "Socrates refuses to separate the way of understanding from what is understood, so that the question 'What is it?' is always accompanied by the question 'What good is it?'" *The Being of the Beautiful: Plato's "Theaetetus," "Sophist," and "Statesman"* (Chicago, 1984), III, p. 69; cf. *Socrates' Second Sailing*, pp. 44, 163.

29. Cf. my "Eine theologische oder eine philosophische Politik der Freundschaft?," pp. 170, 179–80, 189; *Die Lehre Carl Schmitts. Vier Kapitel zur Unterscheidung Politischer Theologie und Politischer Philosophie* (Stuttgart–Weimar, 1994; 4th edition, 2012), pp. 84–86, 138–40, 299–300 [*The Lesson of Carl Schmitt: Four Chapters on the Distinction between Political Theology and Political Philosophy*, expanded edition (Chicago, 2011), pp. 50–51, 86–87, 204–5], and *Das theologisch-politische Problem. Zum Thema von Leo Strauss* (Stuttgart–Weimar, 2003), pp. 45–47 [*Leo Strauss and the Theologico-Political Problem* (Cambridge, 2006), pp. 26–28].

30. That all political philosophy in the sense specified here can be called Platonic may have induced Leo Strauss to give the last book that he himself planned the title *Studies in Platonic Political Philosophy*, a collection containing fifteen studies, only two of which are expressly concerned with Plato.

ourselves in the movement of thought that took place within that quadrilateral and takes place in it ever anew.

In the weighting of each of the moments, the individual abilities and experiences of the philosopher find expression as much as his diagnosis of the present, his assessment of the situation of philosophy, and his stance toward the philosophic tradition come into play there. Thus, for example, in times of severe political persecution, not the rational justification but instead the political defense of philosophy will with reason stand in the foreground of the teaching. With respect to a well-ordered political community—whether one actual in the present or one possible in the future—the political defense will avail itself in turn of a rhetoric that is clearly distinct from the rhetoric that may appear appropriate to the defense with respect to a society that is in decline and to a high degree worthy of critique. Where there are powerful enemies of or strong reservations about philosophy, it will look different from how it looks where the appeal to philosophy has become fashionable. Whereas the defense in the one case will exhibit the healthy political influence and the great social utility of philosophy, or will at least assert its compatibility and harmlessness, in the other case it is more likely to emphasize the oppositions, draw out the basic distinctions, and stress the need to justify philosophy in order to protect it from being usurped, losing its contours, or being leveled.

Correspondingly great is the multiplicity of phenomenal shapes that we can observe in the long history of political philosophy since the Socratic turn. In Aristotle we encounter the first attempt on the part of philosophy to assign an independent domain of knowledge to the political things. Assuming and at the same time distancing himself from Plato's founding of political philosophy, he delimits a teachable and learnable political science that can be implemented by the citizens and with which he can win over future statesmen as allies of philosophy, elevating the strict precedence of the philosophic life over the political life to an integral component of the political-philosophic teaching and, as it were, positivizing it for the tradition. From this eminent act of a politics of friendship, we move with historical seven-league boots to Machiavelli's undertaking to regain the *libertas philosophandi* on the path of a radical politicization of philosophy. He, too, attempts to win allies with the aid of a practical science. The alliance he strives for with the sovereign—the prince or the people—is to guarantee the lasting protection of philosophy by means of the effective separation of politics and theology. He subjects the presentation of his political philosophy so thoroughly to the requirements of spiritual warfare that not only does he reject or avoid all the notions, conceptions, and theorems deriving from the philosophic tradition that could offer the adversary a foothold or that could contribute to the softening of future philosophers, but he even refrains from expressly thematizing what the entire undertaking aims at, namely, the philosophic life itself. It would be a mistake, however, to conclude from Machiavelli's concentration on the knowledge of the political things and their political presentation that the other two determinations of the cause lack significance for his political philosophy. Much the same holds for the political philosophies with which Alfarabi and Maimonides answer the challenge of revealed religion six and four centuries before Machiavelli, respectively. They take the changed situation of philosophy into account by moving the foundations of faith in revelation into the foreground. Returning to Platonic political philosophy, they grasp the divine law, providence, and the prophets as subjects of politics. When, with a view to founding the "perfect city," Alfarabi and Maimonides concern themselves with the philosophic justification of the law as founders and lawgivers, they too by no means follow exclusively political ends. For the philosophic justification of the law is for them the place where the question of the right of the philosophic way of life is raised most acutely and thus where the rational justification of philosophy is at stake.

A profoundly altered situation arises for philosophy out of the historical change ushered in by the alliance with the political sovereign that Machiavelli and his successors inaugurated so as to achieve the systematic conquest of nature and the rational reorganization of society. What began as the emancipation of politics from theology leads, after the successful unleashing of a world of increasingly purposive rationality and growing prosperity, to a state in which the demands of politics are rejected with the same matter-of-factness as those of religion. In pursuing an undertaking that was intended to bolster peace and security, philosophy loses the demanding alternatives that compel it to engage in a serious confrontation. Its contours are blurred in the multiplicity of merely personal concerns, in which everything appears to be compatible with everything else. For political philosophy, the question thus arises whether under such conditions the philosophic transgression, the philosophic ascent, must be preceded more than ever by a counterfounding whose originator is the philosopher himself, a founding that re-instills an awareness of the rank of the political, makes the dignity of the political life visible, and leads those who are the fittest to philosophy—by giving their dissatisfaction with the prevailing situation another orientation. In this sense, Rousseau, Hegel, and Nietzsche, for example, advanced political counterprojects in the eighteenth and nineteenth centuries in answer to a process that, according to their diagnoses, led to the rise of the "bourgeois" or of the "last man," to the dominance of an existence that closes itself to all claims that aim at the whole. While taking the political and philosophic consequences of previous counterprojects into consideration, Strauss attempts in the twentieth century to "repeat" the historical foundings and the *querelles célèbres* of political philosophy, that is, to expound their fundamental principles and the intellectual experiences congealed in them in such a way that they gain a new actuality in the present and draw renewed attention to the question of the one thing needful. The emphasis placed on regions of life and provinces of culture by the "philosophy of culture" then predominant had "relativized" that question to such an extent that philosophy ultimately had to fail to answer the question: *Why philosophy?*

Just as little as philosophy marks a province in the realm of culture, but rather is by its natural sense a way of life, likewise political philosophy does not mark a field in the garden of philosophy. It represents instead, as we have seen, a distinctive turn, a change in the direction of view and inquiry that for philosophy makes a difference in the whole. Political philosophy enriches and deepens the philosophic life to the degree that the growth in self-knowledge is able to enrich and deepen life. And it casts the philosophic life in toto in a different light. This may be illustrated by way of one of the most famous descriptions of philosophic self-sufficiency and philosophic happiness left to us by a political philosopher. I am speaking of the *Cinquième promenade* in Rousseau's *Les rêveries du Promeneur Solitaire*. At first glance the philosopher—who follows his "solitary reveries" while letting himself, stretched out in a boat, be carried along by the drift of the water, who watches the flux and reflux of the waves from the banks of Lake Bienne, and who listens to the aimless lapping of a beautiful river or a brook against the shore—seems to be no less remote from any thought of a political philosophy than Aristophanes' pre-Socratic Socrates hanging high above in his basket. Even if we recall that, in the case of Plato's and Xenophon's Socrates, the citizen of Athens by no means absorbs the philosopher, that the new Socrates does not abandon his study of nature, and that Xenophon shows us at one point a Socrates who dances alone and is sufficient unto himself[31]—even if we take all this into consideration, the contrast between the citizen of Geneva, who calls for virtue and points the way to a well-ordered political community, and the philosopher, whom we encounter in the solitude of his leisurely walks, looks to be astonishingly great at first. Whereas the *législateur* Rousseau did all he could to elevate the political

---

31. Xenophon, *Symposium* II, 19.

life by elaborating his political theory, as well as by working out the constitutional projects he was asked to outline for republics in his day, the *promeneur* Jean-Jacques depicts the bliss of a private, secluded, solitary existence, and he praises the pleasure it would have given him to occupy himself with collecting and studying plants and writing a *Flora petrinsularis* to the end of his days. Rousseau describes the perfect happiness he achieved in his "rêveries solitaires" as a state of continuous, fulfilled, timeless present, a state in which the soul finds a solid enough base to rest itself on entirely and to collect its whole being upon. "What does one enjoy in such a situation?" Rousseau asks. "Nothing external to oneself, nothing if not oneself and one's own existence; as long as this state lasts, one is sufficient unto oneself, like God."[32] In the same breath, however, Rousseau adds that this state not only is "little" known to "most men" but "would not even be good" for them "in the present constitution of things" since it would spoil the "active life" for them. It offers Rousseau, by contrast, "compensations" for the persecution that he suffered and that brought him to such isolated places as St. Peter's Island. Just as Rousseau keeps himself in view when occupied with the political things,[33] likewise when he points to his supreme happiness, he does not for a moment immoderately disregard the political references. And no one will be able to disclose the significance *philosophy* has for Rousseau's "bonheur suffisant, parfait et plein," no one will be able to disclose that in which *his* soul finds its "solid enough base," if one stops with the poetic presentation of the *Cinquième promenade* and does not seek to pursue the argument step by step that Rousseau unfolds on his walks before and after it. For the *Rêveries*, which Rousseau died writing, prove on careful inspection to be a masterpiece of political philosophy. The defense of philosophy, the confrontation with the most demanding alternative, and the self-knowledge of the philosopher are unified in this work in a special way, enchanting both philosophers and nonphilosophers. Of its rank are few.

---

32. Rousseau, *Les rêveries du Promeneur Solitaire* V, *Œuvres complètes* (Paris, 1959–95), 5 volumes, Bibliothèque de la Pléiade (*OCP*), I, pp. 1043, 1045, 1046–47. For this now in thorough detail: *Über das Glück des philosophischen Lebens. Reflexionen zu Rousseaus "Rêveries" in zwei Büchern* (Munich, 2011), especially, First Book, Chapter IV [*On the Happiness of the Philosophic Life: Reflections on Rousseau's "Rêveries" in Two Books* (Chicago, 2016).]

33. See the concluding chapter of *Du contrat social* (IV, 9; *OCP* III, p. 470), on which Hilail Gildin has splendidly commented in *Rousseau's Social Contract: The Design of the Argument* (Chicago, 1983), pp. 190–91. The first word of the *Contrat social* is *Je*, the last *moi*.

CHAPTER TWO

The Renewal of Philosophy and the Challenge of Revealed Religion: On the Intention of Leo Strauss's *Thoughts on Machiavelli*

Zwei so grundverschiedene Menschen, wie Plato und Aristoteles, kamen in dem überein, was *das höchste Glück* ausmache, nicht nur für sie oder für Menschen, sondern an sich, selbst für Götter der letzten Seligkeiten: Sie fanden es im *Erkennen* ... Ähnlich urteilten Descartes und Spinoza.

Friedrich Nietzsche, *Morgenröthe*

Thoughts on Machiavelli has a special place in the œuvre of Leo Strauss. It is the only book for which Strauss chooses a title that refers to his own activity and, insofar as thinking designates the central activity in the life of the philosopher, points to the center of his life. At the same time, it is the book in which Strauss confronts revealed religion in the most detailed way. Again, the title gives important hints. It invites comparison with the most famous title that announced *thoughts* of an author. They concerned religion. Strauss, however, neither holds out the prospect of *Thoughts on Religion*, nor leaves it at *Thoughts* without further specification. He will communicate his thoughts about religion by speaking about Machiavelli. He will present his confrontation with revealed religion in the guise of an interpretation of the thought that determined the life of a predecessor. Thus he will be compelled as commentator and as critic to lend his voice to one with a reputation for evil.[1] In *Thoughts on Machiavelli*, unlike Pascal's *Pensées*, we have before us, not a collection of disparate notes, but rather a theologico-political treatise, secured through commentary and critique and written with the greatest care.

As he does in almost all his writings, Strauss appears in *Thoughts on Machiavelli* with the persona of the traditional interpreter. Yet the first mention of Machiavelli apart from the title already makes clear that here a philosopher speaks and that his interpretation envisages an entirely nontraditional Machiavelli. In the preface, Strauss expresses thanks to the sponsor of the 1953 lecture series at the University of Chicago from which the book emerged "for giving me the opportunity to present my observations and reflections on the problem of Machiavelli."[2] In *Thoughts on Machiavelli*

---

1. Among the devices of which a master in the art of careful writing avails himself, in the first chapter Strauss mentions: "An author may reveal his intention by the titles of his books." This statement is clearly not relevant for Machiavelli, since Strauss continues: "The titles of Machiavelli's two books [*Il Principe* and *Discorsi sopra la prima deca di Tito Livio*] are most unrevealing in this respect." It is most relevant, however, for the book in which the author offers this self-referential hint—along with numerous others. *Thoughts on Machiavelli* (Glencoe, IL, 1958; second edition, Seattle and London 1969; the final edition reviewed by Strauss, in which a few typos and oversights were corrected, is identical in pagination with the first edition), I, 27 (37). I cite according to chapter (I, II, III, IV, or where appropriate preface, introduction) and paragraph; page numbers are in parentheses.

2. Preface, 2 (5).—In the preface to *Natural Right and History* (Chicago, 1953) the corresponding passage, in what are otherwise exactly the same words of thanks to the same sponsor, reads "for inducing me to present coherently my observations on the problem of natural right" (p. vii). Nobody needed to *induce* Strauss to present his "observations *and reflections* on the problem of Machiavelli." "Reflections" stands in for "thoughts" in the title of the book. Strauss's thoughts on religion have found a place in his reflections on Machiavelli and gain expression in them.— That an unconventional author knows how to use a conventional genre for his own purposes, be

Strauss places the problem of Machiavelli on the philosophic agenda as Nietzsche did seventy years before in *Götzen-Dämmerung* with the problem of Socrates. By declaring Machiavelli to be a problem, Strauss singles him out as in his other writings he singles out only Socrates.[3] He elevates him to a historical key figure, the adequate understanding of which is a task of philosophic importance. In fact, in *Thoughts on Machiavelli* he engages the thought of Machiavelli as no one before who wrote about Machiavelli engaged his thought. And he speaks of him as Machiavelli was never spoken of before. Strauss takes Machiavelli seriously as a philosopher. This explains the exceptional character of his book among all books about Machiavelli. And Strauss is the first philosopher who not only reads Machiavelli as a philosopher, but also calls Machiavelli a philosopher.[4] In this lies an innovation that is, as no one knew better than Strauss, of importance beyond his own œuvre.

Thoughts on Machiavelli is the work of an innovator. It is part of Strauss's enterprise of the renewal of philosophy. Stated more precisely, it is one of the most prominent parts of this enterprise, which Strauss preferred to present as a revival of the philosophic tradition. Not surprisingly, his followers and his enemies for the most part share the opinion that Strauss was concerned with the return to "the teaching of the ancients," or with the restoration of a position for which he himself coined the expression "classical political philosophy." Yet the revival of a tradition by a philosopher necessarily includes a critique of the tradition needing such revival. What he restores in particular and what he leaves aside comply with his insight. The deviations in the presentation and the conceptual innovations he carries out are due to the judgment at which he arrives in view of the historical situation of philosophy. Faced with an avowed proponent of the tradition, one easily loses sight of these deviations and innovations. In the case of Strauss, that holds precisely for the innovations, without which his enterprise would not be thinkable at all. I mention three aspects of his innovations, which Strauss makes prominent in rapid succession during the 1940s, and which will come to have considerable significance for all that follows. (1) Strauss is the first philosopher to give a coherent presentation of the art of careful writing, of which the philosophers of the past availed themselves, and a

---

it a dedication, be it thanks to a sponsor, is a point to which Strauss also calls the reader's attention in the first chapter: "if not everyone, certainly an uncommon man is free to invest a common practice with an uncommon significance" I, 8 (20).

3. *Socrates and Aristophanes* (New York, 1966), p. 6.
4. Introduction, 2 (10); III, 30 (127); III, 59 (173); IV, 84 (294).

philosophic grounding of the exoteric-esoteric mode of presentation, which from the end of the eighteenth century was increasingly forgotten.[5] (2) No philosopher before Strauss stressed with similar emphasis that philosophy has to be conceived as a way of life, and few have so sharply grasped the philosophic life and separated it from edifying trivializations or pious appropriations as Strauss does in the very same essay in which he introduces the concept for the first time.[6] (3) The concept of the philosophic life stands in the closest connection with the concept of political philosophy, which was almost not to be found in the tradition and which Strauss makes into the veritable guiding concept of his œuvre. Once again the essay in which he introduces the concept takes up the sharpest, philosophically most demanding determination, repudiating most clearly all the nonphilosophic adaptations. Strauss indicates the necessary interconnection of the two concepts when he has the first part of the essay culminate in the assertion that the highest subject of political philosophy is the philosophic life, and when in the second part he assigns to political philosophy the task of the political defense and rational justification of philosophy, consequently answering the question, *Why philosophy?*[7] All three innovations—making prominent the

---

5. "Persecution and the Art of Writing," *Social Research* 8, no. 4 (November 1941): 488–504. (Strauss wrote the text in the period from November 10 to November 25, 1940. It is based on lectures that Strauss had given in October and December 1939 as well as in February, March, and April 1940.) Revised reprint in *Persecution and the Art of Writing* (Glencoe, IL, 1952), pp. 22–37. The earliest publication in which Strauss made the distinction between esoteric and exoteric communication the subject matter of a case study and explained the connection between the *art of writing* and *persecution* was devoted to Xenophon's *Constitution of the Lacedaemonians*: "The Spirit of Sparta or the Taste of Xenophon," *Social Research* 6, no. 4 (November 1939): 502–36 (written in the period from January 14 to April 7, 1939); see in particular pp. 528–32 and 534–35.

6. "The Law of Reason in the *Kuzari*," *Proceedings of the American Academy for Jewish Research* 13 (1943): 47–96 (written "December 1941–August 1942—with many long interruptions"), reprinted in *Persecution and the Art of Writing*, pp. 95–141. Strauss employs the expression "the philosophic life" there six times: paragraphs 11, 20, 24 note 77, 29, 43 (twice), pp. 106, 117, 121, 126, 138. In "The Spirit of Sparta or the Taste of Xenophon" Strauss already spoke three times—still without the use of the definite article—of "philosophic life" (par. 35, pp. 531–32). But it is only in "The Law of Reason," one of his most intransigent essays, taking a most radical approach, that he introduces the philosophic life as a philosophic concept in the demanding sense and develops by means of precise determinations the characterization that the essay from 1939 outlined in three approximations—the philosophic life is *fundamentally different from political life*, it is *of necessity private*, and it implies *the denial of the gods of the city*. Concerning Strauss's attempt to guard against a dogmatic misuse of the concept in the future and to counteract early its confusion with a way of life to which the status of a new kind of religion is assigned, consider p. 117.

7. "On Classical Political Philosophy," *Social Research* 12, no. 1 (February 1945): 98–117, revised reprint in *What Is Political Philosophy? and Other Studies* (Glencoe, IL, 1959), pp. 78–94. The first part of the essay, paragraphs 2–31 of the final version, develops the concept of political

exoteric-esoteric distinction, making the philosophic life central, and introducing the concept of political philosophy—take into account the historical situation of philosophy. Strauss responds to the challenge of historicism, which identifies philosophy with the time-bounded character of its teachings and has philosophic activity merge with the doctrinal contents that it underlies. He encounters the danger of decisionism and irrationalism, which have made inroads in philosophy and deny or misunderstand that philosophy must justify its right and its necessity if it is going to be adequate to itself. He opposes the pusillanimous character of the philosophy of culture, which parcels out human life into a plurality of autonomous domains and assigns to philosophy a narrowly circumscribed field in the realm of cultural provinces coexisting separately and peacefully. Strauss demonstrates the fruitfulness of his innovations in a long series of penetrating studies, in which he subjects to revision the history of philosophy and its unfinished disputes from Heidegger to the pre-Socratics. In particular, however, he exemplifies it in his interpretation of three authors, whom he wins over first and foremost for philosophy or retrieves for the history of philosophy, one a philosopher of the Middle Ages, one ancient, and one modern: First Maimonides,[8] whom Strauss in his first book did not yet recognize as a philosopher.[9] Then Xenophon,[10] whom barely anyone since the eighteenth century regarded as a philosopher. And finally Machiavelli.

To draw attention to philosophers who previously were not conceived of as philosophers or who long maintained a shadowy existence in the tradition is an effective move for a philosopher in order to indicate the thrust of his

---

philosophy from a hermeneutics of political life and tries to demonstrate the demand for political philosophy from the perspective of the citizen. The second part, paragraphs 32–36, shows the necessity for the turn to political philosophy on the basis of philosophy and develops the concept from the perspective of the philosopher.

8. "The Literary Character of the *Guide for the Perplexed*," in *Essays on Maimonides*, ed. Salo Wittmayer Baron (New York, 1941), pp. 37–91, reprinted in *Persecution and the Art of Writing*, pp. 38–94. The essay was worked out by Strauss in 1938. Preceding it were several preparatory studies—including *Philosophie und Gesetz. Beiträge zum Verständnis Maimunis und seiner Vorläufer* (Berlin, 1935), and "Quelques remarques sur la science politique de Maïmonide et de Fârâbî" from 1936—which are collected in volume 2 of *Gesammelte Schriften* (Stuttgart–Weimar, 1997).

9. *Die Religionskritik Spinozas als Grundlage seiner Bibelwissenschaft. Untersuchungen zu Spinozas Theologisch-politischem Traktat* (Berlin, 1930), reprinted in volume 1 of *Gesammelte Schriften* (Stuttgart–Weimar, 1996), pp. 208, 238, 254. Cf. the editor's preface in *Gesammelte Schriften*, volume 2, pp. xxii–xxv.

10. "The Spirit of Sparta or the Taste of Xenophon" from 1939 and *On Tyranny: An Interpretation of Xenophon's "Hiero"* (New York, 1948). These are, respectively, Strauss's first essay and first book on the work of an ancient philosopher.

enterprise of the renewal of philosophy and to allow its contours to emerge vividly. Conversely, the philosophers brought to light in this way take on such weight for the enterprise itself that the question to what extent they correspond to its founding determinations comes to be more than a merely historical question. By calling Machiavelli a philosopher, Strauss places demands on Machiavelli's thought, on Machiavelli's self-understanding, and on Machiavelli's own enterprise, whose fulfillment must be a central subject of his book. How is Machiavelli's enterprise related to the political defense and rational justification of philosophy? What status does the philosophic life have in Machiavelli's thought? How do things stand with Machiavelli's art of careful writing? These questions, which Strauss's œuvre occasions, point the way to the intention that led Strauss to put the problem of Machiavelli on the philosophic agenda. And access to an adequate understanding of the problem is opened up by the intention of *Thoughts on Machiavelli*.

I

The answer to the question about the art of careful writing in the case of Machiavelli seems to be obvious. What reader of *Thoughts on Machiavelli* could fail to see that Strauss presents Machiavelli as a master in the art of writing? But the purpose to which Machiavelli put this art is in no way obvious. Did it stand entirely in the service of Machiavelli's "spiritual warfare"?[11] Was it exhausted by political cunning and a strategically targeted practice for the deliberate conquest and final transformation of the world? Or are the *Prince* and the *Discourses* also "written speeches caused by love"?[12] Stated otherwise: who is the primary addressee of Machiavelli's books, whom Strauss circumscribes with the expression "the young," and by using this uniform designation seems to present as one? For while the philosophers before and after Machiavelli who avail themselves of the art of careful writing seek to reach with their esoteric communication one addressee, "the young" in the sense of the potential philosophers, it turns out on closer consideration that Machiavelli's presumably one addressee actually comprises two addressees.[13] Accordingly, Machiavelli's exoteric-esoteric presentation is directed to not two addressees, an exoteric and an esoteric, but rather at least three distinct addressees. The twofold addressee of Machiavelli's esoteric address might be the reason that in *Thoughts on Machiavelli*, in which the art of writing plays a greater role than in any other of his books, Strauss speaks nowhere of the exoteric-esoteric distinction.[14] The demonstrative avoidance of the traditional talk of exoteric and esoteric points to Machiavelli's deviation from the traditional practice of careful writing, which Strauss nowhere makes explicit, an ambiguity that is nevertheless of extremely far-reaching significance for the understanding of *Thoughts on Machiavelli*.

Not making the twofold addressee concealed in the expression "the young" explicit is all the more remarkable since Strauss makes *twofoldness* into the key to his interpretation of Machiavelli and the structural principle

---

11. Cf. I, 24 (35); III, 14 (102); III, 36 (138); III, 58 (171–72); IV, 43 (231); IV, 84 (293); IV, 87 (298–99).

12. *Persecution and the Art of Writing*, p. 36.

13. I, 37 (53); III, 16 (105); III, 29 (126–27); III, 56 (168–69) and see III, 56 (170); consider I, 35 (50); II, 20 (77); II, 24 (81–82); IV, 81 (290); and see IV, 45 (233).

14. "The silence of a wise man is always meaningful. It cannot be explained by forgetfulness" I, 18 (30). In one of the headings that Strauss wrote for his own use above each of the paragraphs of the book in the manuscript, "exoteric" appears (II, 18: "exoteric character of the particular counsel in ch. 24 [of the *Prince*]"); in another he uses the term "esotericism" (IV, 1: "Captatio benevolentiae for myself and for M.—esotericism and philosophy"). A footnote in chapter I refers the reader to *Persecution and the Art of Writing* (note 50, p. 304).

for the composition of his theologico-political treatise. The interplay between twofoldness and division into two, between duality and doubling, determines the structure and the orientation of the entire book. Beginning with the duality of Machiavelli's *thought* and *teaching*, which from the introduction on are carefully distinguished;[15] to the programmatic exposition of the twofold character of Machiavelli's teaching in chapter I; the doubling of Machiavelli's *intention* in the two central chapters II and III; and the twofold treatment of Machiavelli's *teaching* that the titles of chapters I and IV announce; up to the duality of Strauss's *thought* and *teaching*, which is constitutive for *Thoughts on Machiavelli* and develops within the span of the arc that marks the title and conclusion of the book. The first chapter, which explicitly deals with the twofold presentation of Machiavelli's teaching and is devoted to Machiavelli's art of writing, consists of two parts. While the second part provides an answer to the hermeneutic question, how to read Machiavelli, and culminates in the discussion of ten devices to which the reader of the *Prince* and the *Discourses* has to pay attention—devices that also are employed in *Thoughts on Machiavelli*[16]—the first part shows that the hermeneutic question is the actual philosophic question. This first part exemplifies, in the problem that the "surface" of Machiavelli's œuvre contains, the significance of the sentence with which the first part of the introduction concludes: "The problem inherent in the surface of things, and only in the surface of things, is the heart of things."[17] Strauss begins with a problem that is so obvious it could not remain hidden from any interpreter, namely, the difficult relationship between the *Prince* and the *Discourses*. In

---

15. Machiavelli's *thought* appears seven times in the introduction, Machiavelli's *teaching* four times: introduction, 4 (10–11); 8 (12); 9 (13); 10 (14); 7 (12); 9 (13); 12 (14). The ascent of the first part of the introduction (pars. 1–9) leads from "the old-fashioned and simple opinion according to which Machiavelli was a teacher of evil" (par. 1, first sentence) to the view of what, according to Strauss's judgment, "is truly admirable in Machiavelli: the intrepidity of his thought, the grandeur of his vision, and the graceful subtlety of his speech," and in the same breath to the designation of the goal that Strauss envisages with his interpretation: "Not the contempt for the simple opinion, nor the disregard of it, but the considerate ascent from it leads to *the core of Machiavelli's thought*" (par. 9, my emphasis).

16. The first part of chapter I comprises paragraphs 1–16, the second paragraphs 17–37. For the devices to which Strauss calls attention, cf. Footnotes 1, 14, 25, 29, 65, 74, 110, 146, 150.

17. Introduction, 9 (13); consider IV, 47 (237). The substantive connection between the initial meaning of the sentence—to indicate to the reader that the nature of things is articulated in the opinions about things and is not accessible other than by starting from what is first for us—and the application to the literary character of philosophic works consists in the fact that the art of careful writing makes it possible for the reader, in the confrontation with the philosophic work as an articulated whole, to have the very same experiences in thinking, understanding, and knowing that are decisive for the confrontation with the whole that is not subordinate to any intention.

contrast to most interpreters, who seek to resolve the question of how the two books are to be brought into harmony with one another, either through historical constructions or through a hierarchy based upon Machiavelli's political conviction, Strauss sharpens the problem of the twofold presentation by being the first to offer the argument that Machiavelli asserted in the dedicatory letters of both books that each of them contains everything the author knows. If Machiavelli makes a comprehensive claim both for the *Prince* and for the *Discourses*, the "surface" of the one as well as of the other work compels the reader to pose the question of the intention that underlies both, but that can be identified with neither alone. But if the question of the intention that moved Machiavelli to present his teaching in twofold shape is posed in all seriousness, Machiavelli's thought is shifted into the center. Strauss's choice of the starting point serves his approach to "what is truly admirable in Machiavelli." Conversely, the same holds for the rejection of the common practice of identifying Machiavelli's perspective with the perspective of the *Prince* or of the *Discourses*. The hasty identification of Machiavelli with either of the two perspectives—for some considerable time mostly with the "republican" *Discourses*—reduces the Florentine to a political partisan or to an ideologue.[18] The inadequate hermeneutic blocks access to the philosopher Machiavelli, whom Strauss, with his insistence on the twofold character of his teaching, has in view from the very beginning.

The structure of *Thoughts on Machiavelli* emerges from the result of chapter I, "The Twofold Character of Machiavelli's Teaching."[19] Since Machiavelli presents his teaching not as a whole but in parts, each of which claims to be a whole in itself, Machiavelli's teaching can be arrived at only by means of a detailed study of these parts, which Machiavelli's art of writing brought forth as works, each with its own aim and particular "surface." The detailed study demands recourse to the intention of the author as the organizing principle that makes the work into an independent whole. Accordingly, the headings of chapters II and III read "Machiavelli's Intention: The *Prince*" and "Machiavelli's Intention: The *Discourses*." Only the twofold focus on the intention that determines the *Prince* and the intention

---

18. "We are compelled to raise the question as to whether Machiavelli's perspective is identical with that of the *Prince* or with that of the *Discourses* or whether it is different from both perspectives. *Under no circumstances are we permitted dogmatically to assume*, as most contemporary students do, that Machiavelli's point of view is identical with that of the *Discourses* as distinguished from that of the *Prince*" I, 16 (29), my emphasis.

19. Strauss spoke in the manuscript at first of the "dual character" and then replaced *dual* with *twofold*.

that determines the *Discourses* allows Strauss to advance to the intention that underlies both works. Only the demonstration that he is able to do justice to Machiavelli's twofold teaching in his interpretation of the *Prince* and the *Discourses* gives Strauss the warrant, that is, the necessary means, to present in chapter IV "Machiavelli's Teaching" and thereby to do what Machiavelli himself did not do. Machiavelli's teaching emerges in Strauss's thinking, which proceeds from the problem in the surface to the core of the teaching. In opposite directions, from the teaching to the intention and from the intention to the teaching, Strauss's movement of thought meets that of Machiavelli.[20] Strauss thinks Machiavelli by subjecting the latter's thinking to the requirements it must satisfy if it is to correspond to the subject to which Machiavelli's intention is directed. The shared subject of thinking is the ground of possibility of Strauss's presentation of Machiavelli's teaching. But it is Strauss who presents Machiavelli's teaching, and he is himself determined as much by his intention as Machiavelli was by his intention in the twofold presentation. After he has discussed in chapters II and III Machiavelli's plan, which the *Prince* and the *Discourses* follow respectively, in chapter IV Strauss follows his own plan. The presentation and integration of "Machiavelli's Teaching," by far the longest chapter of the book, conforms to the purposes of Strauss's *Thoughts*.

The twofold character of Machiavelli's teaching is not exhausted by the twofold presentation of the *Prince* and *Discourses*. Unlike what Machiavelli's statements in the dedicatory letters or Strauss's explanations in chapter I suggest, it is not even clear whether the two books suffice to construe Machiavelli's teaching as a whole. With the opening words of chapter I, "Machiavelli presented his political teaching in two books," Strauss subtly calls attention to the question. For although Strauss leaves no doubt

---

20. On the philosophic implications of Strauss's hermeneutics, see *Die Denkbewegung von Leo Strauss. Die Geschichte der Philosophie und die Intention des Philosophen* (Stuttgart-Weimar, 1996), pp. 41–43 [*Leo Strauss and the Theologico-Political Problem*, pp. 71–73]. *Thoughts on Machiavelli* is Strauss's only book that makes the intention of a philosopher explicitly the subject matter of a chapter, and does this twice. Strauss uses the expressions "movement of thought," alternatively "movement of fundamental thought," three times: the former twice, IV, 30 (213) and IV, 75 (278), the latter once, IV, 56 (223). He already used it in his essay "On the Basis of Hobbes's Political Philosophy," which exhibits in further respects important similarities with *Thoughts on Machiavelli*. The essay was first published in a French translation in *Critique* (Paris) 83 (April 1954): 338–62. The English original appeared in 1959, with a significant expansion in note 2, in *What Is Political Philosophy?*, pp. 170–96. Strauss carefully distinguishes between Hobbes's *thought* und Hobbes's *teaching*, see pp. 170, 173, 174, 177, 181, 182, 189, 190, 196, in particular the first and the last paragraph of the essay, and he speaks of the "movement of Hobbes's thought" (p. 173, French p. 340).

in the course of his presentation that the *Prince* and the *Discourses* present far more than Machiavelli's political teaching in the narrow sense, i.e., more than his teaching regarding the subject matter of politics, religion, and morality,[21] the suprapolitical contours of the teaching of the *Prince* and the *Discourses* may become at least more distinctly visible insofar as additional works come into view. Strauss silently answers the question not just by repeatedly drawing upon other writings and even Machiavelli's letters, but by devoting distinct paragraphs to *La vita di Castruccio Castracani da Lucca* and *La Mandragola*, which form important hinges in the development of his philosophic argument.[22] The twofoldness of the *Prince* and the *Discourses* serves Strauss as a constructive minimum, in order to demonstrate that the unity of Machiavelli's teaching is not given but must rather be thought. Thinking the unity presents a more complex and challenging task to the extent that the reader engages with the hermeneutic endeavor of *Thoughts on Machiavelli*. For Strauss shows in chapters II and III that the *Prince* and the *Discourses* in turn are each determined by an inner twofoldness, so that the twofold character of Machiavelli's teaching, which manifests itself in the twofoldness of the books, finds a repetition in each of them and undergoes an intensification. In the case of the *Prince*, the demand arises to think the unity out of its twofold appearance as *treatise* with a theoretical claim to truth and as *tract for the times* with a practical goal. Once again taking as his starting point a problem that the "surface" makes available, Strauss extracts from the rhetoric of the twenty-sixth chapter, Machiavelli's famous "exhortation to seize Italy and to free her from the barbarians," the decisive aspects needed to disclose the interplay of *treatise* and *tract for the times*. He works out the double function that the concluding chapter of the *Prince* fulfills, on the one hand, of allowing the general teachings of the preceding twenty-five chapters to appear in the eyes of the readers to be grounded or justified by the particular purpose and, on the other hand, of bringing the reader, with a view to the presumed practical goal, to connect the theoretical theses, to apply them experimentally, and as it were to put them into motion in order to draw for himself the conclusions and

---

21. "It is certainly imprudent to assume that his knowledge of the things of the world is limited to things political and military in the narrow sense. It is more prudent to assume that his knowledge, and hence his teaching in either the *Prince* or the *Discourses*, is all-comprehensive." ". . . we have learned from Socrates that the political things, or the human things, are the key to the understanding of all things." I, 6 (19); cf. I, 35 (51) and I, 37 (53).

22. IV, 37 (223–25) and IV, 79 (284–85).

consider the consequences that the author leaves unspoken.²³ In the case of the *Discourses*, whose title refers explicitly to the first ten books and whose articulation into 142 chapters refers implicitly to Livy's work as a whole, which is articulated in 142 books, the demand arises to think the unity of the teaching from the use that Machiavelli makes of his "Bible" or "Anti-Bible." How the *Discourses* bring Livy into play, what they take up and what they pass over in silence, in what way Machiavelli indicates the plan of his book by appealing to Livy, following Livy or deviating from Livy, how Machiavelli has the historian of Rome serve his enterprise of renewal by using him as mouthpiece or distancing himself from him in open criticism—these are all questions that point the reader to *Ab urbe condita* as a second book or as a kind of separated or included text of the *Discourses*.²⁴

Yet even with the double division into two or the twice-doubling of the *Prince* and the *Discourses* we have not yet reached the basis of the twofold character of Machiavelli's teaching. We arrive at this basis only on the level of the twofold discussion and twofold statement that is common to both books and that has a twofold addressee. We arrive at it, in other words, only when we move on the firm ground that the art of careful writing successfully cultivated long before Machiavelli. In fact, everything that Strauss says regarding the theme of *twofold discussion* and *first and second statements* in Machiavelli accords seamlessly with what he showed previously in his writings on the philosophers of the Middle Ages and antiquity. The repeated discussion of the same or closely related subject matters and the sequence of first and second statements, judgments, and observations about the same subject are proven means of giving different addressees to understand different things. The addressees are distinguished according to the level of their capacity to conceive of the difference that lies enclosed in the repetition and to translate the sequence of first and second observations into a deepened understanding of the subject. For Machiavelli's art this means that the addressees actively distinguish themselves in virtue of their ability to

---

23. "both the explicit general teaching and the explicit particular counsel conveyed by the *Prince* are more traditional or less revolutionary than both the complete general teaching and the complete particular counsel. The two pairs of opposites which are characteristic of the *Prince*, namely, its being both a treatise and a tract for the times and its having both a traditional exterior and a revolutionary center, are nicely interwoven. The *Prince* is altogether, as Machiavelli indicates at the beginning of the second chapter, a fine web. The subtlety of the web contrasts with the shocking frankness of speech which he sometimes employs or affects" II, 13 (69).

24. "The peculiar charm and the peculiar remoteness of the *Discourses* are due to the fact that a part of their teaching is transmitted not only between their lines, but as it were between the covers of the *Discourses* and those of Livy's *History*" III, 26 (121).

think for themselves the "twofold character" of the teaching. Chapter I of *Thoughts on Machiavelli* draws a line from Machiavelli's twofold presentation of his political teaching in the *Prince* and *Discourses* to the twofold addressee to whom the presentation of his teaching is directed and whom Strauss separates into the "young" readers and the "old." As soon as we have understood that the twofold presentation and the sequence of *first and second statements* should demand from the true addressee the effort to think for himself and make possible for him the experience of progress in his own understanding, we understand the progress indicated by the fact that in the first sentence of the chapter Strauss calls the relationship between the *Prince* and the *Discourses* "obscure," while in the last paragraph, in contrast, he characterizes it as "enigmatic."[25]

If the twofold character of the teaching has its deepest reason in the distinction between the addressees, it is reserved for the true addressee to survey and to understand the teaching as a whole. For that he must adopt the highest perspective, from which the author can understand himself. Are "the young," whom Machiavelli seeks to win over for the purposes of "spiritual warfare," in the position to do that? Certainly not, insofar as they are the soldiers and officers who are supposed to serve at some point in Machiavelli's army and fight with zeal. Yet how do things stand with future captains, who out of insight make Machiavelli's enterprise their own in order to lead it to success? Evidently the answer depends on what meaning they assign to the campaign inaugurated by Machiavelli and their own task in it. The question of the primary addressee of Machiavelli's *teaching* is tied as closely as possible to the question of the status that Machiavelli's *enterprise* acquires in Machiavelli's *thought*. If the enterprise of a political new founding, of the discovery and implementation of *modi e ordini nuovi*, of a thoroughgoing change of the world, is supposed to be the highest perspective for Machiavelli, if Machiavelli is supposed to understand himself essentially as *principe nuovo*, then the philosopher-warrior, philosopher-prince, philosopher-craftsman, consequently a new kind of philosopher, seems to be the primary addressee of his teaching. Precisely this is the conclusion that *Thoughts on Machiavelli* invites the reader to draw. In its most exposed passages the book depicts the image of an enterprise that is ruled by the absolute primacy of practice and pursues resolutely the instrumentalization of philosophy for the purpose of the transformation of human living conditions, that conforms to the absolute will to rule, that relies on propaganda

---

25. I, 1 (15); I, 4 (17); I, 37 (53).—"the surface of a book as intended by its author, belongs as much to the book as does its substance" I, 12 (24).

as the decisive weapon in the struggle against the power of Christianity and has for its true goal the establishment of a stable order on a solid foundation grounded in sober knowledge. As the reception history shows, many readers round out this image by explaining the readiness to serve, astonishing for a philosopher—for whoever wants to rule must serve—through an appeal to the founder's hope for immortal glory. Others convince themselves of the coherence of the image by tracing Machiavelli's endeavor back to the passion of "anti-theological ire," seizing upon a formulation of Strauss's that, although it does not appear in *Thoughts on Machiavelli*, has such suggestive power that it contends with the famous "teacher of evil" of the opening sentence of *Thoughts on Machiavelli* for the rank of Strauss's most quoted saying about Machiavelli.[26] Since Strauss elevated Machiavelli to the founder of modern political philosophy, we have every reason to consider his treatment of Machiavelli's *enterprise* more precisely.

Strauss offers a twofold presentation, the one striking, the other subtle. The striking one flows into a grand historical narrative. The subtle one refers back to Machiavelli's philosophic reflection. The first presentation makes clear the revolutionary character of Machiavelli's enterprise as it was never before made clear. The second situates Machiavelli within the fundamental continuity that links him to philosophers before and after him. For his spectacular presentation Strauss makes ingenious use of a remark of Machiavelli's that previously played no noteworthy role in any interpretation. It opens the thirty-fifth chapter of the third book of the *Discourses* and in Strauss's translation reads: "How dangerous a thing it is to make oneself the head of a new thing which concerns many people, and how difficult it is to manage it and to bring it to its consummation and, after it has been brought to its consummation, to maintain it, would be too long and too exalted a matter to discuss; I reserve it therefore for a more convenient place." Strauss cites the sentence no less than three times in full length, which is without parallel in *Thoughts on Machiavelli* and underlines the significance that Machiavelli's

---

26. In his essay "What Is Political Philosophy?" from the year 1955, Strauss devoted 13 paragraphs to an exoteric treatment of Machiavelli's teaching. In it one finds the expression "anti-theological ire," which, freed from the reservation or restriction of the original statement, would take off and have a career of its own: "I would then *suggest* that the narrowing of the horizon which Machiavelli was the first to effect, was caused, *or at least facilitated*, by anti-theological ire—a passion we can understand but of which we cannot approve." *What Is Political Philosophy?*, p. 44, my emphasis. The thirteenth sentence of the paragraph at whose end one finds the winged words reads: "He *seems to have diagnosed* the great evils of religious persecution as a necessary consequence of the Christian principle, and ultimately of the Biblical principle," p. 44, my emphasis. In *Thoughts on Machiavelli* Strauss takes it upon himself to develop and substantiate this diagnosis in detail.

remark has for Strauss's presentation.[27] With the third rendering Strauss states explicitly the inner connection between Machiavelli's enterprise and the primary addressee: "the matter too long and too exalted to discuss is his own enterprise insofar as it depends upon the cooperation of 'the young.'" In the same passage he provides an answer to the question of the appropriate place for the discussion of the enterprise. "We believe him on his word that he will not 'discuss that long and exalted matter.' But is there no mean between discussion and complete silence? Is there no 'place' other than the lines of a book? Is a series of intimations not 'a convenient place' for transmitting 'a matter too long and too exalted to discuss'?" Immediately following the evocation of the addressee "the young," we are referred to three places for the closer study of Machiavelli's intimations. First we hear: "In a word, we believe that the last section of the *Discourses* deals obliquely with Machiavelli's enterprise: he selects from Livy VII–X such stories as properly understood throw light on his strategy and tactics." Then we learn "that the last sections of the First and Second Books have the same theme as the last section of the Third Book." The final sections of the three books of the *Discourses* have Machiavelli's enterprise for their subject matter. While the final section of book III begins with the remark cited three times and spans fifteen chapters (III, 35–49), each of the final sections of book I and book II, as will soon be made clear, consists only of a single chapter (I, 60 and II, 33). Strauss's talk of "the last sections" might therefore, despite its literal correctness, lead one to wonder. It proves to be helpful, however, if we are seeking to understand the plan of *Thoughts on Machiavelli*. For Strauss actually treats the subject matter of Machiavelli's enterprise in the last sections of the three chapters of his book that follow the chapter on the art of writing, in II, 25–26, III, 55–59, and IV, 82–87. Strauss's *last sections* depict his influential image of Machiavelli, the new Prince, who assumes his rule posthumously, the modern Moses who carries with him a new Decalogue, the unarmed prophet who contrives a new strategy of spiritual warfare and forges a new alliance with the people, previously thought to be precluded. They describe Machiavelli's "enormous venture" spectacularly as a "war of the Anti-Christ or the Devil, who recruits his army while fighting

---

27. The three complete renderings of the sentence are found in I, 6 (19), I, 15 (28), and III, 16 (105). In the last version Strauss replaces the formulation of the first two renderings, "would be too *large* and too exalted a matter to discuss," which can be explained by the context of chapter I, with "would be too *long* and too exalted a matter to discuss," which he repeats three times in immediate succession, with a different variation of the wording.

or through fighting against the army led by God or Christ." And they charge Machiavelli's "action" with being in the end "a stupendous contraction of the horizon," an ignoring of the suprapolitical, the suppressing of philosophy. In the center of the thirteen paragraphs that Strauss devotes to his memorable presentation stands the historical positioning of Machiavelli's "enterprise," the break and the beginning that mark Machiavelli as another "turning point and vortex of so-called world history": "Machiavelli is the first philosopher who believes that the coincidence of philosophy and political power can be brought about by propaganda which wins over ever larger multitudes to the new modes and orders and thus transforms the thought of one or a few into the opinion of the public and therewith into public power. Machiavelli breaks with the Great Tradition and initiates the Enlightenment. We shall have to consider whether that Enlightenment deserves its name or whether its true name is Obfuscation." What should we think of a philosopher who would allow his conduct to be determined by the belief that the coincidence of philosophy and political power is to be achieved by way of propaganda or enlightenment? Who would hold the final harmony of philosophy and politics to be even worth striving for, a harmony that could be imagined only as the dissolution of philosophy in politics? Who would choose as the true addressee of his teaching philosophers who are ready and willing to be warriors, princes, craftsmen? Not to mention "those young men or potential princes or the conspirators proper," on whom in addition he would depend for the practical implementation of his project.[28]

Strauss prefaces the three final sections dealing with Machiavelli's enterprise, with which he leaves the reader at the end of each of the three chapters, with three paragraphs (II, 24, III, 54, and IV, 81) that put the reader in a position to see Machiavelli as a philosopher in the demanding sense, and that involve the reader in the subtle presentation of the enterprise that comes to light or reaches its peak in them. Strauss's interpretation of the intention that underlies the *Prince* culminates in the first of the three paragraphs. In the third, which brings together all the lines of interpretation, the exposition of Machiavelli's thinking finds its crowning conclusion. The second concerns the attitude of the philosopher toward the highest authority. It will be discussed in the place that the subject matter demands. II, 24 begins in almost

---

28. III, 16 (105–6). II, 25–26 (83–84); III, 55 (168); 56 (170); 57 (171–72); 59 (173); IV, 85 (295).— "One is *tempted* to describe Machiavelli's relation to the young as a potential conspiracy. That chapter of the *Discourses* which is by far the most extensive is devoted to the subject of the conspiracies, i.e., of more or less violent changes of modes and orders" III, 56 (168), my emphasis.

as many words with the declaration of a primacy of theory for Machiavelli.[29] Combined with it is a new classification, that is, a relativizing of Machiavelli's treatment of praxis, which after Strauss's previous statements on the teaching of the *Prince* must be a surprise for most readers:[30] "once one grasps the intransigent character of Machiavelli's theoretical concern, one is no longer compelled to burden him with the full responsibility for that practical recklessness which he frequently recommends." The judgment about the author's undertaking depends decisively on the understanding of his intention and consequently on the answer to the question of his addressees: "The ruthless counsels given throughout the *Prince* are addressed less to princes, who would hardly need them, than to 'the young' who are concerned with understanding the nature of society. Those true addressees of the *Prince* have been brought up in teachings which, in the light of Machiavelli's wholly new teaching, reveal themselves to be much too confident of human goodness, if not of the goodness of creation, and hence too gentle or effeminate." With his ruthless counsels, Machiavelli pursues first and foremost a pedagogical purpose. They serve the hardening, disillusioning, and strengthening of the true addressees. They are expressed with a view to those who want to *understand* the nature of society. They are addressed to those who are meant to be put in a position to know the truth. To be able to appreciate the import of Strauss's answer to the question of the addressee in II, 24, we have to go back four paragraphs in chapter II. For Strauss's statement about " 'the young' who are concerned with understanding" is a "second statement," which reveals its exact meaning only if one sees it together with the "first statement" with which it needs to be compared. In II, 20 Strauss emphasizes that the author of the *Prince* speaks both in the capacity of a "potential adviser of a prince" and in that of a "teacher of political wisdom" or a theoretician, who teaches "the

---

29. In the previous paragraph, taking up once again statements from the introduction, Strauss says about Machiavelli: "The *core of his being* was *his thought* about man, about the condition of man and about human affairs" II, 23 (80), my emphasis; cf. introduction, 4 (10–11); 9 (13). Paragraphs II, 23 and 24 form a classical *digression*.

30. *Inter multa alia*: "the immoral policies recommended throughout the *Prince* are not justified on grounds of the common good, but exclusively on grounds of the self-interest of the prince, of his selfish concern with his own well-being, security and glory. The final appeal to patriotism supplies Machiavelli with an excuse for having recommended immoral courses of action. In the light of this fact, his character may very well appear to be even blacker than even his worst enemies have thought. At the same time however, we are not forced to leave the matter with the remark that the last chapter of the *Prince* is a piece of mere rhetoric, i.e., that he was not capable of thinking clearly and writing with consummate skill" II, 22 (80); cf. introduction, 1 (9). Concerning the last sentence of the quoted passage, consider introduction, 9 (13) as well as Footnote 15.

truth about the nature of princes." Strauss explicates these two capacities using a rhetorical detail of the *Prince*, which leads him immediately to the determination of the addressees of the writing: "He indicates his dual capacity and the corresponding duality of his addressees by his use of the second person of the personal pronoun: he uses 'Thou' when addressing the prince, and even the man who conspires against the prince, i.e., when addressing men of action, while he uses 'You' when addressing those whose interest is primarily theoretical, either simply or for the time being. The latter kind of addressees of the *Prince* is identical with the addressees of the *Discourses*, 'the young.'" II, 20 is the sole passage in *Thoughts on Machiavelli* that communicates to the reader what is foundational for the understanding of the book: the primary addressee of the *Prince* and of the *Discourses* must be thought as twofold. "The young," those who have a primarily theoretical interest, must be differentiated into those for whom this is true *simply* and those for whom it holds only *for the time being*, as preparation for something that appears to them more important than theoretical knowledge in itself. For the one, what matters is to understand the world, for the other, to change it. Machiavelli's teaching, accordingly, has a conventional addressee, divided into "princes" or "men of action," who are susceptible to counsel, and the people, who are instructed about "the nature of princes." And it has a primary addressee with two branches, future philosophers and prospective philosopher-princes. The first branch want to be "potential princes" or "statesmen" in the Socratic sense, who have at their disposal knowledge of princes without for that reason being interested in assuming their position, unless they are compelled to do so, or they do so playfully, that is, with a serious reservation. With the second branch, things are reversed. They want to become actual or posthumous princes for practical purposes, to the realization of which they commit themselves in all seriousness. When in II, 24 Strauss determines the "true addressees" as "the young," those for whom what matters is *to understand* the nature of society, he does not repeat the qualification he used four paragraphs before. That he thereby intends a determination of the true addressee, rather than avoiding this by using a common name for both varieties of the primary addressee or a transitory agreement between them, is clear from the fact that he explicitly coordinates those "who are concerned with understanding the nature of society" with "the intransigent character of Machiavelli's theoretical concern." Moreover, this point is underlined by an astonishing, not to say shocking, commentary in the same paragraph with which Strauss specifies the pedagogical purpose of the *Prince*: "Not only some of the most comforting, but precisely some of the most outrageous statements of the *Prince* are not meant seriously but serve a merely pedagogic function: as soon as one understands them, one sees that they are amusing and meant to amuse." Only the first of the two primary addressees, only the future philosophers in the serenity of their contemplation will in the end be able to understand the most outrageous and shocking statements as "amusing and *meant* to amuse."[31]

Our interpretation of Strauss's esoteric answer to the question of the true addressee of Machiavelli's teaching, and together with it the philosophic status of Machiavelli's enterprise, finds an additional and concluding confirmation in the consideration of the two passages in which the primary addressee in *Thoughts on Machiavelli* is mentioned for the first and last time. Strauss introduces *"the young"* in a paragraph in which he discusses the use of concealed blasphemies as a device of Machiavelli's rhetoric (I, 35). In the previous paragraph Strauss revealed the "enormous blasphemy" that Machiavelli, using a verse from the Magnificat, placed in *Discourses* I, 26, and showed that Machiavelli "leads us to the conclusion, nay, says in effect, that God is a tyrant" (I, 34), a result that will occupy us still further. In I, 35 we learn that the puzzling blasphemy in *Discourses* I, 26, which through Strauss's famous interpretation of the chapter has achieved almost universal familiarity,[32] "is, so to speak, only the spearhead of a large column," and we receive an explanation of what the author aims to achieve by means of the repeatedly applied device: "By concealing his blasphemy, Machiavelli compels the reader to think the blasphemy by himself and thus to become Machiavelli's accomplice." The reader whom Machiavelli makes into his accomplice, whom he entices "to wander in the forbidden," whom he tries to involve in his thinking, is not the reader in general. It is the reader who understands how to think for himself what the author gives him to think, about whom the author can with reason assume that he will in doing so have experiences closely related to the author's own experiences in think-

---

31. II, 20, (77) and 24 (81–82). Consider IV, 45 (233); 68 (265); 78 (282–84). Strauss inserted in the manuscript only later the words "either simply or for the time being" in the statement from II, 20. They are also missing, as is the last sentence from II, 20, also inserted later, in the advance publication of chapter II in the *American Political Science Review* 51, no. 1 (March 1957): 13–40, here p. 33. When the essay appeared, Strauss had not yet completed the work on the book. At the end of the manuscript Strauss noted: "Finis—Laus Deo. December, 9, 1957."

32. In the exoteric presentation of Machiavelli's teaching that Strauss gave in 1955, he declared: "Machiavelli's originality in this field [sc. the critique of religion, chiefly of Biblical religion] is limited to the fact that he was a great master of blasphemy. The charm and gracefulness of his blasphemies will however be less strongly felt by us than their shocking character. *Let us then keep them under the veil under which he has hidden them.* I hasten to his critique of morality which is identical with his critique of classical political philosophy." *What Is Political Philosophy?*, p. 41, my emphasis. Concerning the rhetorical means that Strauss uses here, cf. *Natural Right and History*, p. 76, and "On the Basis of Hobbes's Political Philosophy," p. 189.

ing. "Machiavelli is anxious to establish this kind of intimacy if only with a certain kind of reader whom he calls the 'young.' Concealment as practiced by Machiavelli is an instrument of subtle corruption or seduction. He fascinates his reader by confronting him with riddles. Thereafter the fascination with problem-solving makes the reader oblivious to all higher duties if not all duties." The reader who is seduced into thinking in such a way that he forgets all higher duties owing to his fascination with the problems with whose solution he is concerned is scarcely chosen to serve in Machiavelli's army, whatever his rank may be. We have no reason to rank Machiavelli's books' true addressee's aptitude for the subordination and devotion required in a military enterprise any higher than that of those youth who were corrupted by conversations with Socrates.[33]

The young are mentioned for the last time in IV, 81, in the last of the three paragraphs that Strauss has precede the three "last sections" on Machiavelli's enterprise. At the end of a detailed interpretation of Machiavelli's self-understanding guided by the theme of his conception of the good life or the life according to nature as one of alternation between *gravity* and *levity*, Strauss places the philosopher before the reader in the shape of the "most excellent man," who rises above the level "on which the political good and the erotic good supplement each other while conflicting with each other," and who, in contrast with the "most excellent captain, or soldier of war or love" determined by the poles of war and love, is able by knowledge to reach "full satisfaction and immunity to the power of chance." Following this characterization, which attributes to Machiavelli in substance a self-sufficiency grounded in knowledge and serenity, in harmony with the philosophic tradition, Strauss turns in the last stage of his interpretation of Machiavelli's conception of an alternation between *gravity* and *levity* to the life of the philosopher. This is the place where the true addressee is brought into play for the last time. "If it remains true that even on the highest level the alternation between gravity and levity is according to nature, one must say that whereas gravity belongs with the knowledge of the truth, levity comes into play in the communication of the truth. The same man who is the teacher of founders or princes and who discovers the true character of 'the world' communicates this truth to the young." The seriousness of the philosopher holds for knowledge of the truth. The communication of the truth to the true addressee, on the contrary, seems for him to be something unserious.

---

33. I, 34 (48–49) and I, 35 (49–50).—"It goes without saying that the man who, from the point of view of the established order, necessarily appears as a corrupter may in truth be the first discoverer of those modes and orders which are simply in accordance with nature" III, 56 (169).

But how is his activity as teacher of "founders or princes," who are explicitly distinguished from "the young," to be classified? How does Machiavelli's enterprise stand in relation to the poles of *gravity* and *levity*? Strauss continues: "In the former capacity," that is as teacher of "men of action," "he is half-man half-beast or alternates between humanity and inhumanity. In the latter capacity," as author who makes the truth accessible to the true addressee, "he alternates between gravity and levity." The surprising return of the alternation between *gravity* and *levity* within what at first came into view as the *levity* strand has two noteworthy implications. On the one hand, Strauss makes clear that he remains silent about the classification of the political enterprise in relation to the perspectives of *gravity* and *levity*. The formulation he chooses instead, "half-man half-beast," might remind the reader that Strauss, in an important discussion of the "most excellent man," argued that the thinker who as political teacher in Machiavelli's sense wants to achieve the highest effectiveness has to undergo what to him must be the most degrading of all servitudes if he is not prompted to this very servitude by *levity*, as an endeavor he permits himself without letting it affect the core of his existence.[34] On the other hand, the repetition of the bifurcation *gravity-levity* corrects the impression of the first statement on "communication of the truth." It is not so much the communication of the truth to the true addressee that is something unserious. What is unserious is the mode of the communication. The truth is communicated indirectly to the true addressee in a guise that shows it by concealing it. The teaching that is directly communicated to the founder or to the prince may, for instance, belong to the indirect manner of Machiavelli's communication. Strauss goes on: "For in the latter capacity he is the bringer of a light which illumines things that cannot be illumined by the sun. The unity of knowledge and communication of knowledge can also be compared to the combination of man and horse, although not to a centaur." In the last sentence of IV, 81 the truth of the alternation between the two poles proves to be the working together of two powers. The alternation between *gravity* and *levity* is on the highest level integrated into a unity. Indirect communication allows the author to protect the light he carries with him so that it illuminates only for that reader for whom it is meant. The philosopher speaks to his addressees without expressing what he forbids himself to express. He is mindful of the enigmatically formulated truth "that what ought not to be said cannot be said," which Strauss in the first paragraph of chapter IV puts

---

34. IV, 51 (244).

in front of the argument that reaches its goal in paragraph 81.[35] By finally characterizing the author of the *Prince* and the *Discourses* with the metaphor of the horseback rider, Strauss places him without qualification in the tradition of philosophers who avail themselves of the exoteric-esoteric art of writing. He reinforces his judgment that Machiavelli is to be considered as the inheritor, "the by no means unworthy heir," of that "supreme art of writing which that tradition manifested at its peaks."[36] For Strauss introduced the metaphor in 1957 in "How Fārābī Read Plato's *Laws*" and coined it for works of Farabi and Plato in order to characterize their *twofoldness*.[37] Machiavelli, who induces one of the two primary addressees of his teaching, the true philosopher of the future, to think through the task of his enterprise as a whole, ranks among the great renewers of philosophy.

---

35. IV, 1 (174). Consider Strauss's treatment of the virtue of the philosopher in IV, 54 (246–47): "Virtue in the highest sense, 'extraordinary virtue,' grandeur of mind and will, the pre-moral or trans-moral quality which distinguishes the great men from the rest of mankind, is a gift of nature. Such virtue, which is not chosen, compels a man to set himself high goals, and since such virtue is inseparable from the highest prudence, to set himself the wisest goal possible in the circumstances . . . In the case of men of extraordinary virtue or prudence, 'Is' and 'Ought' coincide: they cannot do what they ought not to do and they must do what they ought to do; in their case the dictates of prudence have compulsory power."

36. III, 26 (120).

37. "Just as Plato before him, Fārābī does not permit himself the seeming generosity of trying to help all men toward knowledge but employs a kind of secretiveness which is mitigated or enhanced by unexpected and unbelievable frankness. Accordingly his resolution is two-fold: his summary of the *Laws* is meant 'to be a help to him who desires to know [the *Laws*] and to be sufficient to him who cannot bear the toil of study and of meditation' (4, 20–21). Those who desire to know the *Laws* form a different class from those who cannot bear the toil of study and of meditation . . . One can articulate the twofoldness of works of this kind by comparing them to men on horseback: to seeming wholes which consist of a discerning and slow ruler and a fast and less discerning subject, and which are well fitted for unexpected attack as well as for flight." "How Fārābī Read Plato's *Laws*," in *What Is Political Philosophy?*, pp. 137–38.—For the contrast between the horseback rider and the centaur, Strauss was apparently prompted by Xenophon's *Cyropaedia* IV, 3, 17–21.

II

At the center of interest of *Thoughts on Machiavelli* stands the confrontation with revealed religion. The interest is twofold. It concerns first the historical answer to the altered political situation that the rule of revealed religion created. Above all, however, it pertains to the philosophic answer to the challenge implied by the claim to truth of revealed religion. The primarily historical interest links Machiavelli with Farabi, the first new founder of political philosophy subsequent to the appearance of revealed religions.[38] The genuine philosophic interest connects Machiavelli no less with Plato, for it is not dependent on the historical appearance or disappearance of revealed religions. Faith in an omnipotent God as creator of the world, ruler and judge of human beings, which constitutes the core of revealed religion, presents an objection to philosophy that demands a response. It accompanies philosophy as a permanent possibility, regardless of the victories or defeats that its historical embodiments have achieved or will suffer. Strauss leaves no doubt that he focuses special attention on the philosophic response when he persistently traces back the Christian religion and the Christian God, with which Machiavelli saw himself confronted as a political actor, to the "Biblical religion" and the "Biblical God" and when he replaces Christian revelation with revelation tout court. The teacher of "potential princes" might have conceived of a spiritual warfare in which an army under the anti-Christian banner confronts an army under the Christian banner. On the other hand, Strauss attests to the thinker in the strongest terms that he "takes seriously the claim to truth of revealed religion by regarding the question of its truth as all-important."[39] If Strauss had not seen himself as being in a position to say of Machiavelli that for him the question of the truth of revealed religion

---

38. See "Quelques remarques sur la science politique de Maïmonide et de Fârâbî" (written in the period from August to October 1935), *Gesammelte Schriften*, vol. 2, pp. 129–30 and 156–58; "Farabi's *Plato*" (written in the period from November 12, 1943, to March 29, 1944), in *Louis Ginzberg Jubilee Volume* (New York, 1945), pp. 378, 382–84; *Persecution and the Art of Writing*, pp. 15–18 and 21; "How Fārābi Read Plato's *Laws*," pp. 144, 152–54.

39. I, 35 (51). Strauss says in the same place about Machiavelli's unbelief: "if, as Machiavelli *assumes*, Biblical religion is not true, if it is of human and not of heavenly origin, if it consists of poetic fables, it becomes inevitable that one should attempt to understand it in merely human terms. At first glance, this attempt can be made in two different ways: one may try to understand Biblical religion by starting from the phenomena of human love or by starting from political phenomena. The first approach was taken by Boccaccio in his *Decameròn*, the second approach was taken by Machiavelli." (My emphasis.) Compare the later statement: "It is hardly necessary to add that Machiavelli's explanation in merely human terms of the root of Biblical belief presupposes *his denial, his destructive analysis* of the phenomenon known to us as the conscience" III, 42 (148–49), my emphasis.

is *all-important*—an expression Strauss does not employ very often[40]—he would not have elevated Machiavelli to the rank of a political philosopher, let alone have brought the problem of Machiavelli into the same constellation as the problem of Socrates. Strauss's undertaking to think Machiavelli as a philosopher and to present his teaching as a whole presupposes that Machiavelli can be interpreted within the horizon of the indispensable necessities and highest requirements that he must satisfy. Strauss's approach is expressed nowhere more manifestly than in the passage, in chapter III, in which he introduces "the central theme" of the *Discourses*: "The characteristic theme of the *Prince* is the prince in the most exalted sense, the bringer of new modes and orders or the founder. The characteristic theme of the *Discourses* is the people as the maintainer of established modes and orders, or as the repository of morality and religion. If it is true, as I believe it is, that the Bible sets forth the demands of morality and religion in their purest and most intransigent form, the central theme of the *Discourses* must be the analysis of the Bible."[41]

Given the emphasis of Strauss's reference to the Bible when the demands of morality and religion are up for discussion, it is not surprising that his presentation of "Machiavelli's teaching" in its most important parts has for its subject matter, explicitly or implicitly, "the Biblical teaching" or "the teaching of the Bible."[42] For the chapter "Machiavelli's Teaching" appears to divide into two equal parts, symmetrically arranged, IV, 1–42 and 46–87, which, following a distinction of Strauss's, are devoted respectively to "Machiavelli's teaching regarding religion and his teaching regarding morality." According to the pronouncement of the previous chapter, "the Bible" is thus supposed to be the central theme of chapter IV. We have reason to expect a treatment of the Biblical God and the Biblical commandment. At the same time, the pronouncement in III, 32 makes us aware that the sequence from

---

40. Five years later Strauss ended *The City and Man* (Chicago, 1964), p. 241, with the sentence: "Only by beginning at this point [sc. the understanding of the divine inherent in the prephilosophic city] will we be open to the full impact of the all-important question which is coeval with philosophy although the philosophers do not frequently pronounce it—the question *quid sit deus.*"

41. III, 32 (133). Regarding the first part of the summary statement on the *Prince* and the *Discourses*, consider Strauss's reading guide: "In reading Machiavelli's statements about the prince or a prince, one must always consider what they would mean if they were applied to God" IV, 17, note 54 (332).

42. In the first half of "Machiavelli's Teaching" Strauss employs the contrasting counterconcepts "the Biblical teaching" nine times: IV, 3 (176), IV, 12 (186, 187, 189) (four times), IV, 16 (197) (twice), IV, 22 (203) (twice); "the teaching of the Bible" three times: IV, 3 (176); and "the characteristic teachings of revelation" once: IV, 2 (175).

religion to morality, which reverses the sequence morality-religion from the discussion of the *Discourses*, needs an explanation. Strauss offers a less subtle hint about his own activity, which raises the question of his intention and his plan, at the end of the first half of the chapter when, anticipating an obvious objection of common readers, he explicitly declares: "We have devoted what at first glance seems to be a disproportionately large space to Machiavelli's thought concerning religion. This impression is due to a common misunderstanding of the intention, not only of Machiavelli but also of a whole series of political thinkers who succeeded him." Strauss underscores the deviation of his own spatial arrangement by adding shortly thereafter that in Machiavelli "the explicit discussion of religion occupies much less space than the explicit discussion of morality."[43] Finally, it cannot remain hidden from any reader just how far removed Strauss is from Machiavelli's reticence in the treatment of the central theme: While Machiavelli mentions the Bible and the Old Testament by name only one time each in the *Discourses* and the *Prince*, respectively (*Discorsi* III, 30, *Principe* XIII), in *Thoughts on Machiavelli* such references are omnipresent, as it were, over long stretches. In the last paragraph of the introduction to chapter IV alone, in which Strauss concedes that the common misunderstanding of Machiavelli's confrontation with revealed religion "is justified to some extent by his reticences," the Bible is mentioned ten times. Strauss makes Machiavelli speak where he is silent. He assists him with arguments where Machiavelli is satisfied with insinuations. However, what Strauss said about Farabi holds for the author of *Thoughts on Machiavelli*: He exploits the specific immunity of the commentator or the historian in order to express in a historical work what he thinks about a serious matter.[44] Under the title "Machiavelli's Teaching," Strauss the commentator and historian presents in the first part of chapter IV "Machiavelli's *thought* concerning religion." And he does this avowedly with recourse to Machiavelli's *intention*.

The plan that the philosopher Strauss follows in chapter IV is, nevertheless, insufficiently described by the division into two halves devoted to religion and morality. The central theme is also in need of a more exact determination. The 87 paragraphs of the chapter are articulated into 11 sections. The eleventh section (IV, 82–87), which, like the last sections of chapters II and III, is concerned with Machiavelli's political enterprise, summarizes the criticism Strauss makes of Machiavelli's teaching with regard to its world-

---

43. IV, 43 (231) and IV, 44 (231–32).
44. "Farabi's *Plato*," p. 375.

historical consequences. Next to the opening of the book, the conclusion is the most exoteric part of *Thoughts on Machiavelli*. It contributes principally to the obfuscation of the suprapolitical content of Machiavelli's thought, which the ten previous sections have brought to light and formulated. For the true theme of paragraphs 1–81, which connects, penetrates, and overarches all the others, is the philosopher: his nature and his virtue, his self-assertion and his self-understanding within the horizon of the tasks and claims of politics, religion, morality. The beginning and the end of these ten sections are joined together in the characterization of the key role that falls to adequate hermeneutics in the recovery of the understanding of "what philosophy originally meant" (IV, 1). The first paragraph classifies the *Discourses* and the *Prince* among those books that do not freely disclose "their full meaning as intended by the author unless one ponders over them 'day and night' for a long time" (IV, 1), and the last is the only paragraph in chapter IV that refers by name to the addressee for whom philosophic books of this kind are written (IV, 81). At the beginning of the sixth section (IV, 43–45), in the first paragraph of a parenthetical consideration that forms a bridge between the two "halves," Strauss draws the reader's attention, as he does in the first paragraph of the first section and in the last paragraph of the tenth section, to the form of communication, which has to be carefully considered if one wants to understand the intention of the philosopher. It is here, in the center of the hermeneutic three steps of chapter IV and in the context of enlightenment about a widespread misunderstanding of the intention "not only of Machiavelli but also of a whole series of political thinkers who succeed him," that Strauss emphatically reminds one of "the art of allusive and elusive writing."[45] Simultaneous with the triad concerning the philosophic art of writing in sections 1, 6, and 10, Strauss articulates the theme of the chapter by the succinct designation he offers of the philosophic author in precisely these sections. The introductory section (IV, 1–3) represents Machiavelli as one of "the wise of the world," whom Savonarola opposes following the model of the Apostle Paul. He counts him among the

---

45. "We no longer understand that in spite of great disagreements among those thinkers, they were united by the fact that they all fought one and the same power—the kingdom of darkness, as Hobbes called it; that fight was more important to them than any merely political issue. This will become clearer to us the more we learn again to understand those thinkers as they understood themselves and the more familiar we become with the art of allusive and elusive writing which all of them employ, although to different degrees. The series of those thinkers will then come to sight as a line of warriors who occasionally interrupt their fight against their common enemy to engage in a more or less heated but never hostile disputation among themselves" IV, 43 (231).

"Averroists," who "reject not only the myths of the pagans, but above all revelation and the characteristic teachings of revelation." He extends the line from Machiavelli backward to the *falāsifa*, the philosophers at whose beginning Farabi stands (IV, 2).[46] Then, in the bridge section Machiavelli stands in appearance as the founder of modern political philosophy (IV, 43). And in the tenth section (IV, 69–81), which has to do with philosophy as the striving after the common good in the precise sense and the life according to nature, Machiavelli finally becomes visible as a philosopher, determined by no historical index, and grasped by no extension backward or forward.

As soon as we recognize that the philosopher is the true theme of chapter IV, we can answer the question why Strauss inverts the sequence in it from morality to religion. While it makes good sense in the case of the political analysis of the people as the preserver of the mores, opinions, and orders of morality to concede the priority of morality over religion with regard to need as well as effect,[47] the philosophic self-understanding shifts religion into the first place, since the demands of morality presuppose the truth of religion, without whose main concept and center they lose their obligatory character.[48] Moreover, in a presentation of Machiavelli's thought that makes the self-understanding of the philosopher its theme, religion is afforded the priority, since philosophy sees itself seriously challenged only by the claim to truth made by religion.[49] It is to Machiavelli's treatment of religion in the immediately political respect that Strauss devotes the fifth section (IV, 38–42), which is the last and, after the introduction, the shortest section of the first half. With this he indicates the weight that would be assigned to religion as a sociological phenomenon in a presentation of Machiavelli's teaching that focuses on its content and scope as "political theory" in the conventional sense. The five paragraphs in *Thoughts* IV, 38–42, which correspond in a clearly delineated way to the famous group of five on religion in *Discourses* I, 11–15, suffice to outline the teaching of the advantage and disadvantage of religion for politics.

A different distribution of space, weight, and emphasis results if what is at issue is the confrontation of the philosopher with revealed religion. It is

---

46. As the heading for the middle paragraph of the introduction of chapter IV, Strauss noted: "M. not a 'pagan' but a savio del mondo, i.e. a faylasûf [written in Arabic]."
47. Cf. "The Law of Reason in the *Kuzari*," pars. 13, 34, 45, pp. 109, 130, 140.
48. Cf. "The Law of Reason in the *Kuzari*," pars. 12, 19, 24, 25, 28, 44, pp. 106–8, 115, 121, 122, 124–26, 139. Consider Friedrich Nietzsche, *Götzen-Dämmerung*, "Streifzüge eines Unzeitgemässen" 5, *KGW* VI, 3, pp. 107–8.
49. See "Reason and Revelation," in Heinrich Meier, *Leo Strauss and the Theologico-Political Problem*, p. 149.

initially the subject matter of the eleven paragraphs that follow the introduction of chapter IV. At the end of the second section (IV, 14), Strauss offers a substantial characterization of the philosopher that shows the perspective from which the preceding treatment of religion has to be read: as from the beginning on related to the philosopher, taking its bearings from him, and attending to the conditions of his existence. The second section (IV, 4–14) begins with Christianity. It starts with the power that, regarding politics as well as philosophy, decisively stamps the historical condition of the moderns ("the moderns are primarily the Christians") and in both respects is for them the main obstacle that blocks the return to the ancient virtues ("the decisive reason for the failure to imitate the ancients properly is precisely Christianity"). The prelude forms a discussion that, viewing the center from the periphery or advancing from the outside to the inside, begins with the effect of Christianity on the world in order to approach what Strauss three times calls "the essence of Christianity."[50] Machiavelli's diagnosis of the effect of Christianity on the world may be encapsulated by saying that it has made the world weak or maintained it in its weakness. Strauss lays out three rings concentrically: World, people, man under the rule of Christianity are essentially "unarmed." The Christian prohibition or counsel not to resist evil is *contra naturam* and must therefore bring forth disastrous consequences.[51] Christianity has lastingly undermined esteem for "the honor of the world," which strengthened the action of many and supported the dedication of the citizens to the political community. Christianity, however, had the truth on its side when it destroyed the belief that honor is the highest good. The innermost ring provides Strauss with the opportunity to establish with all distinctness that Machiavelli "is undoubtedly concerned with teaching the truth and the true way," and in this context, in direct confrontation with the truth of Christianity, to quote "the strongest statement regarding truth which he ever makes": "It is truer than every other truth that where men are not soldiers this is due to a fault of the prince." Strauss comments on the sentence from *Discourses* I, 21 in the arithmetic middle of his

---

50. IV, 4–6 (176–80). Strauss draws in these three paragraphs upon *Discourses* I, Proemio; II, 2 and III, 1 consecutively, of which he says that they are "the three passages explicitly dealing with the essence of Christianity" (176). The *essence of Christianity* is a formulation that Strauss introduces into the discussion.

51. ". . . Machiavelli shows that the neglect of law enforcement, of human punishment, leads to the consequence that either the evils will be eventually corrected with non-legal violence or else that society will perish . . . Non-resistance to evil would secure forever the undisturbed rule of evil men. Resistance to evil is natural to man as well as to any other living being. The counsel against resisting evil can therefore lead only to evasion of that counsel" IV, 6 (180).

discussion of the essence of Christianity: "That most perfect truth upholds the demand for the strength of the world. Hence if Christianity has led the world into weakness, it cannot be true. There is essential harmony between truth and worldly strength: 'all those modes and those opinions deviating from the truth arise from the weakness of him who is lord.'" Strauss leaves unmentioned that Machiavelli avails himself in his critique of Christianity of an ad hominem argument, since he can presuppose as generally familiar Christ's saying from the Sermon on the Mount, *You shall know them by their fruits*. But now he not only attests to Machiavelli's awareness of the claim to truth of Christianity, but also wants us to know with the explicit reference to the truth of Christianity—the truth that concerns the glory of the world as the presumably highest good—that Machiavelli "has come to grips with that claim." The fruit from which Machiavelli infers that Christianity "cannot be true" seems to grow from the fact that Christianity regards "humility, abjectness and contempt for things human" as the highest good. The ground in which the present weakness of the world is rooted is, however, not yet reached. In order to reach it and to expose the core of Christianity, Strauss goes one step further than Machiavelli. He expresses what Machiavelli does not allow himself to express. First he directs the reader's attention to Machiavelli's superseding of his statement that the religion of the ancients regarded "worldly honor" as the highest good by a second statement, according to which the religion of the ancients regarded "greatness of mind, strength of the body and all other things which are apt to make men very strong" as the highest good. Subsequently, he combines with this substitution, which puts the religion of the ancients in the service of the strengthening of man and places its truth in the development of his mental and bodily capacities, an analogous operation with the contrary result, which is inspired by Machiavelli: "He thus suggests a corresponding improvement of his statement concerning the highest good as understood by Christianity: the highest good is God, who assumed humility and weakness and thus consecrated humility and weakness."[52]

The "weakness of the modern world," for which Machiavelli holds Christianity responsible, is far from being exhausted by a diagnosis of decadence. It must be conceived, as Strauss shows in the three paragraphs about the essence of Christianity and in the second section altogether, as the expression of a fundamental alternative. Christianity proves to be the main obstacle to the renewal of the ancient virtues, not only with regard to the

---

52. IV, 5 (178–79). See Matthew 7: 16 and 20. Consider Footnotes 41 and 48.

facticity of current circumstances but above all owing to its teaching of the highest good and with that the accompanying demotion of those virtues, if not the negation of their being virtuous altogether. It is not a historical decline in itself, but rather the central place of Christian *humilitas*, to give an example that is more than an example, that blocks access to classical *magnanimitas*. Strauss sharply emphasizes the underlying conflict by conceiving Machiavelli's response to the *unum est necessarium* of faith in the answer "good arms." In a footnote that he adds to the "strongest statement" of Machiavelli's about truth, Strauss calls his sentence "good arms are the one thing needful," which in the text of *Thoughts on Machiavelli* appears once before and once after this citation, "the anti-Biblical truth par excellence."[53] It is obvious that the expression "good arms" refers as little merely to politics or warfare under the conditions of the Christian era as something like the distinction between the strength and the weakness of the world under ancient conditions would apply merely to the political freedom of the republics of the West and the despotic servility of the monarchies of the East. Strauss's argument operates on more than one level. We have reached the decisive level when his statements and determinations are applied to philosophy and the life of the philosopher. On this level, the one thing needful means insight, grounded on the free use of one's own reason, at the head of the virtues that make possible a self-sufficient life, and "good arms" in particular are good reasons to defend this life. A life that wants to understand itself on the basis of the obedience of faith denies the philosophic life in its raison d'être. Even and precisely where it makes a place for contemplation for the sake of the glory of the highest authority, it cannot help but negate the central activity of the philosopher as an activity that is not bound in advance to any obedience. Finally, concerning humility, which Strauss has immediately precede weakness in the designation of the core of Christianity, it is according to the Christian understanding essentially obedience and the complete denial of the philosophic thesis that virtue is knowledge. It is virtue to the extent that it does not know itself as virtue. For if it were to know itself as virtue, it would not be free from pride and could not count as the highest Christian virtue.[54] In the thirteenth paragraph, which immediately

---

53. IV, 5, note 10 (330); II, 24 (82); IV, 30 (212); cf. IV, 13 (189) and IV, 18 (199). See Luke 10: 42.

54. Martin Luther names humility "the supreme virtue." He says about it: "God alone knows humility / he alone judges, too, and reveals it / so that man never knows less about humility / than precisely when he is properly humble." And he explains: "Proper humility never knows that it is humble / for whenever it were to know it / so would it become arrogant by viewing the same beautiful virtue / but rather with heart / mind / and all the senses /it clings to the lesser things / it has them incessantly in view." *Das Magnificat verdeutschet und ausgelegt*, ed. Otto

precedes the concluding paragraph of the second section on the "most excellent men," Strauss translates the anti-Biblical truth par excellence as follows: "According to Machiavelli, man will not reach his highest stature if he himself does not demand the highest from himself without relying on support from powers outside of him, and if he cannot find his satisfaction in his achievement as his own achievement. Not trust in God and self-denial but self-reliance and self-love is the root of human strength and greatness." And further: "Consciousness of excellence on the part of excellent men must take the place of consciousness of guilt or sin."[55]

But let us return to the course of the argument in the second section. The first part (IV, 4–8) is devoted to the challenge of revealed religion in the historical shape of Christianity. The Bible, Biblical religion, the Biblical God, Biblical commandment or Biblical morality are not mentioned in this part. Yet already the first note suggests to the reader that he consult an earlier passage in *Thoughts on Machiavelli*. There one finds talk of "Biblical demands for humility and charity," which require of Machiavelli the proof that the virtue of the ancients, which he commends to the moderns, is "genuine virtue." Strauss leaves the reader with no lack of clarity about what such a proof implies for the philosopher: "To prove that ancient virtue can be imitated and ought to be imitated is tantamount to refuting the claims of Biblical religion." The rejection of the demands of Biblical morality requires the refutation of the demands of Biblical religion, that is, the invalidation of its claim to truth and obedience.[56] Thus we are prepared for Strauss to advance briskly from Christianity to Biblical religion. The transition from the particular historical manifestation to the fundamental principle occurs in the center of the second section. Together with this transition, Strauss no longer speaks of the "weakness of the modern world," but rather envisages the "weakness of the world." The transition is marked by the last word of the eighth paragraph, "Jerusalem," which not only connects Christianity with

---

Clemen II, pp. 148, 150; *Weimarer Ausgabe* VII, pp. 560, 562. Consider in connection with this determination of humility as the "highest virtue" Luther's critique of the virtue of Socrates at the beginning of *Vorlesung über den Römerbrief 1515/1516*.

55. IV, 13 (189–90). Shortly before, in the same paragraph, Strauss formulates the Biblical counterposition: "one ought to put one's trust less in flesh and blood, in men's will, and ultimately in one's own arms, virtue and prudence than in prayer and in God. If one were to follow the Bible, one could not count Moses among those new princes who acquired their power by their own arms and their own virtue. One would have to say that he deserves admiration 'only with regard to that grace which made him worthy to speak with God'" (189).

56. IV, 4, note 5 (329); III, 3 (86). Cf. I, 35 (51) and see IV, 5, note 10 (329–30).

Judaism and divides the two, but also stands for revealed religion simply.⁵⁷ The transition from the essence of Christianity (IV, 5) to the center of Biblical religion (IV, 12) begins with a brief look back to the origin (IV, 9) and ends with a concise sketch of the victory of Christianity (IV, 11). In the center stands a sharp critique of the "essentially tyrannical" rule that is characteristic of the "Biblical polity" (IV, 10). The political approach that Strauss, proceeding from Machiavelli, outlines for the analysis of the emergence and development of revealed religion in IV, 9–11 reminds us of the critical or genealogical investigations in Spinoza's *Tractatus theologico-politicus* and Nietzsche's *Antichrist*,⁵⁸ not to mention Hobbes, Rousseau, or Julius Wellhausen. Agreement regarding the most important points speaks less for the success of a conspiratorial enterprise than for the objectivity of the analysis.⁵⁹ "Christianity stems from the servile East . . . It stems more particularly from a weak Eastern nation which had a very defective polity." Unlike the citizens of the Roman republic, who gained their freedom supported by good arms and good laws in their inner struggles and asserted it in victorious wars, unlike the Roman people, who won from political participation the confidence to make the public cause their cause and to identify themselves with the fatherland, for the Jewish people, because of the lengthy time of oppression or exile, the land of the fathers was an object of longing and not a space of lived freedom and experienced self-determination. The longing for the promised land is transformed in Christianity into the longing for the heavenly fatherland and translated into the dualism of heavenly and earthly fatherland: "the true Christian is an exile on earth who lives in faith and hope and who arouses these passions in others."⁶⁰ In historical reality belief in the dualism of heavenly and earthly fatherland anchors the

---

57. IV, 8 (182). Strauss refers to Jerusalem only once more in the text, namely, in the next paragraph in the phrase "the temple in Jerusalem," saying something that Machiavelli, as he adds, refrained from saying: IV, 9 (183). Machiavelli mentions Jerusalem once in *Discourses* II, 32.

58. From the *Tractatus theologico-politicus*, which is not mentioned in *Thoughts on Machiavelli*, Strauss incorporates in IV, 18 (199) a modified citation ("nam nulla divinae justitiae vestigia reperiuntur, nisi ubi justi regnant"), which fourteen years later in his final essay on Machiavelli he will designate as a saying of Spinoza's. "Niccolo Machiavelli," in Leo Strauss and Joseph Cropsey, eds., *History of Political Philosophy*, second edition (Chicago, 1972), p. 274. Cf. Spinoza, *Tractatus theologico-politicus* XIX, ed. Carl Gebhardt, p. 231, 30–31.—*Der Antichrist* is one of two books of Nietzsche's that Strauss explicitly mentions and cites: IV, 17, note 52 (332). Nietzsche introduces the terms "war" and "propaganda" of Christianity or of "Christian propaganda" in the center of a treatise that, in the guise of a writing with the purpose of anti-Christian propaganda, addresses the question, What is a philosopher? *Der Antichrist* 31, *KGW* VI, 3, pp. 199–200.

59. Cf. III, 52 (163–64); III, 58 (171); IV, 43 (231).

60. IV, 9 (182–83).

dominant influence of transpolitical religion on politics and secures direct or indirect rule of the priests in the political community. Priestly rule is the most important political legacy of the "Biblical polity," which continues to have its influence in the *respublica christiana* and binds it to its origin, not only for historically contingent reasons. The criticism of the rule of priests, who trace their authority to the highest authority of revealed religion, unites Machiavelli with all political philosophers who come after him. "The chief reason why Machiavelli opposed the direct or indirect rule of priests was that he regarded it as essentially tyrannical and even, in principle, more tyrannical than any other regime. Commands which are alleged to be derived from divine authority or given by virtue of divine authority are in no way subject to approval by the citizen body however wise and virtuous." Strauss's presentation of Machiavelli's criticism of political theology brings to light the succinct political meaning of the "anti-Biblical truth" that good arms are the one thing needful.[61] Strauss does not hesitate to bring into play, at the arithmetic middle of his discussion of Machiavelli's principled opposition to the most tyrannical regime, the "classical tradition" of philosophy: "In his judgment on the rule or supremacy of priests Machiavelli merely follows the classical tradition. Plato's rule of philosophers is meant to replace the Egyptian rule of priests." Strauss testifies that Machiavelli, in a question of the greatest political significance, is of one mind with Plato and Aristotle, who is named immediately thereafter in this connection. The criticism of the rule of priests also unites Machiavelli with all political philosophers who came before him. The appearance of Plato and Aristotle—it is the first in chapter IV—immediately before Strauss's explanation of the factors that led to the historical victory of Christianity reminds the reader above all, however, that the tradition Strauss typically distinguishes with the title "classical political philosophy" did not know how to prevent the unprecedented rise of priestly rule with which Machiavelli saw himself confronted, and Machiavelli consequently might have had good reason to bring about a revision of the "classical tradition" and deviate from it in order to renew it. Actually, Strauss indicates in his genealogy that

---

61. Strauss writes at the end of IV, 10 (185): "If a government is based on divine authority, resistance is in principle impossible; the rulers have nothing to fear. On the other hand, if a government is based on arms and if the citizen body is armed and virtuous, misgovernment can easily be prevented." In the first half of the paragraph he declared: "If the fundamental alternative is that of rule of priests or rule of armed men, then we understand why Machiavelli suggested that the truth 'where men are not soldiers, this is due to a fault of the prince' is the greatest truth" IV, 10 (184).

classical philosophy not only did not prevent the triumph of Christianity but rather, without intending to, contributed to it. He takes upon himself the task of explaining, in Machiavelli's place, how Christianity, which made the world weak, achieved the development of its own power: "We must try to show how he could have accounted on the basis of his principles for the victory of Christianity." In the paragraph heading he wrote down for himself, Strauss calls the explanation he gives in paragraph IV, 11, one of the shortest and one of the few without any notes, simply "Rational account of victory of Christianity." If the weakness of the world necessitates a return to Jerusalem, the ascent of Christianity to power requires a look back to Rome. It was the Roman empire that prepared the ground for Christianity politically, morally, and strategically. "Rome had destroyed freedom and the spirit of freedom in the only part of the world in which freedom ever existed. Rome itself had become corrupt. The Romans had lost their political virtue. Roman men and especially Roman women became fascinated by foreign cults." The empire expanded the initial conditions of the "servile East" in cosmopolitan measure. "Christianity originated among people who completely lacked political power and therefore could afford to have a simple belief in morality. The severe morality preached and practiced by the early Christians created respect and awe especially in those subjects of the Roman empire who equally lacked political power." The preaching of religious humility strengthened the politically humiliated and elevated the servants over their masters. The security of faith resisted and was nourished by the insecurity of the order. Out of the weakness of the world grew the strength of Christianity. "It thus was enabled to inherit the Roman empire and *whatever* remained of the classical arts and sciences. *In this shape* it confronted and over-awed the young and vigorous if rude nations which conquered the Roman empire." The legacy of the ancients, the arts, the sciences, and, at their center, philosophy, discreetly omitted by Strauss, gave Christianity the knowledge and education to carry out its mission in all heavenly directions, the arms and instruments to establish its rule for the next millennium.[62]

Strauss follows the sketch of the historical victory that Christianity achieved with a pointed characterization of the rule it exercised during Machiavelli's time. He emphasizes "pious cruelty" as the trait in which the moderns proved themselves to have surpassed the ancients, and draws upon the expulsion of the Marranos by King Ferdinand the Catholic as a contemporary

---

62. IV, 11 (185–86), my emphasis.

example in which this trait found its expression.[63] Machiavelli's critique of "pious cruelty" serves Strauss as a starting point in a paragraph that begins with "Machiavelli" and ends with "God," in order to advance to "a deeper level of Machiavelli's argument." He returns in IV, 12 from political praxis to the religious principle, from "pious cruelty" to the "Biblical teaching" and finally to the "Biblical command"—the mention four times of "Biblical teaching" and the fourfold deployment of "Biblical command" correspond to the fourfold appearance of "pious cruelty"—which allows "pious cruelty" to appear "as a duty," that is, as pleasing to God, and gives a good conscience to the believer in the zeal of his action. "According to the Biblical teaching, love of the neighbor is inseparable from love of God whom one is commanded to love with all his heart, with all his soul, and with all his might." In his discussion of the *Discourses* in chapter III, Strauss already illuminated the connection between the obedience of faith to "the jealous God of the Bible who demands zealous love" and the political excesses of "pious cruelty or pitiless persecution."[64] Still, the core of the confrontation does not come up for discussion until chapter IV, in which the philosopher is the theme and the raison d'être of his existence is at issue. The deepest level of the argument is exposed when, in the twenty-seventh sentence of chapter IV, 12, Strauss says to himself and to us about Machiavelli: "We must try to understand what he meant by indicating that the Biblical God is a tyrant."[65] The

---

63. In the fifty-second paragraph of "What Is Political Philosophy?" from 1955, at whose end the expression "anti-theological ire" is found, Strauss likewise made clear the new quality of "pious cruelty": "Moral virtue had been transfigured into Christian charity. Through this, man's responsibility to his fellow men and for his fellow men, his fellow creatures, had been infinitely increased. Concern with the salvation of men's immortal souls seemed to permit, nay, to require courses of action which would have appeared to the classics, and which did appear to Machiavelli, to be inhuman and cruel: Machiavelli speaks of the pious cruelty of Ferdinand of Aragon, and by implication of the inquisition, in expelling the Marannos from Spain. Machiavelli was the only non-Jew of his age who expressed this view. He seems to have diagnosed the great evils of religious persecution as a necessary consequence of the Christian principle, and ultimately of the Biblical principle" (pp. 43–44).

64. III, 48 (157). See in addition III, 39 (143), III, 51 (160), and III, 54 (167). Francis Bacon, following in Machiavelli's line of succession, refers concisely to the difference between the pagan Gods and the Biblical God, and consequently between the ancients and the moderns, in *De sapientia veterum* XVIII, Diomedes sive zelus: "dii ethnici zelotypia, quod est Dei veri attributum, non tangerentur" (ed. Spedding, Ellis, Heath, vol. 6, p. 658).

65. In note 33, which Strauss appends to the twenty-seventh sentence, he refers the reader to the interpretation of *Discourses* I, 26 he furnished in chapter I, 34 (49) (see P. 42 and Footnote 32).—Numbers play a conspicuous role in IV, 12: "the Biblical God" in the twenty-seventh sentence is the sixth of altogether eleven uses in total of "Bible" and "Biblical" and the single use of "Biblical God." "Tyrant" is the seventeenth word of the twenty-seventh sentence. "God" appears in the paragraph seventeen times.

formulation Strauss chooses is evidently parallel to the task specified in the preceding paragraph: "We must try to show how he could have accounted on the basis of his principles for the victory of Christianity." Once again Strauss willingly takes on himself the task to speak for Machiavelli and in his stead to illumine what needs to be illumined. In both cases, it has to do with giving a *rational account*, alternatively a *reasoning*,[66] a presentation and a justification satisfactory to reason. In IV, 11 it concerns an event of considerable political significance; in IV, 12 it concerns a judgment of the greatest political and philosophic weight. In the thirteen sentences following the twenty-seventh sentence, Strauss supplies the justification that Machiavelli withholds. In the beginning stands the command, which is revelation, authority, which demands obedience not only in action but above all in faith and which makes thoughts, which cannot be commanded, into a sin, which makes disobedience, which thinking is, into a crime. The prelude shows that Strauss's justification has in view the central activity of the philosopher and, consequently, the necessary conflict with his nature. "The Biblical command is revealed; its acceptance is based not on reason but on authority; authority will not be accepted in the long run by many people if it cannot use compulsion 'in order to keep firm those who already believe and in order to make the unbelievers believe'; for not only actions but beliefs are demanded. To demand belief is to stamp as criminal or sinful thoughts of a certain kind which man cannot help thinking precisely because of the unevident character of what man is commanded to believe; it means to induce men to confess with their tongues what they do not believe in their hearts; it is destructive of generosity."[67] The generosity on which the Biblical command has such a destructive effect is easy to understand as the readiness of the philosopher to communicate the truth. Pointing this out confirms that the statements in Strauss's argumentation reveal their full meaning only when they are applied

---

66. Consider IV, 21 (202).

67. IV, 12, 28–29 (188). The citation Strauss uses in the first of the thirteen sentences is the only citation from Machiavelli (*Prince* VI), who is never mentioned by name in the justification. Four of the first six sentences, 1, 3, 4, and 6, begin in the same way: "The Biblical command..."— Cf. Thomas Hobbes, *Leviathan* IV, ch. 46: "There is another error... which they never learned of Aristotle, nor Cicero, nor any other of the heathen, to extend the power of the law, which is the rule of actions only, to the very thoughts and consciences of men, by examination, and *inquisition* of what they hold, notwithstanding the conformity of their speech and actions. By which, men are either punished for answering the truth of their thoughts, or constrained to answer an untruth for fear of punishment." "... to force him to accuse himself of opinions, when his actions are not by law forbidden, is against the law of nature; and especially in them, who teach, that a man shall be damned to eternal and extreme torments, if he die in a false opinion concerning an article of the Christian faith" (ed. Michael Oakeshott, p. 448).

to the philosopher. That the statements hold for the philosopher in the highest measure gives the argumentation its particular stringency and its immunity from historical contingencies of every kind, since they are grounded in the self-knowledge of the philosopher. Thus, the philosopher knows how to explain that which remains for the obedience of faith an article of faith, which rests upon a deeply unsettling mystery: that and why man, confronted with the command of the Biblical God, must become disobedient. "The Biblical command cannot be fulfilled: all men are sinners; the universality of this proposition proves that all men are necessarily sinners; this necessity must derive from a disproportion between the command and man's nature or original constitution." Despite the discrepancy between the Biblical command and nature, in which the rebellion against the God of revelation has its basis, and notwithstanding the Biblical teaching that disobedience to and estrangement from God are in themselves absolute misery, obedience of faith is compelled to insist that in addition rebellion as a crime has to be punished. However, a crime against the holy God demands an eternal, infinite punishment. "The God of Love is necessarily an angry God who 'revengeth and is furious' and 'reserveth wrath for his enemies,' a consuming fire, who has created Hell before he created man, and the fire of Hell is reflected in the fire with which the enemies of God are burned at the stake by faithful men."[68] With the jealous God, the center of Biblical religion has been reached. With the appearance of hell, which he introduces in the last of his thirteen sentences, Strauss, deviating from Machiavelli,[69] makes vivid the connection between the Biblical teaching and pious cruelty. The political-theological context, which is illuminated by the reflection of the fire in which the enemies of God burn at the stake, which their persecutors prepare for them, is the spectacular concluding point of Strauss's justification. It is, however, not its most important aspect. What proves far more important is its yield for the philosophic argument of Natural Theology.

The argument of Natural Theology is not developed in *Thoughts on Machiavelli* in one context, but instead is presented in pieces, which the reader, if he wants to understand it, has to put together himself. Consequently, the argument remains his work. Strauss avails himself of a device of his predecessors Farabi and Machiavelli when he distributes and disperses statements

---

68. IV, 12, 31 and 40 (188), sentences 4 and 13 in Strauss's justification. The citation in sentence 13, the second and last that Strauss uses in the argument, comes from Nahum 1: 2. In the translation of the King James Bible, the complete verse reads: "God is jealous, and the Lord revengeth; the Lord revengeth, and is furious; the Lord will take vengeance on his adversaries, and he reserveth wrath for his enemies."

69. "he never mentions hell" I, 19 (31).

and clues in such a way that their peculiar force does not unfold until they are known and considered in their cohesiveness.[70] For this reason the reader of Strauss's thirteen sentences does not encounter in IV, 12 the decisive attribute of Natural Theology, wisdom. He must wait patiently until the end of the thirteenth paragraph. There for the first time Strauss refers to wisdom, *in statu negationis*. Its sole preceding appearance in chapter IV was the threefold reference to the "wise of the world," who reject "revelation and the characteristic teachings of revelation." In the next to last sentence of IV, 13, we read, then: "a punishment for sin which compels men to sin still more ... does not appear to be wise." A judgment obviously relevant for the core of the conflict that Strauss dealt with in the preceding paragraph. The last sentence underlines this backward reference by recapitulating a cardinal point of the justification of the thirteen sentences: "It is then ultimately the nature of man and of man's situation which accounts for the necessity to sin."[71] The Natural Theology of the philosophers has for its subject matter the question τί ἐστι Θεός, which is coeval with philosophy. To Natural Theology falls the task of reflection on the attributes, discussion of the determinations, identification of the criteria for which the question *What is a God?* asks. It denotes an endeavor of reflection and criticism.[72] A tyrant who is not wise does not live up to the standard of Natural Theology. Owing to his lack of wisdom, the recognition of the philosophers is denied to him.[73] And insofar as he is understood as a tyrant, he loses, moreover, the support of faith. For in the justification of the thirteen sentences, two lines of argument intersect: the argument of Natural Theology, which has its peak in the attribute of wisdom, and an ad hominem argument that has in view the attributes that faith in revelation proclaims. The meeting of the two lines of argument is prepared in the central paragraph of the four chapters of *Thoughts on Machiavelli*.

70. See I, 34 (48–49) on *Discourses* I, 25 *in fine* and 26 as well as *The Prince* XXVI.

71. IV, 13 (192). The seventeenth sentence already reads: "Man is by nature compelled to sin." In IV, 13 "nature" appears nine times, "God" four times.

72. *Natural Theology* is not to be confused with *Natural Religion*, which deals with a teaching philosophers offer in order to provide the need for belief with what reason can give it. Natural Religion has its raison d'être consequently in the belief of the addressees of the teaching, while Natural Theology in contrast has its raison d'être in the self-understanding of the philosophers. On the distinction between Natural Theology and Natural Religion see the second book of my *Über das Glück des philosophischen Lebens*, especially pp. 295–96, 300, 305, 327–35, 339–43, 348–49, 362–63, 371, 406–10, 438 [*On the Happiness of the Philosophic Life*, pp. 223–24, 227–28, 231–32, 249–57, 259–63, 267–68, 278–79, 285, 314–17, 340].—Concerning the question *What is a God?*, its history and its subject matter, cf. *Die Lehre Carl Schmitts*, pp. 138–41 and 3rd edition 2009, pp. 299–300 [*The Lesson of Carl Schmitt*, pp. 86–88 and 204–5] as well as *Das theologisch-politische Problem*, pp. 45–47 [*Leo Strauss and the Theologico-Political Problem*, pp. 26–28].

73. Consider *Socrates and Aristophanes*, p. 33.

Strauss gives expression in that passage to Machiavelli's *thought* about the relationship between the Biblical writers and the Biblical God: "The Biblical writers present themselves as historians, as human beings who report what God said and did, while in fact they make God say and do what in their opinion a most perfect being would say and do; the ground of what presents itself as the experience of the Biblical writers is their notion of a most perfect being; that notion is so compelling that the 'Ought' comes to sight as 'Is'; this connection is articulated by the ontological proof; there is no way which leads from 'the things of the world' to the Biblical God; the only proof which commands respect, although it is not a genuine proof, is the ontological proof."[74] The ontological "proof" commands respect because and to the extent that it takes as its starting point the perfection of God and allows a discussion of the all-important question in light of the criteria that are demanded by the determination of perfection. The examination of the attributes that must be assigned to a being that is supposed to count as perfect in the highest sense stands in the center of the philosopher's confrontation with the claim to obedience of faith in revelation.[75] It connects the argument of Natural Theology with the ad hominem argument of philosophic dialectics, the former presenting the attributes of wisdom, of self-sufficiency, of goodness, the latter dealing with the attributes that faith ascribes to a perfect being, especially its justice, its love, its jealousy.[76] Hence Strauss draws our attention to the nerve of Machiavelli's argument when in IV, 12 he brings together the two approaches in order to unite them in a single concept and urges us: "we must try to understand what he meant by indicating that the Biblical God is a tyrant."[77] The only beings of which Strauss will say in *Thoughts on Machia-*

---

74. III, 42 (148). On the continuation of the passage, see Footnote 39.—III, 42 is the 105th of 209 paragraphs of chapters I–IV (37 + 26 + 59 + 87).

75. Concerning the consequences that follow if the attribute of existence is denied to the "most perfect being," although it is not a genuine attribute, see *Socrates and Aristophanes*, p. 143, and consider "Reason and Revelation," p. 163.

76. Cf. I, 35 (50–51) on the one hand, III, 45 (152) on the other, and see Footnote 64.

77. Some have tried to reinterpret Machiavelli's fundamental criticism of the Biblical God, which Strauss first made famous, as a compliment to the Christian God. Underlying this misguided attempt is the opinion that the term "tyrant" for Machiavelli is a term of esteem, that Machiavelli intended the transformation of the world by future tyrants and that he imagined himself as a tyrant who by means of his teaching would establish rule that to his glory would last for centuries. Machiavelli's confrontation with Christianity appears according to this opinion as an essentially historical conflict, in which one will to power opposes another will to power, one tyrant competes with another tyrant, a new order is at strife with an old order. The opinion presupposes that Machiavelli takes the *principe nuovo* to be the highest type, that he allows himself to be determined by the primacy of praxis, that he was no philosopher. Strauss's approach is entirely different. He uncovers the "enormous blasphemy" in *Discourses* I, 26 not in order to impress the

velli that for them Is and Ought coincide are "men of extraordinary virtue or prudence." By means of extraordinary virtue, grounded in their nature, it holds for them that "they cannot do what they ought not to do and they must do what they ought to do; in their case the dictates of prudence have compulsory power." The highest prudence, however, is "to set oneself the wisest goal" possible under given circumstances. The highest prudence proves itself, in other words, in the firm orientation to wisdom. There can be no doubt that Strauss's talk of the coincidence of "Is" and "Ought," brought about by the highest prudence, has the philosopher in view. In perfect agreement with the underlying argument, the philosophers also mark the concluding point of the important second section of chapter IV. Of the "most excellent men" it is attested in IV, 14 that they are not shaken by the whims of fortune; that thanks to their knowledge of the world, their knowledge of nature, their insight into necessity, they lead their life in an even temper, without hope and without fear or trembling; that they might feel regret but they sense no need

---

reader with a spectacular uncovering, but rather to make visible step by step that in his confrontation with revealed religion Machiavelli makes use of an argument that takes the claim of revealed religion seriously and rejects it with reasons. For Strauss it is a matter of thinking Machiavelli as a philosopher. That is also why he speaks in the twenty-seventh sentence of IV, 12 of the Biblical and not of the Christian God, just as in *Discourses* I, 26 what is indisputably at issue is the Biblical God.—In his last publication on Hobbes Strauss provides hints concerning the argument of Natural Theology, which in light of the second section of chapter IV become much more clear. A year after the detailed treatment and historical classification of Hobbes's political philosophy in *Natural Right and History*, Strauss begins anew in 1954 in order to address its *basis*. The central part of "On the Basis of Hobbes's Political Philosophy"—it encompasses paragraphs 16–21 (pp. 182–89), which, incidentally, are marked in the French first edition as the third of five sections of the text—is devoted to Hobbes's confrontation with revealed religion. In the middle of the section, Strauss suggests two possible approaches of Hobbes's. First (par. 18, p. 186), he treats the attempt to give a political answer to the philosophic question, i.e., to vanquish Christianity in the joint working of political sovereignty and enlightenment, to hollow out religion by the transformation of human living conditions as a whole, and ultimately to dispose of the challenge of revealed religion historically. In regard to such an enterprise of solving or circumventing the theologico-political problem, the early Strauss once spoke of a "truly Napoleonic strategy" (*Philosophie und Gesetz*, p. 21). Subsequently (pars. 19–20), he turns his view in the direction of Natural Theology, whose argument he ostentatiously omits. ("According to Hobbes . . . , if 'the things' do not supply a sufficient reason for assent, the understanding, if awake, necessarily doubts, and this doubt is not subject to the will . . ." "Hobbes argues against the possibility of revelation *also* in this way . . ." "Hobbes attempts to refute revealed religion more specifically by attempting to prove that the content of the Biblical revelation is against reason. We mention *here only* what he indicates in regard to the relation between the Biblical teaching and 'the morality of natural reason,'" p. 187, my emphasis.) The addition Strauss made in 1959, after the publication of *Thoughts on Machiavelli*, in note 2 of the essay (see Footnote 20 above), to whose significance he referred emphatically twice later, in 1964 in the German foreword to *Hobbes' politische Wissenschaft* and in 1971 in the "Preface to the 7th Impression" of *Natural Right and History*, belongs likewise within the ambit of Natural Theology.

for repentance or redemption. "Imitating nature, they will be filled with both gravity and levity but they will be free from fanaticism. They will not expect to find perfection or immortality anywhere except in works of art." In this remarkable characterization, which anticipates the concluding treatment of the "most excellent man" in IV, 81, at the end of the tenth section, we are permitted to associate the endeavor of the perfection of one's own nature by means of art, in particular the art of writing, with the *gravity* pole, and the expectation of immortal glory, which either arises or does not arise from the products of this art, with the *levity* pole. The last sentence of the section unmistakably refers back to the criticism of the Christian virtue of humility or of perfect obedience: "They will regard as the virtue opposite to pride or arrogance, not humility, but humanity or generosity."[78]

Having concentrated in the second section on the center and context of the philosophic confrontation with the Biblical teaching, Strauss turns in the third (IV, 15–25) to Machiavelli's criticism of individual doctrines, starting with conscience (IV, 15), proceeding through providence (IV, 16–19) and the immortality of the soul (IV, 19), to the creation of the world out of nothing (IV, 20), with which he connects a discussion of the range of this criticism (IV, 21–25). The opening of IV, 15, in which Strauss for the first time in chapter IV explicitly refers to Machiavelli's teaching, raises the question why Strauss, in his march through the doctrines, begins with conscience and not for example with providence, which rules the whole, or creation, which is the beginning of all things: "This is the place to survey Machiavelli's teaching regarding the conscience." Why is the prelude of the new section the right place to make conscience the theme? The obvious answer seems to be that Machiavelli's explanation of faith in revelation, as Strauss confirmed in the middle of the four chapters, presupposes "his destructive analysis of the phenomenon known to us as the conscience." Indeed, in IV, 15 Strauss provides clues relevant for that analysis. The anthropological function of good conscience, for example, which opens up for moral man the possibility of feeling satisfaction or admiration for himself. Or the prudence in the bad conscience of the Christian, who believes himself to be vulnerable to a witness with unlimited access to his innermost self and to a judge with a power of punishment that cannot be resisted. Finally, Machiavelli's denial of the cognitive significance the moderns attach to the expressions of conscience. However, it is no less true that Strauss poses fundamental questions, that he seeks in three attempts to encompass "what Machiavelli thought about the

---

78. IV, 54 (246–47); cf. IV, 1 (174). IV, 14 (192–93); for the last sentence of chapter IV, 14 cf. the twenty-sixth sentence of IV, 5 (179) and the second of the thirteen sentences in IV, 12 (188).

status of the conscience," in order to inform us: "To answer these questions, one would have to summarize Machiavelli's analysis of morality."[79] Machiavelli's "destructive analysis" of conscience cannot be treated adequately, in other words, without providing an account of his analysis of morality as a whole, which cannot be separated from it, but which Strauss defers until the second half of the chapter. The assertion of the opening, "This is the place," makes us aware, in light of what follows, that Strauss has a particular reason to invoke conscience already now in immediate connection with the argument of the second section. The logic of the sequence is discernible when we read in IV, 15: "The conscience of a man is the witness within him; this witness is in many cases the only witness to what he does and, so to speak, in all cases the only witness to what he believes." It is the dispute between belief and unbelief that connects conscience most closely with the chain of thought of the preceding section. More precisely, it is the question whether the disobedience of thought has to fear the objection of conscience at its own peril. Or whether conscience would counsel against philosophy as a persistent repetition of the Fall. The answer emerges if one applies Strauss's justification in the thirteen sentences directly to conscience, and it presupposes in itself no roundabout analysis of morality as a whole. "If man is compelled to sin," that is, if he is compelled to it by the necessity grounded, as he understands clearly, in the nature of the matter, "there is no reason why he should have a bad conscience for sinning." By placing conscience at the head of his march through the Christian and Biblical doctrines of the third section, Strauss indicates that by beginning with the innermost and ending with the most external, proceeding from the nearest to the farthest, he follows the perspective of the philosopher. The guiding point of view—at which I will have to leave it here—is the set of objections for which the philosophic life has to be prepared, the sanctions to which it can succumb, the obstacles that threaten its failure.

The criticism Strauss levels against Machiavelli's teaching concerning the subject matters discussed in the third section develops on three levels. (1) In regard to Machiavelli's denial of creation and endorsement of the eternity of the world, Strauss remarks that almost all of Machiavelli's relevant statements express mere judgments or conclusions, but do not communicate the

---

79. "We are led to wonder what Machiavelli thought about the status of the conscience: Does it belong to man's natural constitution or to the natural constitution of men of a certain type or is it the work of society, if not of societies of a certain kind? With a view to what does the conscience decide on what a man ought to do? What is the relevance of a man's condemnation by his conscience? To answer these questions, one would have to summarize Machiavelli's analysis of morality. At present we note . . ." IV, 15 (194).

reasoning that leads to them and on which they rest. In the presentation of important parts of his teaching, Machiavelli leaves out the underlying arguments. He conceals, consequently, their philosophic character. Likewise, he dims down philosophy to the best of his ability, obscures the philosopher, and veils the philosophic life. The advantages and disadvantages of this strategy will concern us more closely later. In the present case, however, Strauss goes one step further. He makes clear that Machiavelli refers to the Averroists without mentioning them by name, on the one hand, in order to make known his own position, and on the other hand, to be able, for the purpose of its justification, to have recourse to the teachings of the Averroists as a kind of available supplement of his presentation. That would be the case not only for the denial of creation, but likewise for the denial of providence and the denial of the immortality of the soul. "The fundamental tenets of Averroism were as well known to intelligent men of Machiavelli's age as the fundamental tenets of, say, Marxism are in the present age. We must turn to the books of the 'Averroists' in order to complete Machiavelli's intimations and to fill in the gaps between the seemingly unconnected denials without which his political teaching as a whole would be baseless."[80] With this pointed comment, Strauss firmly anchors Machiavelli, as it were in passing, in the philosophic tradition, knowing full well that many a reader will find his opinion strengthened that Machiavelli is a derivative thinker. Strauss's provocative contention will be productive if it induces us to fill in ourselves "the gaps between the seemingly unconnected denials." It misleads if it nourishes the belief that Machiavelli's edifice of thought presupposes the doctrines of the Averroists and without those lacks any philosophic basis.[81] Strauss does not turn subsequently to the books of the Averroists to secure that basis. Instead, in the second section he has dem-

---

80. IV, 21 (202–3). Strauss takes up in IV, 21 three of the six statements he formulated in IV, 2 (175) with reference to Savonarola, in order to characterize the "wise of the world" or the *falāsifa* or the "Averroists," and determines them as views of the Averroists, furnishing these views with his own explanations or translations: "Machiavelli draws our attention to 'those philosophers' who taught that the world is eternal, *or, in other words, that there is no efficient cause of the world*. Savonarola mentions contemporary 'worldly wise' men who assert that God is not the efficient but the final cause of the world as well as that there is only one soul in all men, *i.e., that there is no immortality of individual souls*. The men who held these views were the Averroists" (202, my emphasis). Are the three statements, which Strauss does not repeat, not specific views of the Averroists, but rather the common property of the philosophers?

81. Strauss previously indicated that Machiavelli does not even have to presuppose the "Averroist" *doctrine* of the eternity of the "world," but rather may very well with Lucretius have recourse to the eternity of "matter." See IV, 20 (201) and cf. IV, 36 (222). Consider Strauss's explanation of the teaching of the eternity of the world in Footnote 80.

onstrated *ad oculos* how the reasoning is to unfold that Machiavelli in fact cannot do without. (2) In the center of Strauss's critical interrogation stands the reproach against dogmatism or a demand for evidence that rests on a *petitio principii*. Strauss formulates it after he has attributed to Machiavelli the position that there is no evidence supporting the Biblical teaching. And he formulates it as follows: "He may be said to exclude dogmatically all evidence which is not ultimately derived from phenomena that are at all times open to everyone's inspection in broad daylight." Is what is said about Machiavelli here correct? The historical origins of revealed religions would elude an inspection that can be carried out by everyone at any time in broad daylight. As would expressions of conscience. Likewise, miracles and signs reported by tradition. Strauss reminds one in the immediate sequel of Machiavelli's effort to illuminate, by his study of Roman history, the historical beginnings and the development of revealed religion. The insights to be won in this way might not be sufficient to end the dispute over the phenomena at issue. However, the undertaking of the *Discourses* does not testify to their dogmatic denial. Something similar can be said about a critique of miracles that refers comparatively to claims about miracles at different times and places, miracles rejected by the revealed religions. Whoever believes in the greatest of all miracles, creation out of nothing, has no reason to reject any miracle as impossible. Concerning Machiavelli's attitude toward the dictates of conscience, Strauss's last word in our context runs as follows: "we become inclined to believe that, according to Machiavelli, every articulation of the dictate of the conscience needs a support different from the conscience itself. In accordance with this, traditional theology had a proper regard for the objective evidence concerning the beginnings of revealed religion."[82] (3) At the beginning of IV, 16 Strauss speaks twice of "the inadequacy of Machiavelli's argument," without communicating what the inadequacy consists in. The conclusion of the immediately preceding paragraph about conscience reads: "For the time being we suggest that Machiavelli tried to replace the conscience, or religion, by a kind of prudence which is frequently indistinguishable from mere calculation of worldly gain: 'the true way' consists, not in obeying God's invariable law, but in acting according to the times." In IV, 16 "the inadequacy of Machiavelli's argument" is

---

82. IV, 22 (203–4); cf. IV, 23–24 (204–7). For another attempt to explain the origin of revealed religion, see "Zur Genealogie des Offenbarungsglaubens," in *Das theologisch-politische Problem*, pp. 49–70 ["On the Genealogy of Faith in Revelation," in *Leo Strauss and the Theologico-Political Problem*, pp. 29–43].

not determined more closely.[83] However, at the end of the third section, in IV, 25, Strauss inserts a concise comment that is of considerable importance for every attempt to replace religion by a mere calculation of worldly gain: "Biblical religion is characterized by dissatisfaction with the present, by the conviction that the present, the world, is a valley of misery and sin, by longing for perfect purity, hence by such a noble scorn for the world and its ways as to pagans was bound to appear as hatred for the human race, and by a hope which derives from the promise or certainty of ultimate victory."[84] Does the inadequacy of Machiavelli's argument lie in not doing sufficient justice to the power of the need for security, for a security in which all the security of the world is destroyed, and to the depth of the longing for purity, for a moral order of absolute validity? A need and a longing that Biblical religion lives up to and that finds its fulfillment in faith in the Holy God?

The teaching about God is the subject of the fourth section (IV, 26–37). In it Strauss treats Machiavelli's theology or quasi-theology with constant regard to the philosophic tradition and above all to Aristotle, whom he takes up directly in the first and in the last paragraph. The twenty-sixth paragraph of chapter IV, which not only brings together Machiavelli and Aristotle but also has the God of the Bible encounter the God of the philosophers, can be considered with reason as the culmination of *Thoughts on Machiavelli*. At the same time, the paragraph, kept free of any note, is one of the most enigmatic in the book. The prelude to the fourth section places in the foreground the attitudes of humility, humanity, and magnanimity. It looks, thereby, as similarly displaced as the prelude to the third section did. For, like the latter, the prelude to the fourth section appears to begin a discussion that belongs to the second half of the chapter, the discussion of morality. Yet in IV, 15, with the assurance that "This is the place," Strauss drew attention especially to the "displacement" whose perception opened the way to the actual agenda, while now he presupposes that the reader has been warned and pays attention to the particular place in order to pose the question of the decisive point of view. "The peculiar difficulty to which Machiavelli's criticism of the

---

83. In IV, 16 Strauss contrasts Machiavelli's positions almost throughout with those of more recent theology, a comparison that works in favor of Machiavelli. In the center stands the following contrast: "Recent theology tends to solve the difficulty inherent in the relation between omnipotence and omniscience on the one hand and human freedom on the other by reducing providence to God's enabling man to work out his destiny without any further divine intervention except God's waiting for man's response to his call. Machiavelli's indications regarding providence are concerned with *that notion of providence* according to which God literally governs the world as a *just king* governs his kingdom." IV, 16 (197), my emphasis. See Pp. oo–oo.

84. IV, 15 (196); IV, 16 (196–97); IV, 25 (207).

Bible is exposed is concentrated in his attempt to replace humility by humanity." What is the measure of the peculiar difficulty spoken of in the first sentence? Does Strauss take as the measure the political purpose of Machiavelli's criticism? Does he have in view the consequences for philosophy? Does he take account of the morality of the attempted replacement? Strauss continues: "He rejects humility because he believes that it lowers the stature of man. But humanity as he understands it implies the desire to prevent man from transcending humanity or to lower man's goal." The three sentences prove no incoherence as measured by the political purpose—to elevate man as citizen, to strengthen his self-esteem, his confidence, his independence, and at the same time to oppose "pious cruelty," to guard against fanaticism, and to promote sobriety. But is the stature of man exhausted by the stature of the citizen or of the prince? And does the intention of humanizing politics demand that man be defined by humanity, a moral attitude beyond which nothing further is permitted to him? Would humility have this advantage over humanity in the end, that it points man beyond himself? Would Machiavelli's teaching, with its attempt to replace one attitude by another, thus end up lending support to the exclusion of the most rare, the satisfaction with what is suitable in general, the limitation in the face of the highest possibilities? By a sharp turn that—although it does not come unprepared given the earlier references to the "Averroists"—at this place and in its wording occasions wonder, the fourth sentence assimilates Machiavelli's criticism of the Bible to the criticism of the Bible in the teaching of Aristotle: "As for the other elements of his criticism of the Bible, it would be useless to deny that they were implicit in the teaching of Aristotle and developed by those intransigent Aristotelians who knew the Bible." The last four sentences elucidate the agreements and the difference in Aristotle's and Machiavelli's criticism of the Bible, which the first four sentences have brought into view: "Aristotle tacitly denies cognitive value to what is nowadays called religious experience. There is no place for piety in his ethics." Strauss expresses what Aristotle as well as Machiavelli left unexpressed, their denial of the cognitive significance of conscience and of the call that faith believes it hears in conscience. And readers who should have conjectured, after the first half of IV, 26, that Strauss is concerned with a weakening of the criticism, or with a defense of humility, are faced with an Aristotle who is summoned only as a more stringent critic of the highest Christian virtue: "According to him, humility is a vice. On the other hand, he identifies the virtue opposed to humility not as humanity but as magnanimity." The end, which returns to the beginning, contains the puzzle that opens up the paragraph: What is the meaning of the talk of magnanimity? The contrast between Machiavelli, who is concerned with replacing humility by humanity, and Aristotle, who positions the virtue of magnanimity against the vice of humility, seems to direct us to a difference in the moral teaching. Since the agreement in the classification of humility is emphatically stressed, the difference is apparently to be sought in the evaluation of magnanimity. Up to this point, however, Strauss has not indicated that Machiavelli fails to provide an evaluation of magnanimity, or that he denies its character as a virtue altogether. On the contrary, previously he attributed to the "most excellent men," in almost as many words, *megalopsychia* or *magnanimitas*, namely, "a proper estimate of their worth," or consciousness of their excellence. And what in our context is no less pertinent, the opposition to "humility and weakness," which he made central to his discussion of the essence of Christianity, would not be difficult to formulate as "magnanimity and strength."[85] For this reason, the talk of magnanimity in IV, 26 must have a more specific sense. It does not have to do with magnanimity or greatness of soul in general, but rather refers with the highest precision to the teaching about God. The last word of the paragraph aims at its center. For we have left out the fifth of the nine sentences: "The Aristotelian God cannot be called just; he does not rule by commanding, but only by being the end; his rule consists in knowing, in his knowing himself." In the center of IV, 26 the Aristotelian God responds to the Biblical God of the twenty-seventh sentence of IV, 12. Put briefly, the center of the center, the middle of the tripartite sentence, contains the core of the philosophic alternative to the Biblical teaching and its core, which was the subject of the thirteen sentences. The magnanimity of Aristotle shows itself in a teaching about God that does not conceal philosophy but rather points to the philosophic life. At the same time, Aristotle transforms fundamental insights of Natural Theology into a traditional doctrine, capable of being handed down to serve the philosopher as a medium of self-reflection, self-interpretation, and self-criticism.

Machiavelli's teaching about God or, more precisely, the doctrine he presents in his own name, in contrast with the doctrine of Aristotle, flows not from magnanimity but rather from humanity.[86] In his doctrine of divine

---

85. IV, 14 (192); IV, 13 (190); IV, 5 (179).

86. To paragraph IV, 26—above which he wrote as a heading: "Practically the whole criticism of *revelation* is Aristotelian—only the opposite of humility is not humanity but magnanimity"—Strauss makes the following connection in the first sentence of the next paragraph: "In order to bring out more clearly *the* difference between Machiavelli and Aristotle, we must consider Machiavelli's *doctrine* regarding God and his attributes" IV, 27 (208). And later he speaks explicitly of "Aristotle's *doctrine* of God," which had been understood in highly diverse ways: IV, 36 (221–22). In each case my emphasis.

things, the philosopher does not grant himself what befits him. He is determined by philanthropic considerations, political purposes, and strategic deliberations. This is the case both for the outlying district, the heavenly signs, which are brought up in *Discourses* I, 56, and for the citadel of the doctrine, Fortuna, which makes its great appearances in *Discourses* II, 29 and in *Prince* XXV. The reference to the "heavenly signs," which warn men of accidents of public importance, and which Machiavelli, alluding to an unnamed philosopher, links to intelligences in the air as their possible authors, is considered by Strauss within the comprehensive context of Machiavelli's opposition to the belief in the existence and punishing power of angry Gods. The interpretation, according to which the "heavenly signs" are traced to intelligences who are moved by compassion for men to announce an impending misfortune, rather than appearing as messengers of a threatening tribunal, is the example of a salutary doctrine: It calls men not to repentance but to vigilance, and thus can contribute to making men not weak but strong. Moreover, the explanation of the philosopher, which Machiavelli communicates without endorsing, consists, as Strauss emphasizes, "in entire agreement with the intention of his whole work," an intention "sufficiently revealed by his silence in both books regarding devil and hell," or rather by his silence concerning divine punishment. Since shortly before, in regard to Machiavelli's discussion of Roman religion in *Discourses* I, 11–15, Strauss established that fear of the anger of God "can be very useful," the question arises why Machiavelli opposes the belief in angry Gods so strongly that Strauss is able to see the intention of Machiavelli's whole work in conjunction with this opposition. Three reasons may be mentioned, a political, a pedagogical, and a philosophic one: Belief in divine punishment furnishes the interpreters and the representatives of a transpolitical religion a sharp weapon, of which they avail themselves for the maintenance of the "most tyrannical of all regimes," or which they are able to deploy in accordance with a "foreign power" against the political authority of the political community.[87] Weaning the "young" from the effeminizing effects of the teachings with which they have grown up concerns not only the care but equally the punishing power that these teachings ascribe to providence.[88] Finally, angry Gods do not satisfy the criteria of Natural Theology.[89]

---

87. Cf. III, 20 (111); III, 21 (112–13); III, 24 (117–19); IV, 10 (184–85); IV, 41 (229–30).
88. Cf. II, 24 (81–82) and IV, 15–20.
89. See Pp. 60–64.—See IV, 27 (208); IV, 29 (209–11). The conclusion of IV, 29 casts additional light on the political approach of genealogical reconstruction in IV, 9–11 (182–86): "Weakness is not only the effect but the very cause of the belief in angry gods."

The doctrine of Fortuna is developed by Strauss in three steps in three consecutive paragraphs (IV, 31–33). Fortuna thus takes shape in three highly diverse manifestations, which are evidently meant for three distinct addressees. Strauss's triple talk of Machiavelli's "quasi-theology" corresponds to Machiavelli's threefold doctrine. At the outset Fortuna is represented as a willing and thinking being, the only intentionally acting superhuman being whose existence Machiavelli asserts in the *Discourses*, bowing to the authority of Livy or exploiting it for his purposes. This first figure of Fortuna takes the place of the Biblical God. She elects and condemns according to her unfathomable counsel. Her scope, however, is limited to the world of men. She is, in other words, not omnipotent. Fortuna I should inspire hope, indifferent to reason, or in any case awaken more hope than fear. She has the people as addressee. In the middle, Fortuna appears as the enemy of men, whose project must be wrested from her, whose interests must be asserted against her. If she is no longer seen as a superhuman being, she can be defeated in battle. This second figure of Fortuna draws her power from the lack of virtue, prudence, and rational institutions on the part of her opponents. Like the belief in heavenly intelligences that warn men with good intention, Fortuna II is meant to incite men to vigilance, virtue, and the development of all capacities, even if the doctrinal approach seems to run to the contrary. She has the politically active, in particular the excellent ones, as addressee and embodies the truth of the maxim: Good arms are the one thing needful. In the end, Fortuna proves to be accident, on which the success or failure of an enterprise depends. The third figure of Fortuna has its efficacy in the agreement or disagreement between the capacities of an individual and his time. In herself the expression of natural necessity, she stands in for the difference between nature and historical practice. Fortuna III is able to foster insight into the impossibility of conquering one's own nature and the limitation of all practical power to shape what is given. She has the few as her addressee who, by knowledge of "the world," can achieve "ultimate superiority to every fear and every hope" or ataraxia.[90] The addressee of the third and last manifestation of Fortuna is underdetermined. It can include future princes as well as the philosophers of the future. The doctrine, which does justice to the role of chance, corresponds to the inner freedom that outstanding individuals know how to preserve both in political life and in the philosophic life. Strauss indicates the overlapping that goes together with the fundamental ambiguity of the addressee of Machiavelli's teaching when in his explication he speaks only of "excellent men"

---

90. Cf. IV, 33 (218) in connection with I, 6 (17–19).

and not of "most excellent men": "Excellent men will rise above chance. Chance will have no power over them, over their minds. While their fortune varies, they will always remain the same. The dignity of man consists, not in conquering chance, but in independence." Independence may to a certain degree be common to the prince and to the philosopher. Self-sufficiency that is grounded in contemplation and knowledge of himself distinguishes the philosopher. In Machiavelli's doctrine of Fortuna, in the triad "God," "enemy," "accident," the God of the philosophers has no place. Therefore, it is a matter of a "quasi-theology." The threefold doctrine gives men a differentiated orientation for their action and their attitude toward the fundamental character of their existence, exposedness. And it serves the protection of the philosophers. But it offers the philosophers only a limited possibility of self-understanding. Strauss has this lessening in view when pointing the reader to the replacement of *magnanimity* by *humanity*. In a closely related sense, with the same intention though less enigmatically presented, at the end of his life he will put forward another replacement and close his penetrating essay on Nietzsche with the sentence formulated by himself in German: *Die vornehme Natur ersetzt die göttliche Natur.*[91]

Strauss's treatment of the teaching about God provides us with the occasion to make three observations that immediately concern the confrontation with revealed religion. (1) It is not only with a practical intention that Machiavelli's doctrine of Fortuna is decisively related to the God of revealed religion, calling upon man in his exposedness to become aware of his own power and strength. At the same time, with a theoretical intention, it seeks to respond to the assertion of unfathomability by taking it up and translating the *Deus absconditus* into the triad God-Enemy-Chance, in order to make visible the implications of the assertion of the opponent, if his appeal to unfathomability does not serve him solely to break off the confrontation concerning his claims. Accordingly, the threefold doctrine would confirm that Machiavelli did respond to the objection to his ad hominem argument about God's justice, always already brought by "thinking believers," their objection, namely, that recognizable injustice, i.e., the deviation from the moral order of the world, is "an essential part of the mystery of the providential

---

91. "Note on the Plan of Nietzsche's *Beyond Good and Evil*," in *Studies in Platonic Political Philosophy* (Chicago, 1983), p. 191. (The essay was written in the period from March 18, 1972, to February 2, 1973.)—IV, 29 (211); IV, 31–33 (213–18). The triad of God, Enemy, and Chance in Machiavelli's doctrine of Fortuna is once again the topic of discussion in IV, 35 (220–21) in connection with *Prince* XXV. In this context Fortuna II is explicitly characterized as *angry*: "Fortuna is the enemy of man. Fortuna exercises her power only when she is angry, when the times are turbulent or difficult" (221).

order."⁹² (2) With the proclamation of the divinity Fortuna, Machiavelli is following his "Bible," *Ab urbe condita*. In the first step he bows to the authority of Livy. In the second he turns against it. And in the third he frees himself from it in order to follow reason alone. This is the place to recall that in chapter III Strauss has investigated in great detail how Machiavelli used the work of Livy and its subject matter, the ancient Romans, as a model, in order to demonstrate *in corpore vili* the requirement and the possibilities of criticism of the Bible. An aspect that is of extraordinary significance in Strauss's interpretation of the *Discourses*. I limit myself to the most important point, liberation from the principle of authority, and leave it with brief hints concerning two passages appropriate for shedding light on Strauss's position regarding the theologico-political problem. In III, 50, regarding Machiavelli's questioning of the highest authority, Strauss remarks: "He acquired the right to question that authority by first surrendering to it without any reserve." In order to acquire the right to put into question the highest authority, which demands absolute obedience, or in whose name such a claim to obedience is raised, the philosopher must surrender himself without any reserve to the highest authority, i.e., he must radically take this claim to authority seriously and himself invest it with validity. He must support authority with reasons by means of his own reason. He must supply the best reasons in order to go beyond the principle of authority. Strauss indicates the twofold shape, political and theological, in which the claim of the highest authority is able to encounter and challenge the philosopher when he shortly afterward speaks of those authorities "to whom a thinker as thinker could be subject," in order to identify them for the Machiavelli of the *Discourses* as "the authority of the Romans and the authority of Moses." In III, 54, in order to make accessible to the reader a sufficient understanding of "Machiavelli's thought," Strauss explains what the principle of authority implies and what consequently is at issue in the liberation from that principle: "The principle of authority finds its primary expression in the equating of the good and the ancestral. This equation implies the assumption of absolutely superior or perfect beginnings, of a golden age or of a Paradise. The ground or origin of the perfect beginning is the supremacy of the Good or of Love, or, as we might also say, the rule of Providence. The origin of evil is a fall. Progress is return, betterment is restoration." Subsequently, clarifying his statement concerning the criticism of the highest authority in III, 50, he holds that the "comprehensive theo-cosmological scheme" that he has just outlined must

---

92. Cf. IV, 16 (197) and IV, 31 (214–15).

be rendered more precise and narrowed down "in order to become salutary." The scheme must be reduced to the concrete authority that can raise a claim to validity. In the case of Machiavelli this means to the authority of the Romans and the presumed return to them, or to the authority of Moses, or to the authority of Livy: "Bowing to the principle of authority is sterile if it is not followed by surrender to authority itself, i.e., to this or that authority. If this step is not taken one will remain enmeshed in the religious longing or the religiosity so characteristic of our centuries, and will not be liberated by religion proper."[93] (3) Machiavelli's doctrine of Fortuna is a doctrine of disillusionment. According to its inner threefold articulation, and no less in regard to its answers. It disillusions the longing for purity, since it rejects belief in a moral world order. It disillusions the need for security, since it rejects the belief in an intention that is the origin of the whole, that rules it and cares for all its parts, as well as the belief in a goal to which the whole is directed and in which it finds its support. At the same time, it disillusions the hope of being able to control chance, which is bound up with belief in Gods,[94] but also with the thoroughgoing intelligibility of the world. The fundamental movement of thought, which Strauss confirms in conclusion in IV, 36, from God through Fortuna to chance understood as nonteleological necessity, leaves no doubt that Machiavelli does not presuppose the doctrines of the Averroists or of the Aristotelians as the basis of his edifice of thought.[95]

The section on the teaching about God begins and ends with Aristotle. If the prelude in IV, 26 stands for Strauss's "gravity," the conclusion in IV, 37 illustrates Strauss's "levity." Strauss makes *La vita di Castruccio Castracani da Lucca* into the subject of a virtuoso interpretation that corroborates the teaching of Machiavelli he has gleaned from the *Prince* and the *Discourses*.[96] In the center of the interpretation stand thirty-four sayings,

---

93. III, 50 (158) and III, 54 (165–66). For this consider Strauss's discussion of what he calls the "Tacitean subsection" of the *Discourses* (III, 19–23) in III, 51–53, which is relevant for the overcoming of the principle of authority and develops the argument that underlies the two passages in III, 50 and III, 54.

94. Men are "anxious to foresee what is unforeseeable either in itself or for them. For this purpose they as it were postulate beings of superhuman perfection which can predict to them the future; once they believe that there are gods who can predict to them their future good and evil, they readily believe that those gods cause their good and evil. They thus arrive at making foreseeable the unforeseeable and at transforming the simply unintended into something intended." IV, 34 (219); cf. "An Untitled Lecture on Plato's *Euthyphron*," *Interpretation* 24, no. 1 (Fall 1996): 18. (The lecture was written at the beginning of the 1950s and delivered at St. John's College, Annapolis, in February 1952.)

95. IV, 34 (218–20) and IV, 36 (221–23).

96. The first sentence reads: "Machiavelli has indicated his *fundamental thought* also in his *Life of Castruccio Castracani*," IV, 37 (223), my emphasis.

which Machiavelli places in the mouth of the hero of his biography. Thirty-one of them Strauss traces back to sayings of philosophers transmitted by Diogenes Laertius. Strauss's analysis exposes a core in the arrangement of the sentences, constituted by a saying of Aristotle's surrounded by two utterances in each case, to the left and to the right, of Bion, a pupil of Theodorus and Theophrastus (numbers 17–21). On one side of the group of five stand eleven utterances of Aristippus, a pupil of Socrates, on the other side fifteen utterances of Diogenes of Sinope. The importance of Aristippus and Diogenes, who shared "an extreme contempt for convention as opposed to nature," and the prominent placement of Bion, who was "so shameless as to behave like an atheist," Strauss refers to as an "ironical but not misleading expression of Machiavelli's innermost thought." He concludes: "That expression is not misleading since it points to a thought at the core of which Aristotle is kept in bounds or overwhelmed by Bion and the periphery of which consists of a shocking moral teaching." Strauss takes all precautions in order not to shock anyone and nevertheless to make explicit that in the innermost core of Machiavelli's thought we encounter Aristotle. A brief exchange of words ascribed to Aristotle, which makes no reference to any Aristotelian doctrine but simply reflects the superiority of the philosopher, suffices for Strauss to draw our attention once again to the most important common feature that links the thought of Machiavelli with the thought of Aristotle. We have reason to determine the vanishing point of this common feature as the God of the philosophers.[97]

The philosopher maintains his presence even in the comparatively short section that treats religion in an immediately political respect and completes the first half of chapter IV. In the center of IV, 38–42 Strauss calls to mind the political interest the philosophers have in the establishment and defense of *libertas philosophandi*, by returning to Machiavelli's praise of the "golden time" under the Roman emperors from Nerva to Marcus Aurelius, in which "perfect freedom of opinion" ruled. Already in I, 22 Strauss showed the hyperbolic praise of the non-Christian emperors that leaves out the restrictions on which every regime must insist, in order to present what great significance Machiavelli bestows on "freedom of thought or of discussion" and how Machiavelli indicates to the reader the rarity of this freedom, which was not to be found in his time. In IV, 40 he does not repeat the specification of the general "freedom of opinion" as the "freedom of thought or of discus-

---

97. IV, 37 (223–25).

sion" pertaining to the philosophers in particular. Instead, when he speaks of the "five good emperors," he now calls Marcus Aurelius a philosopher.[98] Not only does he thus explicitly maintain the presence of the philosopher in the group of five, IV, 38–42, but more precisely he brings the question raised at the center—whether in a political community the fear of God can be replaced by the fear of a virtuous prince—implicitly into conjunction with the question of the wisdom and humanity of the philosopher, who makes it his task to become a prince or a teacher of future princes in order to establish a genuinely political rule.[99] The question whether the fear of God can be replaced by the fear of a prince without political damage cannot be answered either by reference to the philosopher-emperor Marcus Aurelius or by an anticipation of the "enlightened despotism" of a Frederick the Great. Neither the Roman philosopher from Machiavelli's "golden time," nor the Prussian king who authored an *Antimachiavel* before he assumed the throne, ruled over a people in which the fear of God and piety played no role. Both incidentally were at first princes owing to the belief in the legitimacy of their coronation.[100] The answer rests all the more on the more far-reaching question of whether religion is politically dispensable. And this is even more the case for the question, which underlies the two others, whether politics has the means to overcome religion. Religion and its political significance are not exhausted by the fear of God. The fear of God, which for its part can be traced back to a more deeply rooted fear, goes together with a reverence and devotion, no less deeply rooted, which are directed to something higher and nobler than the individual is capable of, something absolutely valid and permanent.[101] Machiavelli obviously takes this into account when he declares religion to be indispensable in the case of the republic. The republic demands belief in the common good, which is to be realized in it. Its well-being is based on the commitment of the citizens and dependent on the

---

98. Strauss uses *philosopher* within the fifth section only this one time in IV, 40 (227). Consider the sequence "Marcus Aurelius," "the philosophic Marcus Aurelius," "the philosopher Marcus Aurelius," in I, 22 (33); III, 52 (163); IV, 40 (227). Cf. *Il Principe* XIX, which contains the one mention of *filosofo* in the book.

99. IV, 40 marks the last link in a chain of argument that reaches back over the pivotal point IV, 26 to IV, 12. The triad IV, 12, 26, 40 is separated and connected by intervals of 13 paragraphs in each case.

100. Cf. III, 52 (163) and consider III, 32 (133).

101. Strauss grasped both roots in the formulas *Timor fecit deos* and *Amor fecit deos*. See his treatment of the question *What is a God?* in the letter to Seth Benardete of January 22, 1965, reproduced unabridged in *Das theologisch-politische Problem*, p. 81 [*Leo Strauss and the Theologico-Political Problem*, p. 50]. Cf. IV, 25 (207) and Pp. 67–68.

reputation of the representatives of the political class for acquiring glory and honor in service to the republic. If Machiavelli holds that, in the case of the principality, the fear of God can be replaced by fear of a prince of outstanding virtue, at the same time he makes emphatically clear how important it is for the princes to guard the appearance of being religious. Or should the advice to political actors to maintain the religious semblance be provisional and be valid only for as long as religion still has power over men? In other words, did Machiavelli believe, regardless of the assurance of the indispensability of religion in republics, and despite the dictum of its periodic renewal, which occurs two or three times in 5,000 or 6,000 years (*Discourses* II, 5), that religion could be overcome? And was he of the opinion that it should be overcome? Strauss approaches these questions indirectly. He touches upon them when in conclusion he treats the question of the utility of religion for "the people," on the one hand, and for "the great" on the other.[102] "The people, in contradistinction to the great, make very modest demands on their rulers; they merely desire that their lives, their small properties and the honor of their women be respected. Yet *as human beings* they are necessarily dissatisfied with what they possess more or less securely. Being by nature compelled to crave a satisfaction which is impossible, they will be fundamentally in a situation no less desperate than that in which the Samnites were"—who sought refuge in religion—"when they longed for independence after having suffered many disastrous defeats. The great no less crave a satisfaction which is impossible, but wealth, pre-eminence and glory supply many comforts of which the many are necessarily deprived." Would the power of religion over the people dwindle if the people were freed from their "desperate" situation and politically strengthened? And does the first of the three comforts, with which the great console themselves while "the many are necessarily deprived" of them, show the way to completely break the power of religion? How, if wealth—in a certain sense also glory[103]—does not have to be withheld from the many? What if one were to succeed in "pushing back" ever further "the boundary of nature," according to the promise of the nineteenth century, to create a society of affluence, to bring about a realm of universal freedom? Assuming that the imagined process were successfully carried out,

---

102. In the first sentence of IV, 42 Strauss asks "whether Machiavelli was convinced that religion fulfills an important function." He asks further "whether according to him religion is more than a necessary consequence or product of the mind of 'the vulgar'—an enormous rock which cannot be removed or split, which is useless and with which one must reckon." He continues: "This doubt however goes too far. Since according to Machiavelli the locus of religion is the multitude, one must consider his opinion of the multitude or the people" (230).

103. Cf. III, 30 (130).

that it were to manifest itself in a never-before-seen expansion of production and consumption, commerce and participation, would it give reason to expect that religion, starved out and enfeebled, would finally die? Such a belief would stand in opposition to Strauss's indication of the longing for a satisfaction that is impossible, a longing that affects "the people" as well as "the great," since its unfulfillability is inherent in the human condition.[104] But let us return from these historical excesses of imagination to Machiavelli's sober diagnosis. In his contrasting consideration, Strauss arrives at the result: "Society would be in a state of perpetual unrest, or else in a state of constant and ubiquitous repression, if men were not made incorrupt by religion, i.e. if they were not both appeased by religious hopes and frightened by religious fears."[105] For political wisdom, therefore, not the overcoming but rather the regulation of religion is on the agenda. The attempt to transform transpolitical religion into a civil religion, or to constrain revealed religions by a Natural Religion, in any case to subject the ruling religion to political rule. The intention to help establish the primacy of politics over religion Machiavelli has in common with his successors and his most important predecessors.

---

104. If theoretical reason should combine the expectation of a final refutation of the claim to truth of faith in revelation with the prospect of a historical overcoming of religion, the expectation would be discernibly misguided, i.e., independent of the result of the historical experiment it would be unfounded. The objection in principle, made in the name of the omnipotent God of revealed religions, against the right and the necessity of philosophy is in need of an answer from philosophy, even if that objection were to fall silent in history, even if in the present it is put forward only indistinctly or not presented at all. See Footnote 77.

105. IV, 42 (230), my emphasis.

III

The renewal of philosophy is the reason Strauss puts the problem of Machiavelli on the philosophic agenda in the closest proximity to the problem of Socrates. At the same time it is the unifying point where the two problems meet. The renewal that a long tradition associates with the name "Socrates" defended philosophy against political-theological attacks and introduced philosophy into political communities by ascribing the highest virtue to the philosophic life, by giving it the reputation of what is pleasing to the Gods, if not of what is divine, and by making it appear to the citizens as worthy of reverence. The renewal that goes back to Machiavelli protected the philosophic life by concealing it as far as possible and by forging strategic alliances in order to subdue its most powerful enemy. Instead of calling for philosophizing and praising philosophy, it gave the impression that philosophy stands in the service of political humanitarian purposes and gains its justification from its social utility. One can bring the problem of Socrates and the problem of Machiavelli into two concise countervailing formulas, that essentially private philosophy comes to be a public power, which by means of its universal claim and subversive effect undermines the political communities and finally delivers them to an enemy takeover, and that the reestablishment of politics succeeds only at the price of an obfuscation of philosophy. These formulas express, in a first approximation, that the problem of Socrates was an integral part of the problem with which Machiavelli saw himself confronted. For Machiavelli's problem remains insufficiently determined as long as one has in view only the altered situation that the rule of revealed religion created. The irruption of revealed religions is the most massive fact that separates Machiavelli historically from Socrates. Yet the Socratic turn to political philosophy, which Plato and Xenophon put to work,[106] founded a tradition that, with all the metamorphoses it underwent, contributed not inconsiderably to Machiavelli's altered situation. Beyond the repercussions of the political tectonics already mentioned, the tradition had concepts and doctrines at the ready that Christianity knew how to use as

---

106. Strauss makes this aspect of the problem of Socrates explicit when, in *What Is Political Philosophy?*, he says of Socrates: "Classical political philosophy . . . *was originated* by Socrates," while regarding Machiavelli he asserts: "The *founder* of modern political philosophy *is* Machiavelli" (pp. 38 and 40, my emphasis). Cf. the two openings of *Socrates and Aristophanes* (p. 3) und *Xenophon's Socratic Discourse* (Ithaca, 1970, p. 83): "Our Great Tradition includes political philosophy and thus seems to vouch for its possibility and necessity. *According to the same tradition*, political philosophy was *founded* by Socrates." "The Great Tradition of political philosophy was *originated* by Socrates." (My emphasis.) Consider *Socrates and Aristophanes*, p. 314.

weapons and instruments in order to establish and solidify its rule over the centuries. Machiavelli responds to this, for instance, by conspicuously avoiding any talk of the soul and immortality, of contemplation or the highest good. The philosophic tradition needed a critical revision, with regard to both the political consequences and the philosophic conclusions to be drawn from dealing with its teachings and experiencing its implications. This was the case above all for the Aristotelian branch of the tradition. With its easily comprehensible distinction between independent spheres of acting and knowing and a doctrinal edifice as extensive as it is elaborate, which apparently could be disengaged without difficulty from the philosophic life, it proved to be in considerable measure historically adaptable. The Aristotelian presentation of the *bios theoretikos*, which gave the philosophic life an unpolitical, in the precise sense pre-Socratic appearance, was assimilated by the teachers of the church to the Christian *vita contemplativa*. In it and in the cloisters, which were instituted for its regulation, the theoretical life was supposed to find its fulfillment and perfection. In such a condition there were good reasons for concealing the philosophic life and protecting it from confusion with a life that is based on obedience and breathes piety. The exhortation to the *vita activa* and depreciation of the *vita contemplativa* serve the same purpose. Access to the philosophic life is made difficult. All should be diverted from it and kept at a distance. With the exception of philosophic natures.

Thoughts on Machiavelli demonstrates *ad oculos* that the problem of Machiavelli poses extraordinary challenges but does not make the ascent to philosophy impossible. Strauss's "observations and reflections" give an unrestricted view of a philosopher who gives absolute priority to knowledge, who is moved from within by the pleasure of thinking, who sees the common good in nothing other than in truth. The primacy of knowing and comprehending gets expressed in an as it were "inhuman detachment or neutrality" of the political adviser, an inhumanity that must disturb the great majority of his readers. The particular attention of the author is directed to those readers among the young who share with him the "primarily theoretical interest" not only "for the time being," and of whom he can therefore expect that they will understand what belongs to the *gravity* and what to the *levity* pole in his life. They will know how to estimate correctly, regarding the "enterprise" that will be the basis for his glory, what meaning it has for his thought and teaching, i.e., what purpose it serves, before and after it has been historically realized.[107] The briefly recapitulated view of the philosopher designates the

---

107. IV, 69 (266); IV, 73 (274); IV, 78 (282–84). Introduction, 9 (13); I, 35 (50); II, 20 (77); II, 23 (80); II, 24 (81–82). See the interpretation on Pp. 36–45.

highest perspective that engages the problem of Machiavelli. It allows one to consider from a single point of view both the challenge to which Machiavelli's innovations respond and the challenge his innovations will become for future generations. Accordingly, Strauss's criticism of the founder of modern political philosophy constantly keeps in view the effects on philosophy. The widely received and generally applied formulas of the Straussian doctrine about "ancients and moderns," from "the narrowing of the horizon" to "the lowering of the standards," aim throughout at philosophy: its suppression, the reduction of its rank, the contraction of its scope, the abandonment of its claim. The same holds, as we have seen, for the replacement of magnanimity by humanity. Here it remains to add that Strauss's consideration of that replacement stands in a connection, not yet illuminated, with the orientation toward the subhuman, which he emphasizes as characteristic for Machiavelli and the moderns. The connection is below the surface in *Thoughts on Machiavelli*; for the treatment of the problem of Machiavelli, however, it is significant. It leads us back from IV, 26 to II, 21, where Strauss interprets Machiavelli's reference to the centaur Chiron in chapter XVIII of *The Prince*. The centaur, whom the ancients presented as a God and to whom they referred as a teacher of princes, is profaned by Machiavelli into a being that is half beast, half man, and that he recommends to princes for imitation. Strauss exploits the transformation of Chiron and the counsel for the new prince to use the natures of the fox and the lion for a statement as fundamental as conceivable: "The imitation of the beast takes the place of the imitation of God. We may note here that Machiavelli is our most important witness to the truth that humanism is not enough. Since man must understand himself in the light of the whole or of the origin of the whole which is not human, or since man is the being that must try to transcend humanity, he must transcend humanity in the direction of the subhuman if he does not transcend it in the direction of the superhuman. *Tertium*, i.e., humanism, *non datur*." The replacement of *magnanimity* by *humanity*, which concerns the philosopher's teaching about God, thus meant in the last analysis the replacement of the orientation toward the superhuman by the orientation toward the subhuman. Strauss follows the sentence about the excluded middle of humanism with a threefold prospect: "We may look forward from Machiavelli to Swift whose greatest work culminates in the recommendation that men should imitate the horses, to Rousseau who demanded the return to the state of nature, a subhuman state, and to Nietzsche who suggested that Truth is not God but a woman." Each of the three examples are clearly in need of explanation, since according to Strauss's judgment, Swift in the famous "querelle" is precisely not to be counted among the partisans of the moderns, and since the metaphor of the "woman" does not exactly provide evidence for Nietzsche's orientation toward the subhuman, not to mention the return Rousseau demanded to the state of nature.[108] The three authors have in common that the orientation and anchoring of their teaching is stamped by the challenge of Christianity. Concerning the anchoring, one can say that it begins at a deeper level, concerning their orientation, that it is subphilosophic. Strauss continues: "As for Machiavelli, one may say *with at least equal right* that he replaces the imitation of the God-Man Christ by the imitation of the Beast-Man Chiron."[109] The displacement of the discipleship of Christ by the discipleship of "Chiron" proves to be the *verità effettuale* of the replacement of God by beast. Machiavelli can come forward in the mask of a new Chiron. The proclamation of Christ to be the way, the truth, and the life for all who have a human face blocks Machiavelli's return to the divine philosopher.

Obfuscation is the sign of the problem of Machiavelli. The obfuscation of philosophy, which Machiavelli's innovations have for their result, and the obfuscation of the philosopher Machiavelli, which makes it difficult to envisage the core of his being. Accordingly, Strauss's central characterization of Machiavelli's enterprise culminates with the expression "obfuscation," the last word that immediately precedes his presentation of Machiavelli's teaching. The term "obfuscation" gathers and bundles together the most striking criticism in *Thoughts on Machiavelli*.[110] Considered from the

---

108. Concerning Strauss's judgment on Swift, cf. along with note 51 (309), which he appends to the statement in the text, *The Political Philosophy of Hobbes: Its Basis and Its Genesis* (Chicago, 1952), Preface to the American Edition, p. xix, *Natural Right and History*, p. 252, *What Is Political Philosophy?*, p. 25, as well as the letters to Gerhard Krüger of December 25, 1935 (not sent) and to Karl Löwith of August 15, 1946, in volume 3 of *Gesammelte Schriften* (Stuttgart–Weimar, 2001), pp. 450, 641. As for Rousseau und Nietzsche, to whom Strauss adds no clarifying notes, two hints might suffice: In "Persecution and the Art of Writing" (first publication in 1941, p. 503, note 21), Strauss philosophically summons Rousseau's state of nature in one breath with Aristotle's *Physics*, and Nietzsche's last word, as Strauss knows, appealed to the God Dionysus, whom in the same place he called a philosopher.

109. II, 21 (78), in the last sentence my emphasis. Cf. IV, 86 (296–97).

110. III, 59 (173); see P. 39. The most striking criticism in the book in the last section of chapter III is taken up and surpassed by the most vehement criticism in the book in the last section of chapter IV: " as our presentation could not help showing, *one is entitled to say* that philosophy and its status is *obfuscated* not only in Machiavelli's teaching but in his thought as well. That moral virtue is a qualified requirement of society is infinitely clearer to him than that it is a requirement of philosophy or of the life of the mind. As a consequence he is unable to give a clear account of his own doing. What is greatest in him cannot be properly appreciated on the basis of his own narrow view of the nature of man" IV, 85 (294), my emphasis. Between the two sections criticizing Machiavelli's enterprise lie the paragraphs IV, 1–81, which allow the reader to come to his own judgment whether what "one is entitled to say" counts for the philosopher or not, and in particular whether one must say, in light of the interpretation of Machiavelli's thought

highest perspective the book exhibits, the obfuscation of philosophy can nevertheless be understood as an expression of caution and restraint.[111] From the immoderation of Machiavelli's enterprise it is possible to read moderation on a deeper level. The boldness of the political man points to the moderation of the philosopher, who emphasizes in the enlightenment he initiates the practical utility of theory, professes its compatibility with society, and lays stress on its philanthropic gain. What is shocking can serve pacification, what is provocative, diversion. Political boldness and philosophic moderation can contribute equally to obfuscation. That Strauss, who does not have the reputation of ascribing moderation to Machiavelli's speech, should nonetheless acknowledge its moderation in the most important respect, namely, in the obfuscation of philosophy, appears less paradoxical if we recall that in another place, he manages to connect moderation very well with obfuscation, defining "obfuscation" as "acceptance of the political perspective" by the philosopher. The explicit correlation is, however, not found in *Thoughts on Machiavelli*, and is not discussed in connection with any modern. Strauss introduces it in the interpretation of Plato, and the effect that the speech about wine drinking in the *Laws* has on the Athenian Stranger serves as his example.[112]

Strauss's enterprise of renewal responds both to the tradition that Machiavelli founded and to the tradition that originates with Socrates and to

---

that Strauss gives in the eighty-one paragraphs, that Machiavelli is not in a position or that he is not willing to give a clear presentation of what he does and what he omits. Strauss begins the next paragraph with an example that what "one is entitled to say" could be better said and consequently brought closer to the truth: "Instead of saying that the status of philosophy becomes *obscured* in Machiavelli's thought, *it is perhaps better to say* that in his thought the meaning of philosophy is undergoing a change" IV, 86 (295), my emphasis. See Pp. 39–45.

111. "Machiavelli is justly notorious or famous for the extraordinary boldness with which he attacked generally accepted opinions. He has received less than justice for the remarkable restraint which he exercised at the same time. This is not to deny that that restraint was, in a way, imposed upon him" I, 22 (32).

112. "If the philosopher is to give political guidance, he must return to the cave: from the light of the sun to the world of shadows; his perception must be dimmed; *his mind must undergo an obfuscation*. The vicarious enjoyment of wine through a conversation about wine, which enlarges the horizon of the law-bred old citizens, *limits the horizon of the philosopher*. But *this obfuscation, this acceptance of the political perspective,* this adoption of the language of political man, this achievement of harmony between the excellence of man and the excellence of the citizen, or between wisdom and law-abidingness is, it seems, the most noble exercise of the virtue of moderation: wine-drinking educates to moderation. For *moderation is not a virtue of thought*: Plato likens philosophy to madness, the very opposite of sobriety or moderation; thought must be not moderate, but fearless, not to say shameless. But *moderation is a virtue controlling the philosopher's speech.*" *What Is Political Philosophy?*, p. 32, my emphasis. The passage belongs to the second and by far most important part of the tripartite essay. Cf. Footnote 110.

which Machiavelli responded. It takes into account the effects and consequences of both traditions, reflects on the advantages and disadvantages of obfuscation as well as ennoblement when it exposes philosophy in a way that heretofore has been unknown. After the entanglement of the traditions with one another brought in its wake an obliviousness to "what philosophy originally meant," Strauss's enterprise moves the philosophic life into the center, seeking to free it from the accretions of the tradition and to immunize it against its confusion with what does not belong to it or is incompatible with it. It gives the philosopher a new visibility by making the concept once more into a concept of distinction and by helping to provide it with concrete clarity through exemplary confrontations, whether with Machiavelli or with Socrates. In light of the dominant prejudice that excludes a return to the ancients and regards their philosophy as obsolete, it takes it upon itself not only to show that regarding what is most important the return is possible, but beyond that to awaken the opposing prejudice, that a return to the ancients and above all to the thought of Plato is needed.[113] But the return that Strauss sets in motion appropriates the criticism that his predecessors presented, and it is a highly nontraditional Plato into whose ambit Strauss enters. Finally, political philosophy, the guiding concept of the renewal, sharpens by its knowledge of the requirement for the political defense and protection of philosophy awareness of the repercussions that every public presentation has on philosophy. Prior to *Thoughts on Machiavelli*, in his dialogue with Alexandre Kojève, Strauss drew attention to the problem inherent in the "resounding success," which echoes up to the present, of Plato's defense of philosophy before the tribunal of the city. In regard to the religious and moral accommodations that Plato, Cicero, Farabi, and Maimonides decided to make in order to create respect for philosophy in the political or religious communities in which they lived, Strauss states: "Contrary to what Kojève seems to suggest, the political action of the philosophers on behalf of philosophy has achieved full success." Then he adds: "One sometimes wonders whether it has not been too successful."[114] The

---

113. In a related sense the young Strauss, on his way to an adequate understanding of "what philosophy originally meant," sought to offer a prejudice in favor of Maimonides, having explained at the beginning of *Philosophie und Gesetz*: "Maimonides' rationalism is the true natural model, the standard to be carefully protected from any distortion, and thus the stumbling block on which modern rationalism falls. To awaken a prejudice in favor of this view of Maimonides, *or rather to arouse suspicion against the powerful opposing prejudice*, is the aim of the present writing" (p. 9, my emphasis).

114. "Restatement on Xenophon's *Hiero*," in *What Is Political Philosophy?*, pp. 126–27 (written in 1950 and first published in *De la tyrannie* [Paris, 1954], p. 333). On the most important

defense of philosophy might be called too successful if its political dissemination serves as the standard. The accommodation must be judged as too successful if it robs philosophy of the sting of resistance, puts it into a condition in which it becomes an unquestioned matter of course, and leaves it vulnerable to cooptation by what is hostile to it. *Thoughts on Machiavelli* approaches the problem of the double tradition with a double strategy. On the one hand, the tradition of the moderns is subjected to an explicit criticism, for which the construction of "classical political philosophy" provides the contrasting foil, while the tradition of the ancients experiences only an implicit criticism, to which the melding of the philosophic and antiphilosophic tradition into the "Great Tradition" refers.[115] On the other hand, the recourse to the philosopher Machiavelli, which the philosophic destruction of the modern tradition demands, requires a detailed interpretation of his thought, which cannot help but bring to light what he has in common with the philosophers of the Middle Ages and antiquity. The demonstration of how much Machiavelli took over from his predecessors, or of how little they fell behind him in the knowledge and understanding of the decisive things, must by itself cast the ancients in a new light.[116] Thus *Thoughts on Machiavelli* counteracts the petrifaction of philosophy in the tradition of the moderns and in that of the ancients at the same time. Corresponding to the insight into the problem of the tradition, which comes to light in the "problem of Socrates" and the "problem of Machiavelli," is the rejection on the doctrinal level of the idea of an excellence that would be free from every defect, or of the concept of a "most perfect being" that could not be the cause of evil.[117]

Having devoted the first half of chapter IV to "Machiavelli's *thought* concerning religion," in the second half Strauss discusses "his *teaching* concern-

---

accommodation, consider the reference "Plutarch, *Nicias* ch. 23," which Strauss has follow in parentheses the mention of Plato's "resounding success."

115. The young Strauss spoke of the "absurd interweaving of a *nomos*-tradition with a philosophical tradition," "a tradition of obedience with a 'tradition' of questioning, which insofar as it is traditional is indeed no longer questioning." Letter to Gerhard Krüger of November 17, 1932, *Gesammelte Schriften*, vol. 3, p. 406. For Strauss's talk of "the Great Tradition," see II, 6 (59–60); III, 26 (120); III, 55 (167); III, 59 (173). The "Great Tradition" is pulled apart in IV, 50 (241–42); cf. III, 54 (167). The explicit criticism of the modern tradition reaches its peak in the eleventh section of chapter IV (IV, 82–87). On the implicit criticism of "classical political philosophy" cf. IV, 84 (293) and IV, 87 (298–99) in connection with IV, 10–11 (185–86). See Pp. 55–57.

116. *Inter multa alia*: IV, 26 (208) and IV, 85 (295).

117. Cf. IV, 51 (244).

ing morality and politics."[118] In contrast with what the pronouncement in III, 32 might have led one to suppose, the confrontation with the Biblical teaching no longer stands in the foreground. Instead, particular attention is paid to the philosophic tradition, and above all to the Aristotelian teaching about politics and morality. Strauss paves the way in the sixth section (IV, 43–45) when he calls to mind Machiavelli's claim that his teaching is "new," limiting the claim and sharpening it in order to establish that Machiavelli's teaching can be considered "wholly new" only in regard to morality and politics, but not to religion: "In his teaching concerning morality and politics Machiavelli challenges not only the religious teaching but the whole philosophic tradition as well." In a single stroke the whole philosophic tradition is put into question. Strauss hastens to make more precise that Machiavelli's claim would be "wholly justified" by the boldness with which he presents his teaching, that is, even if the teaching was familiar to his predecessors and they were in agreement with its positions either in part or in the whole: "that boldness as considered boldness would presuppose a wholly new estimate of what can be publicly proposed, hence a wholly new estimate of the public and hence a wholly new estimate of man." Since Strauss has just before explained, in the center of the bridge section that joins the two halves of chapter IV, that Machiavelli is "less reticent regarding morality than regarding religion," we may assume that the "wholly new estimate of man" operates within comprehensible limits. The lesser reticence Machiavelli imposes on himself in matters of morality in contrast to religion might go together with the expectation that it will not be difficult for the public to assimilate his teaching as moral and to attribute a moral intention to his enterprise as a whole. The greater boldness, which expects more of the nonphilosophers than the tradition expected of them, is cushioned by the emphasis on the practical utility of the teaching, which allows them to find their own purposes in it or their own way to connect with it. In the end, Machiavelli's rhetoric bears witness to his estimate that moral need will forge ahead, despite his public criticism.[119] At the beginning

---

118. IV, 43 (231) and IV, 45 (232), my emphasis. "Thought" and "intention" appear in IV, 43 three times and once, respectively. "Teaching" is not mentioned at all. In IV, 45 "teaching" appears thirteen times (the highest concentration of "teaching" in a single paragraph); "thought" and "intention" remain unmentioned; on the other hand, "classical political philosophy" has a threefold appearance, once accompanied by "traditional political philosophy" and once by "political philosophy of the classics."

119. IV, 44–45 (232–34). Cf. *The Political Philosophy of Hobbes*, Preface to the American Edition, p. xx.—On the estimate of the relation between religion and morality that arises from the Biblical teaching consider: "The integration of morality into religion or the subordination of

of the second half Strauss contrasts Machiavelli's claim to novelty with the claim of "classical" political philosophy to fundamental agreement with "what is generally said about goodness, that is, about moral virtue." The development of the argument in sections 7–10 will prove that the two claims from which it takes its start are in the main misleading. Machiavelli's claim gives Strauss the opportunity to correct the understanding of the philosophic tradition, and the claim of "classical" political philosophy puts him in the position to treat Biblical morality even where it is not explicitly mentioned. Sections 7–10 of the second half would deserve a no less detailed consideration than sections 2–5 of the first, to which they stand in a relationship of multifarious correspondence. We concentrate on those aspects that are of particular importance for the self-understanding of the philosopher.

The treatment of goodness and virtue, to which the seventh section (IV, 46–51) is devoted, is dominated by Machiavelli's agreement with the Socratic equation "virtue is knowledge," which Strauss already anticipates in the introduction to *Thoughts on Machiavelli* when he quotes "the words ascribed to Machiavelli" by Marlowe: "I hold there is no sin but ignorance."[120] The agreement with the Socratic tradition, which Strauss makes visible, concerns, however, not only the end, knowledge, on which virtue is based, and more precisely the insight that rules the right use of the moral virtues and vices, but also the beginning of the investigation, the point of departure it takes from the *endoxa*, starting with the "surface" of the opinions, and advancing to the contradictions that are inherent in the opinions about "goodness" and that come to light in the *logoi*, in the speeches praising the relevant actions.[121] Strauss uses the middle and most extensive part of the section for Machiavelli's complex confrontation with the common understanding of moral virtue, which found its "classical expression" in Aristotle's thesis that virtue is the middle or the mean between two defective extremes or vices opposed to one another. Strauss shows how Machiavelli, on the one hand, is able to build on the praise of the mean; thus it makes good sense to determine political freedom with common sense as a mean between tyranny and license. He shows how, on the other hand, Machiavelli can begin with the dominant belief and

---

morality to religion leads to the consequence that morality appears to be less comprehensive and hence less fundamental than religion" IV, 44 (232). See P. 50.

120. Introduction, 9 (13). In *Natural Right and History* Strauss cited Marlowe as follows: "I . . . hold there is no sin but ignorance" and then added: "This is almost a definition of the philosopher" (p. 177). The full citation, with the omission initially noted by Strauss, reads: "I *count religion but a childish toy, / And* hold there is no sin but ignorance." Christopher Marlowe, *The Jew of Malta*, Prologue of Machiavel, 14–15, my emphasis.

121. IV, 47 (236–37); cf. Footnote 17.

its contempt for the middle course of the lukewarm, who seek to evade the all-important either-or, when he opposes *la via del mezzo*. With this he hits upon the case on which for the philosopher everything depends: There is no mean between the obedience and disobedience of thought. With the example of equanimity Strauss puts before us Machiavelli's rejection of the doctrine of virtue as the right mean between two vices, and in doing so he explicates not only Machiavelli's rejection but at the same time also the meaning of Aristotle's teaching. The equanimity of the excellent or great man has for its opposite only a single vice, the vice of the weak, which manifests itself in two defects, arrogance on the one side and humility on the other. "What he means to convey can be stated as follows. The two opposite defects are merely two aspects of one and the same vice which comes to sight in opposite forms in opposite circumstances; one does not understand either defect if one does not see in each the co-presence of the other. The virtue in question on the other hand comes to sight as one and the same in all situations; it is stable and unchanging, for it is based on 'knowledge of the world.'"[122] Further stages of the confrontation with the teaching of the middle course that directly concern the philosopher are the demonstration that justice is impossible as the stable mean between self-denial and injustice, a result that brings to the fore the question of justice toward oneself, or what the philosopher owes himself in regard to his own good; and finally the orientation of life to nature, which demands an alternation between two poles, since nature is itself manifold and variable. "The true way consists therefore in the alternation between virtue and vice: between gravity (or full devotion to great things) and levity . . ." The alternation in harmony with nature, however, consists by no means "in being pushed or pulled now in one direction and then in the opposite direction; it consists in choosing virtue or vice with a view to what is appropriate 'for whom, toward whom, when and where.'" The life according to nature that does justice to the variation of challenges and the change of occasions gains its stability from the orientation toward one's own good. The alternation will, therefore, be different for different natures. In the case of a philosopher the *gravity* pole and the *levity* pole are, as we have seen, necessarily determined differently than they are in the case of a prince. But in the one as well as in the other case, insight or prudence, or what Aristotle set off as dianoetic in contrast with moral virtues, will take the lead: "That alternation is a movement guided by prudence and sustained by strength of mind, will or temper. Prudence and that strength are then always required: whereas in the case of

---

122. IV, 48 (237–38). Consider IV, 14 (193).

the moral virtues it suffices for the prince to possess the appearance of them, in the case of prudence and strength of mind or will he needs the substance. In other words, prudence (judgment) and strength of mind, will or temper are the only generally recognized virtues which truly possess the generally recognized character of virtue in general: they are themselves always salutary. Whereas the moral virtues and vices (e.g. religion and cruelty) can be well and badly used because their use must be regulated by prudence, prudence cannot be badly or imprudently used."[123]

The life according to nature presupposes the philosopher's rejection of the idols that correspond to the longing for perfect purity. The insight into the necessity of nature is incompatible with the notion of a good without mixture, without limitation, without impairment. Machiavelli's rejection is expressed in the last paragraph of the seventh section, which like the last paragraph of section 2 has for its subject matter the "most excellent men." Strauss concentrates on the idols or wishes that primarily concern the philosophers and philosophy: the teachings of the best regime, of perfect happiness that would exclude every evil, and of the universal man. Machiavelli's objection to the tradition and his conclusion, that every kind or degree of excellence is accompanied by a particular defect or specific evil, Strauss explicates using a figure that can count as Machiavelli's counterpart to the philosopher-king and with which—if we want to follow the most prominent reading of *Thoughts on Machiavelli*—Machiavelli identified himself: "The excellence of a man who is the teacher of both princes and peoples, of the thinker who has discovered the modes and orders which are in accordance with nature, can be said to be the highest excellence of which man is capable. Yet this highest freedom cannot become effective if the thinker does not undergo what to him must be the most degrading of all servitudes. Or if, prompted by levity, he would derive enjoyment from undergoing that servitude, he would lose the respect of his fellow men." If Machiavelli as thinker enjoys the highest freedom, but is able to communicate the yield and the experience of this freedom in no other way

---

123. IV, 50 (240–42). Strauss immediately continues: "We must emphasize the fact, which Machiavelli has deliberately obscured by his usage, that his doctrine of 'virtue' preserves the relevance, the truth, the reality of the generally recognized opposition between (moral) virtue and (moral) vice. This fact affords perhaps the strongest proof of both the diabolical character and the sobriety of his thought. This is not to deny but rather to affirm that in his doctrine of 'virtue' the opposition between moral virtue and moral vice becomes subordinate to the opposition between another kind of excellence and worthlessness. Machiavelli expresses the difference between moral virtue and certain other kinds of excellence most simply by distinguishing between goodness (i.e. moral virtue) and virtue or by denying to moral virtue the name of virtue" IV, 50 (242). Cf. introduction, 9 (13).

than in the guise of servitude; if he makes himself into a teacher of princes and peoples in order to speak to his equals; if he laughingly condescends "to play the fool";[124] if in the end he is concerned not with the glory of the world but rather with the judgment of those who seek to understand him as he understands himself, then that changes nothing in Machiavelli's understanding of excellence in general. What changes is only the understanding of his excellence in particular.[125]

The highest excellence comes to light in the coincidence of "Is" and "Ought." For those who possess "extraordinary virtue or prudence" the following holds: "They cannot do what they ought not to do and they must do what they ought to do." The command of prudence has for them compulsory power. The ought that the highest prudence or insight commands is admittedly no Pure Ought or Universal Law. It is measured by "the wisest goal" possible under the prevailing circumstances. It presupposes knowledge and judgment of what necessity allows in the best case and demands in the given case. The highest excellence, which is oriented toward wisdom, is determined by the highest insight. It encompasses not only insight into the necessity that underlies all knowing, but also insight into the necessity that makes one capable of virtue, insight into one's own nature, which in its particularity is not at one's disposal. Strauss stresses emphatically that "grandeur of mind and will," the premoral or transmoral quality that differentiates "great men" from the rest of humanity, is a *gift of nature*. The "great men" apparently include the "excellent men," spoken of elsewhere, or they stand in for them.[126] What Strauss says about Machiavelli's "virtue in the highest sense" can with even greater right be said of the highest virtue, and what holds for the excellent holds all the more for the most excellent. At the peak of the eighth section (IV, 52–60), which investigates freedom and necessity, Strauss offers a hint regarding the ultimate basis for the differentiation of philosophers and nonphilosophers. Strauss will refer to this ultimate basis when, at the end of the book, in a united front with Machiavelli against the idealistic contention of a radical freedom or of an Archimedean point outside of everything given, he asserts "the natural basis of the radical distinction between philosophers and non-philosophers."[127] The eighth section, which, like the corresponding third section that began with conscience, begins with *liberum arbitrium*,

---

124. III, 55 (168).
125. IV, 51 (242–44). Consider III, 54 (165–67) and IV, 25 (207). See Pp. 43–45.
126. See IV, 33 (218) and Pp. 72–73, furthermore IV, 70 (269). Cf. the talk of "great men" and the characterization of Goethe as "great man" in IV, 1 (174).
127. IV, 86 (297–98). Consider the two last sentences of the book (IV, 87).

explicitly maintains that the particular nature of a man, far from being determined by his choice or free will, determines this man, his choice or his "free will." If Machiavelli says "we cannot change ourselves," he knows that the qualities that constitute our particular nature in any given case are partly inherited, partly the result of education, or that nature is modified by habituation. "Still, innate qualities are of decisive importance."[128] In the three paragraphs that immediately follow the peak (IV, 55–57), the attribute *wise* does not appear. These paragraphs deal with men in general, who can be induced to act justly, operate well, or work industriously by external or externally imposed necessity, by fear and hunger, by the terror of nature and the compulsion of the laws. The antagonism between fear of death and ambition or vanity, which Hobbes chooses as the starting point for the order he designs, plays a prominent role. Wisdom returns after Strauss has turned to the "virtuous founders," who act from inner necessity, whether driven by "their natural desire for the common good," or led by the prospect of finding their happiness in "the glory of the world" that their work will earn for them. With the founders, who are to set ends for themselves and others on a large scale and for the long run, choice appears once again in the foreground. The "wise or honorable choice," which "is the prerogative of the prudent and the strong," indicates a higher degree of freedom of action, without thereby leaving the realm of necessity.[129] For insight remains indispensable for the right choice and the final completion of the work for which the great take risks, "animated by ambition or love of glory." "Only men of supreme virtue or prudence are compelled by their desire for glory to operate in the most perfect manner. What they recognize as wise or honorable acts on them with the same compulsory power with which only fear of great, manifest and imminent evils acts on most men." Like the overlapping talk of "great men" and "excellent men," the twice-used formulation "wise or honorable" in IV, 58–59 draws our attention to Strauss's simultaneous treatment of two forms

---

128. IV, 54 (246–47).

129. "Necessity and choice are related to each other as the low and the high." ". . . since there is no perfect good, to choose means at best to choose a good mixed with evil. To choose means therefore in all important cases to take a risk and to trust in one's power to keep under control the evil which goes with the good chosen. The weak lack that trust . . ." "While the desire for glory in its highest form acts with compulsory power, it can be identified with choice or freedom for the following reasons. The compulsion stemming from the desire for glory cannot be imposed on a man as can be the compulsion stemming from fear; the former compulsion arises entirely from within. The man driven by the desire for glory is guided by a pleasing prospect rather than compelled by a harsh present . . ." IV, 58 (250–51) and IV, 59 (251).

or types that are not the same and must be distinguished by the reader. What appears as honorable to the excellent might very well stand in conflict with that which the most excellent recognizes as wise. Whoever elevates honor to the rank of a "necessity" by which he is determined becomes enmeshed in a profound dependence. This has to be kept in mind when Strauss continues: "The necessities, with a view to which men of supreme prudence as such necessarily act, are not so much present as foreseen necessities." When he more precisely contrasts necessities that are known as such with false opinions, with belief or superstition;[130] and when he finally maintains that for Machiavelli, not success but rather the wisdom of an enterprise deserves praise and admiration. Not the smallest part of the wisdom of an enterprise consists in the recognition of the necessity of chance.[131]

The critique of morality in light of the politics of the common good is the theme of the ninth section (IV, 61–68). It is the third section in a sequence that Strauss devotes to the analysis of moral virtue, and the third and last that takes Aristotle as its starting point using almost the very same words.[132] Under the impression given by the opening, which presents the moral-political doctrine of Aristotle with impressive simplicity, we are tempted to take the problem of politics and man to have been in principle solved. Human nature, virtue, and the best regime seem to work together so harmoniously that nothing suggests a conflict between society and the individual, or a necessary dissonance between the political community and the

---

130. "The two kinds of necessity which make men of the two kinds operate well are naked necessities, necessities known as such . . . Only the known necessity compels men to make the supreme effort, not to trust in Fortuna but to try to subjugate her. If men do not know the necessity in question or are under the spell of false opinions denying it, that necessity is counteracted by the compulsory power of ignorance or false opinion; this composite necessity—a wrong kind of 'middle course'—prevents them from operating well" IV, 59 (252). Consider III, 25 (120).

131. IV, 60 (253).

132. "The common understanding of virtue had found its classic expression in Aristotle's assertion that virtue, being the opposite of vice, is the middle or mean between two faulty extremes (a too little and a too much) which are opposed to each other" IV, 48 (237). "The common understanding of goodness had found its classic expression in Aristotle's assertion that virtue is the habit of choosing well and that choosing well or ill as well as the habits of choosing well or ill (the virtues or vices) are voluntary: man is responsible for having become and for becoming virtuous or vicious" IV, 52 (244). "The common understanding of goodness had found its classic expression in Aristotle's assertions that virtuous activity is the core of happiness for both individuals and societies, that virtue or the perfection of human nature preserves society, and that political society exists for the sake of the good life, i.e., of the virtuous activity of its members. In order to fulfill its natural function in the best way, the city must have a certain order, a certain regime: the best regime" IV, 61 (253–54).

philosopher. This beautiful semblance rests above all on the opening sentence, which speaks of "virtue" and "virtuous activity" without differentiating the moral virtues from the virtues of thought. The correction is not long in coming, for a few sentences later we learn: "the best regime *strictly understood* exists very rarely, if it has ever existed, although it is of its essence to be possible." The beginning of the section sets the tone for what follows: Machiavelli's criticism holds for the exoteric teaching of Aristotle, it targets the "common understanding" that that teaching takes up and expresses. This makes it possible for Strauss to let the criticism of the common understanding in its full extent come into its own while nonetheless letting the agreement with Aristotle become visible. Thus, Strauss remarks, immediately following the classical beginning, that Machiavelli emphasizes "the fact of human badness" by contrast with "the classics," in order to emphasize for his own part that "Aristotle *teaches as clearly* as Machiavelli himself that most men are bad as well as that all men desire wealth and honor."[133] The criticism that the ninth section develops holds, against the "classic exponent of moral virtue, i.e., of the highest kind of that virtue which is *not* knowledge,"[134] that the purpose of civil society consists not in virtue or in moral goodness, but rather in the good of each particular political community. It shows republican virtue, which puts itself in the service of the common good, to be the truth of moral virtue. The latter, like the former, understands itself essentially from duty or from the subordination to something higher that appears worth subordination and worthy of devotion. On closer consideration, the purpose that virtue serves proves to be a variety of one's own good, whether aimed at directly or sought in a roundabout way. While moral goodness, however, cannot always be brought into harmony with the common good, republican virtue, or patriotism, which aims at the collective self-interest, is not subject to the same limitation, and the virtue that is knowledge is always needed for the common good. This is the case for the understanding of the political presuppositions to which moral action is bound. It is the case for the insight into the necessity of suspending the rules in extraordinary cases, which can claim validity under ordinary circumstances. And it is true for prudence in making political decisions that are fitting for the concrete situation. For in an extreme situation in which the existence or independence of the political community is at stake, the orientation to the common good can demand deviation

---

133. IV, 61 (254), my emphasis in each case.
134. IV, 64 (258), my emphasis. Cf. *The City and Man*, pp. 26–29.

from the normal rules of justice, without letting the extreme situation be determined in its singularity and the deviation from the rules be regulated in advance. When Strauss succinctly summarizes "Machiavelli's thought" concerning this point, he repeats in substance what he stated regarding the matter in *Natural Right and History* on the occasion of his explanation of the thought of Aristotle.[135] The common good, in its turn, which is the measure of justice, shows itself in the course of the investigation only according to its pretension to be a good common to all, or one in which all participate equally.[136] At any rate, it demands from the constitutive parts of the republic, the ruling elite and the people ruled, different virtues, qualities, attitudes, which correspond to their place or their task within the whole.[137] Insofar as the republic tolerates philosophers in its midst, moderation in particular will be demanded of them. To this belongs the "wise interpretation" of the moral minimum requirements of social life, which commonly, although not in *Thoughts on Machiavelli*, are designated natural law. As Strauss notes, Machiavelli is far from denying that the divorce of "those simple rules of conduct" from "their selfish end" and their elevation to the status of a universally valid, unchangeable law is "wise." He certainly holds that those rules cannot be understood as what they are if one leaves it at their "wise" interpretation.[138]

In the tenth section (IV, 69–81), the common good of politics is subjected to criticism guided by the private good. The section, whose thirteenth and last paragraph puts before us the philosopher Machiavelli in his integral shape, begins with a paragraph that recalls, as the central paragraph of the fifth section on religion did previously, the political interest of the philosopher in the freedom to philosophize. Accordingly, the field is framed within

---

135. IV, 65 (259). *Natural Right and History*, pp. 157–63, especially pp. 160–61. In the paragraphs in the middle of the book Strauss provided only a single reference in a footnote. It refers the reader to Strauss's essay "The Law of Reason in the *Kuzari*" (p. 158, note 32).

136. "since the common good requires that innocent individuals be sacrificed for its sake, the common good is rather the good of the large majority, perhaps even the good of the common people as distinguished from the good of the nobles or of the great" IV, 66 (260).

137. "Machiavelli illustrates this difference of virtues chiefly by examples taken from the Roman senate and the Roman plebs. The characteristic virtues of the senate were prudence and a calculated liberality, dispensing sparingly such goods as had been taken from enemies; also, dignity and venerability; and finally, patience and artfulness. The characteristic virtues of the plebs were goodness, contempt for the seemingly or truly vile, and religion. Goodness is then at home with the people" IV, 68 (263).

138. IV, 68 (264–65). Cf. "The Law of Reason in the *Kuzari*," pp. 136–40; *Natural Right and History*, p. 158.

which the argument advances and the ascent takes place that begins with the claim of the republic to be the custodian of the common good. Strauss has already noted the discrepancy between the claim and the actuality of the republic in the ninth section. The common good presents itself for the most part as the good of the large majority. In the best case it is conceived as the good of almost everyone, not, however, as the good of all or of each individual. Now he makes the gulf manifest in the freedom of the philosophers, for whom the golden times of the Roman emperors were favorable, whereas by contrast the model of republican virtue three centuries earlier had taken care that philosophers found no admission in Rome (*Istorie fiorentine* V, 1). The contrast between the glorious patriot Cato and an emperor in the mold of Marcus Aurelius points to the difference it makes for the philosopher whether he is facing a prince who might have understanding, greatness of mind, strength of will at his disposal, or a regime in which the common good is understood and implemented as the good of the predominant majority or almost all but in which the final say lies with the people. Strauss does not need to bring up the republic *in statu corruptionis*. He does not have to speak of excesses or aberrations. He can also pass over the death of Socrates in silence. Already in the third chapter he characterized the people as the repository of morality and religion. He determined the people as the embodiment of faith in every sense.[139] To the extent that the proclaimed public good of the republic comes to light as the particular good of one or more of its parts, even if it is the good of the common people, the balance shifts in the evaluation of the regimes. The principality gains in stature when the private good moves into the foreground. For instance, as soon as the observer looks for protection from intermediate powers, from "sects" and other social powers. His perception of the prince also changes when, in the representatives of the republic, he recognizes "princes" who work together as a body and solidify their rule. Even for tyranny it can thus be argued that it is exercised in the interest of the majority, even if it is not exercised in alliance with the people against the "great." Finally, the critical analysis of the common good of the republic by recourse to the principality and tyranny serves Machiavelli in bringing to light that the political condition as such is necessarily bound up with coercion, with the duty to obey, with injustice; that society is essentially subject to oppression; that the only natural

---

139. IV, 69 (266); IV, 66 (260); IV, 68 (262). See III, 28 (126); III, 30 (130); III, 32 (133); cf. IV, 11 (185–86); IV, 42 (230–31); IV, 68 (263); IV, 77 (282); *The City and Man*, p. 37.

good is the private good.[140] Knowledge of the natural good underlies Machiavelli's conceptions of a politics oriented toward the common good. It can be read off his paradigmatic presentation of the Roman republic, according to which the precarious public good, and in particular political freedom, rest upon the continuing conflict and unstable equilibrium between the patricians and the plebs. It shows up no less in the practical options he proposes: In a workable alliance of the philosophers with the princes for defense against a rule of the priests and in the appropriate appeal to the people for the arming of a republican order, which would foster the freedom and the self-confidence of the citizens and would in the long run benefit philosophy.[141] Machiavelli's conceptions revolve around the art of building a bridge from the private to the public good. Punishments and rewards serve to link the one with the other. "Fear of government" and "love of government," virtuously deployed and modified, are the means of this art. The royal road it travels begins with the love of glory. "The desire for glory as the desire for eternal glory liberates man from the concern with life and property, with goods which may have to be sacrificed for the common good; and yet glory is a man's own good. It is therefore possible and even proper to present the whole political teaching as advice addressed to individuals as to how they can achieve the highest glory for themselves." Putting love of oneself into service politically by means of the love of glory certainly cannot hide the fact that the reconciliation of the private and the common good can be achieved only at the price of being outside oneself, of dependence and of illusion. The longing for "eternal" glory points to this illusory character.[142] It bears eloquent witness to the fragility of every construction that the political art knows how to create. Even if it takes its point of departure from the selfish desires of the rulers and the ruled and erects its edifice on the "only natural basis of politics."[143]

140. IV, 75–76 (278–80). "Oppression, or injustice, is then coeval with political society. Criminal tyranny is the state which is characterized by extreme oppression. There is then in the decisive respect only a difference of degree between the best republic and the worst tyranny. This difference of degree is of the utmost practical importance, as no one knew better than Machiavelli. But a difference of degree is not a difference of kind" IV, 75 (278).

141. IV, 10–11 (184–85). See Pp. 55–57. Cf. *Persecution and the Art of Writing*, p. 15.

142. IV, 77 (281–83); cf. IV, 25 (207), further IV, 13 (190) and IV, 14 (193) as well as Pp. 63–64. The last sentence of IV, 77 gives expression to the substitute for "eternal glory" on which the great majority remain dependent: "Since the many can never acquire the eternal glory which the great individuals can achieve, they must be induced to bring the greatest sacrifices by the judiciously fostered belief in eternity of another kind." See Pp. 76–79.

143. In the passage in which Strauss designates the core of the "whole political teaching," in the seventy-seventh paragraph of chapter IV, he reminds the reader that Machiavelli's political

The insight into the limits of the common good of politics and consequently into the nature of political life is the presupposition for the approach to the life that is directed toward the common good in the most demanding sense, the truth. The truth is the only good that can be considered without qualification as the common good, insofar as participation in it does not hinder that of any other and one's own share does not reduce the share of anyone else. That one's own appropriation does not lessen the common good of truth does not mean that access to the truth would be good for each under all circumstances and in equal measure. What holds for every good holds for the common good in the most demanding sense: It is good for someone or for something and therefore not free from limitations or from evil. For this reason, the common good "in the strict sense" does not annihilate the distinction between private and public good. Just as little does the life directed to truth leave behind the determinations of political and unpolitical life. In short: the understanding of the common good of philosophy must incorporate the understanding of the common good of politics, which in turn includes the understanding of the necessary tension with the natural good. To make clear to the reader the integration that constitutes the philosophic life, Strauss devotes a paragraph of its own to *La Mandragola*, which provides a "supplement" to the common good of politics. The supplement, "which exists on the same level as the common good, i.e., on a level lower than the truth," is the unpolitical or solitary life, which the song at the beginning of *Mandragola* praises. On closer inspection, the unpolitical life, which in regard to knowledge of the truth Strauss explicitly places on the same level as the political life,[144] is a life of love. The love of a woman appears alongside the care for the state, or the will to rule. The polarity of *gravity* and *levity* returns. But this time Strauss does not leave it at the alternation

---

philosophy is not exhausted in the guidance of "prudent" praxis, but rather is responsible for the political defense and rational justification of "prudence" or insight as such: "*To the extent to which Machiavelli's two books are meant for immediate prudent use rather than for rendering secure the basis of prudence*, their broad purpose is to show the need for reckoning with the selfish desires of the rulers and the ruled as the only natural basis of politics, and therefore for trusting . . . in one's own virtue (if one possesses it) as the ability to acquire for oneself the highest glory and hence to acquire for one's state whatever makes it strong, prosperous, and respected. The *wise rulers* who act with a view to their own benefit will enlist the cooperation of the ruled . . ." IV, 77 (282), my emphasis. See Footnote 77.

144. IV, 79 (284). In the immediately preceding sentence, Strauss distinguishes them in the following way: "The good things of which the political common good consists or which it protects or procures are incompatible with other good things *which are even less common* than the political common good *but which give a satisfaction no less pleasing, resplendent and intense, yet more within the reach of some men than glory*." My emphasis.

between the poles: "The difference between matters of state and matters of love corresponds to the difference between gravity and levity, between the two opposed qualities, the alternation between which, *or rather the union of which*, constitutes the life according to nature. The union of gravity and levity, we suspect, is achieved, according to Machiavelli, by the quest for the truth, or for that good than which none is more common and none is more private."[145] Machiavelli's comedy offers Strauss the opportunity to show what Machiavelli does not show, to connect what Machiavelli leaves unconnected, to express what Machiavelli passes over in silence. After the digression on *Mandragola*, which is assigned a key role in the argument of *Thoughts on Machiavelli*, Strauss inspects anew the two books in which Machiavelli presents his twofold teaching, and demonstrates that the love of glory, which the *Prince* and the *Discourses* highlight, is not sufficient to understand adequately the activity to which the two books owe their existence.[146] The application of Machiavelli's doctrine to himself would result in his identifying his own good with the glory that the future holds ready for him, with the honor the public will accord him some day, or with the recognition his œuvre must earn him from the most discriminating judges. Machiavelli's reward would consist in praise and nothing more. The royal road, which rests on the longing for eternal and immortal glory, abstracts from *eros*. The abstraction from *eros* proves to be the reverse side of the politicizing of the natural good.[147] Strauss draws the line from the mythical founders through the most excellent artists and writers to the discoverer of the all-important truth for man and society, who, as the bringer of the truth

---

145. IV, 79 (285), my emphasis; cf. I, 28 (40); IV, 50 (241). See also I, 35 (52); IV, 51 (244) and IV, 79, the last sentence (285).

146. Strauss underlines the deviation from his maxim, to present Machiavelli's teaching wholly with reference to the *Prince* and the *Discourses*, which paragraph IV, 79 on the *Mandragola* implies, by ironically deploying precisely this maxim against himself at the beginning of the immediately following paragraph: "Some people will think that the obscurities which we were compelled to imitate can be avoided if one simply disregards the *Mandragola* as an extraneous work which belongs to a department wholly unconnected with the department of serious thought, and if one limits oneself strictly to the two books each of which contains in its way everything Machiavelli knows" IV, 80 (285–86). The deviation of IV, 79 on the *Mandragola* in the second half of chapter IV corresponds to the deviation of IV, 37 on the *Vita di Castruccio Castracani* in the first half.

147. "The only selfish desire which can induce men to be passionately concerned with the well-being of remote posterity is the desire for perpetual or immortal glory. The desire for such glory is the link between badness and goodness, since while it is selfish in itself it cannot be satisfied except by the greatest possible service to others. The desire for immortal glory is the highest desire since it is the necessary accompaniment of the greatest natural virtue. It is the only desire of men of the greatest natural virtue" IV, 80 (286). See Footnotes 142 und 143.

regarding the order that is in accordance with nature, can claim for himself the highest glory. To earn this glory, he must place himself—at the same time founder, artist, writer, and discoverer—in the service of the order he wants to create. "He looks at society not theoretically but, being the teacher of founders, in the perspective of founders. The desire for the highest glory, which is the factual truth of the natural desire for the common good and which animates the quest for the truth, demands that the detachment from human things be subordinated to a specific attachment or be replaced by that attachment." Strauss clarifies the impasse Machiavelli would face if he were to maintain the desire for the highest glory as the explanation of the search for truth—a desire that first determines and may later lend wings to the search for truth—in a sidelong glance at Plato's *Republic*, where the love of glory makes the founders of the best city subservient to the common good of their founding and accordingly can explain the transformation of the love of tyranny into the love of justice.[148] But the political transformation there is only the preparation for the "true conversion," which consists in the turn to philosophy and which is brought about by the insight into the necessary limitations of everything political. In contrast with Plato, in Machiavelli the true conversion is not presented. "In Machiavelli the transformation of man through the desire for glory seems to be the only conversion; the second and higher conversion seems to have been forgotten. This conclusion, however, is not compatible with Machiavelli's clear awareness of the delusions of glory and of the limitations of the political. Immortal glory is impossible, and what is called immortal glory depends on chance. Hence to see the highest good in glory means to deny the possibility of happiness." That Machiavelli abstracts from *eros* and does not advocate for the turn to philosophy does not imply that he has forgotten the "true conversion." It means that the reader of the *Prince* and the *Discourses* who has reached the point at which he sees himself confronted with incompatible conclusions and applications of the teaching is compelled to the *periagoge* that remains omitted in Machiavelli's presentation. With explicit reference back to the digression on the *Mandragola*, Strauss sketches the way that leads Machiavelli out of the impasse that must result from the orientation to glory and the abstraction from *eros*. He turns his eye from political life to the "supplement" of

---

148. "By suggesting to his young companions that they should together found a city, Socrates appeals from the petty end of the tyrant to the grand end of the founder: the honor attending the tyrant who merely uses a city already in existence is petty in comparison with the glory attending the founder and especially the founder of the best city. The founder however must devote himself entirely to the well-being of his city; he is forced to be concerned with the common good or to be just" IV, 81 (289).

the unpolitical life and returns to the life according to nature, which for Machiavelli seems to be realized in the alternation between politics and love. "But, as was indicated before, he rises above the plane on which the political good and the erotic good supplement each other while conflicting with each other. The most excellent man, as distinguished from the most excellent captain, or soldier of war or of love, acquires full satisfaction and immunity to the power of chance through knowledge of 'the world.'" Strauss's presentation of Machiavelli's thought culminates, as we saw, at the end of the tenth section with the combining of knowledge of the truth and communication of the truth into a bipolar unity. With the choice of the image of the man on horseback for the elucidation of the unity, Strauss invokes the tradition of the art of philosophic writing. And with the final mention of the "young," the true addressee to whom Machiavelli's art is directed, he recalls the significance of *eros*, without which that unity, and Machiavelli himself, cannot be thought.[149]

The eleventh section (IV, 82–87) is separated from the argument Strauss has developed in the preceding sections, coming to a conclusion in IV, 81, by a caesura that turns the last six paragraphs of the book into a kind of epilogue. At the same time, it is the last of the three "final sections" that Strauss devotes to a criticism of Machiavelli's enterprise. Accordingly, Strauss gathers together in the narrowest space the most important topoi of his doctrine of "ancients and moderns." The criticism of the founder of modern political philosophy, therefore, stands in the foreground of the epilogue. Strauss concentrates not on the intention of the philosopher but instead on the action of the politician. He draws an image of Machiavelli informed by foresight of the historical consequences. He considers Machiavelli as the starting point of a process whose costs to philosophy Strauss reckons at the end of *Thoughts on Machiavelli* and highlights for the common understanding. All this makes the most exposed part of the book into its most rhetorical. Indeed, the rhetoric of the last six paragraphs is especially suited to cover over the most important result of Strauss's philosophical investigation and to blunt the sharpness of its peaks by a historical smoothing over. Strauss leaves the attentive reader with no lack of clarity about the rhetorical character of the epilogue. He inserts statements that noticeably do not correspond to the interpretation he previously presented with reasons. Or he indicates through brief corrections that his discussion is far removed from Machiavelli and has in view, let us say,

---

149. IV; 81 (288–90); cf. *Persecution and the Art of Writing*, p. 36 and "Restatement on Xenophon's *Hiero*," p. 117 (par. 30 *in fine*, par. 31 *in princ.*). On the last paragraph of the tenth section, consider Pp. 43–45.

Locke, Kant, Marx, without mentioning their names.[150] In addition, Strauss can expect that the reader who has followed the argument of paragraphs 1–81 with the required alertness and reflection knows how to apply what he has learned and understood up to this point. Thus, the spectacular pronouncement about Machiavelli's threefold "forgetting"—Machiavelli has forgotten Socrates, tragedy, and the soul—which the reader encounters in the epilogue, will not find him unprepared. He will remember that in the introduction to chapter IV Strauss rebutted the assertion of another threefold "forgetting" of Machiavelli's. He will examine what reasons Strauss offers for the late pronouncement. And finally he will investigate whether Machiavelli's "forgetting" of Socrates, tragedy, and the soul is a case similar to his "forgetting" of the true conversion to philosophy, which Strauss treated in an exemplary way in IV, 81.[151] The core of Machiavelli's action, which the reckoning of the conclusion targets, is the rapprochement with the people or, more precisely spoken, the new politics toward the "*demos* in the philosophical sense, i.e., the totality of the citizens who are incapable or unwilling to defer to philosophy." In order to be able to win over "the most powerful ruler," the philosopher must adapt himself to the ends of the demos and satisfy them. Closely connected with the democratic turn of philosophic politics, which Strauss traces back to Machiavelli,[152] are characterizations such as "lowering of the standards" and "narrowing of the horizon." Looming as its most far-reaching

---

150. "for Machiavelli the pleasure deriving from honor and glory is genuine and perhaps the highest pleasure" IV, 83 (291); cf. IV, 81 (289–90). "As regards chance in general, it can be conquered; man is the master" IV, 83 (292); cf. IV, 33 (218); IV, 35 (221); IV, 54 (246); IV, 60 (253). "his eventual identification of the most excellent man with the most excellent captain" IV, 87 (299); cf. IV, 14 (192–93) and IV, 81 (290). "To return to that manifestation of the new notion of philosophy which appears clearly in Machiavelli's books . . ." IV, 86 (296). "Yet in looking forward to the extreme consequences of Machiavelli's action, we must not forget the fact that for Machiavelli himself . . ." IV, 86 (298).

151. IV, 82 (291); IV, 83 (292); IV, 84 (294); cf. IV, 2 (175); IV, 81 (289). The reader of the epilogue might be least prepared for the central subject of the assertion of Machiavelli's threefold forgetting (but consider I, 28 *in fine*): "In Machiavelli we find comedies, parodies, and satires but nothing reminding of tragedy. One half of humanity remains outside of his thought. There is no tragedy in Machiavelli because he has no sense of the sacredness of 'the common'" IV, 83 (292). The reader who wants to gain greater clarity about Machiavelli's "forgetting" on this point can begin with the question of which philosopher, before or after Kant, made *the sacredness of the common* into his cause.

152. "Through his effort philosophy becomes salutary in the sense in which the *demos* understands, or may understand, the salutary. He achieves the decisive turn toward that notion of philosophy according to which its purpose is to relieve man's estate or to increase man's power or to guide man toward the rational society, the bond and the end of which is enlightened self-interest or the comfortable self-preservation of each of its members. The cave becomes 'the substance'" IV, 86 (296). See IV, 84 (294) and III, 55 (168).

effects are the imposition of the function of religion on philosophy and the final denial of the radical distinction between philosophers and nonphilosophers. Strauss emphasized in the center of chapter III that Machiavelli opposed the "aristocratic prejudice or the aristocratic premise" of "classical philosophy" (III, 30), and he left no doubt that Machiavelli, for political reasons, took the side of the people (III, 31). Preceding this was the presentation of Machiavelli as another Fabius, who prepared the victorious campaign of his brothers by operating unrecognized among their enemies, for which he had to cross a territory thought to be impassable, the Ciminian Forest (III, 17). Machiavelli's allegorical self-presentation, which Strauss extracts from the central of the three "last sections" of the *Discourses* (II, 33) concerning Machiavelli's enterprise, and from details of Livy's underlying story (IX, 36), indicates that the enemies, the *Tuscans*, were of the belief that no "outsider" would ever venture into the Ciminian Forest, and that the Roman Senate forbade the advance into the unexplored territory because it took it to be too dangerous. We can read the allegory in such a way that the "Ciminian Forest" stands for the nature to be cultivated, which is opened up by the use of science and the arts; the fruits of the advance are held out in prospect for the people, who for their part will be cultivated, that is, politically formed; the "Senate" represents the political philosophy of the ancients, which counsels against the opening up and places a narrow estimate on the capability of the people to be formed; the "Tuscans," however, among whom Machiavelli "in a bold disguise" explores the possibility of a successful attack, and who will finally be defeated by the surprising alliance with the people, point to the "foreign power" of the transpolitical religion, whose rule is still unbroken in the *respublica christiana*.[153]

Christianity, revealed religion, and the Bible are never spoken of in the epilogue. It treats the Machiavellian turn without referring by name to the challenge to which it responds. At the end, Strauss seems to have forgotten the central subject matter of the book and to direct all his attention to the break of the moderns from the ancients, in order to demonstrate the superiority and self-sufficiency of the integral position of the ancients. Yet revealed religion asserts its presence in *Thoughts on Machiavelli* even where it is not mentioned by name. Not only must the new philosophic politics remain unintelligible as long as it abstracts from the enemy with whom

---

153. III, 17 (106–7); consider III, 45 (153); III, 47 (153–54). On transpolitical religion, see III, 21 (112–13) and III, 24 (118); on the alliance with the people, III, 25 (119); III, 28 (125–26); III, 30 (128–31); III, 31 (131); III, 55 (168); IV, 68 (263); on the criticism of the ancients, in addition to III, 30 (127) also IV, 60 (253).

it was conceived face to face, so that the reader is compelled to take up once more the thread of chapters II and III and of the first half of chapter IV; the last paragraph of the book opens with a reference to "the necessity" that was determinative for "Machiavelli and his great successors"; Strauss recalls the "powerful adversary" with whom they saw themselves confronted; and after a brief rhetorical interlude he poses the question, no less rhetorically formulated, that will unavoidably involve the "foreign power" in the consideration of the internal relation between modern and ancient philosophers: "we cannot cease wondering as to what essential defect of classical political philosophy could possibly have given rise to the modern venture as an enterprise that was meant to be reasonable." Since historical change is at issue, in regard to the reasonableness of the enterprise of the moderns as well as in respect of the validity of the teaching of the ancients, Strauss returns to the attitude that "the classics" adopted toward inventions and the political or social dynamics that innovations are capable of spurring on: "They demanded the strict moral-political supervision of inventions; the good and wise city will determine which inventions are to be made use of and which are to be suppressed." Assuming there were a constantly well and wisely ruled city or that the philosophers permanently controlled technological change, nothing would seem to stand in the way of the stability of the good and wise city of the classical philosophers. "Yet they were forced to make *one crucial exception*. They had to admit the *necessity* of encouraging *inventions pertaining to the art of war*. They had to bow to the *necessity* of defense or of resistance."[154] With the exception that ruins the stability of the best regime, Strauss has arrived at the very necessity with which he began the paragraph. The necessity that comes from without, which war creates, which is the enemy. Many a reader might gain the impression that Strauss concedes to Machiavelli a point of criticism of subordinate importance when he establishes by way of summary: "The difficulty implied in the admission that inventions pertaining to the art of war must be encouraged is the only one which supplies a basis for Machiavelli's criticism of classical political philosophy." In fact it is an attack of considerable significance on the self-sufficiency of the classical teaching. It concerns not solely the conception

---

154. IV, 87 (298), my emphasis. Strauss continues: "This means however that they had to admit that the moral-political supervision of inventions by the good and wise city is necessarily limited by the need of adaptation to the practices of morally inferior cities which scorn such supervision because their end is acquisition or ease. They had to admit in other words that in an important respect the good city has to take its bearings by the practice of bad cities or that the bad impose their law on the good. Only in this point does Machiavelli's contention that the good cannot be good because there are so many bad ones prove to possess a foundation" (298–99).

of the best regime or the good city and its stability. It holds in particular for the neglect of foreign policy, which for "classical" political philosophy seemed to harbor no controversy of fundamental interest.[155] The situation had to change decisively when, alongside the familiar actors of the cities and empires, a foreign power of a wholly different kind appeared, which in contrast to the particular political communities was characterized by a universal claim to supremacy and a demand for absolute loyalty reaching into the innermost domain of the citizens. The connection between the recognition of the "primacy of foreign policy" and the new situation that the historical irruption of revealed religions implied for politics as well as for philosophy had become clear to Strauss in 1935 in his confrontation with Farabi and Averroes. In *Thoughts on Machiavelli* Strauss alludes to this medieval prehistory with a remark that for most readers remains inaccessible and leaves the theologico-political background in the dark. Without mentioning the *falāsifa*, he laconically states that Machiavelli's teaching cannot "be characterized as the first political teaching which gives its due to foreign policy or which recognizes the primacy of foreign policy."[156] The evocation of the enemy at the end has all the greater significance. The reference to the compulsion that springs from "inventions pertaining to the art of war," in the last paragraph of a book in which "spiritual warfare" plays a prominent role and in which the victory of the successful war party has been explicitly traced back to an invention in the realm of the art of war, to the employment of propaganda, can hardly count as a reference of subordinate significance. "Classical" political philosophy was not able to prevent the victory of the enemy. Instead, it unwittingly contributed to it. By its teaching it bestowed on science a previously unknown visibility and reputation. It prepared the ground for the use of science for practical, political, and military purposes, a use spurned by theory, as Strauss makes sure to remind the reader: "From

---

155. See the essay in which Strauss introduces the concept of classical political philosophy, "On Classical Political Philosophy," pp. 84–85. Cf. "Maimonides' Statement on Political Science" (1953), in *What Is Political Philosophy?*, pp. 164–65.

156. IV, 84 (293). After Strauss had recognized to which deviations from Plato's political teaching the medieval Platonic political philosophers saw themselves forced by the irruption of the revealed religions—from the new evaluation of courage and of war to a new determination of the role of rhetoric—he inserted into the English translation of his book *Hobbes' politische Wissenschaft* a long paragraph about the primacy of foreign policy, which was not contained in the German manuscript (*The Political Philosophy of Hobbes*, pp. 161–63). I have documented the historical details regarding the insight that underlies the treatment in *Thoughts on Machiavelli* of the "primacy of foreign policy," "spiritual warfare," and "inventions pertaining to the art of war" in my prefaces to *Gesammelte Schriften*, vol. 2, pp. xxii–xxiii, and *Gesammelte Schriften*, vol. 3, pp. xxiii–xxiv.

the point of view of the classics, such use of science is excluded by the nature of science as a theoretical pursuit." Its theoretical nature did not protect science from being put into the service of the active transformation of the world. And Machiavelli encountered an adversary who had drawn a large part of his arms from the arsenal of the philosophy of the ancients.[157]

After the exposition of the break, after criticism and countercriticism, after the rupture by and about historical change, the last six sentences of the book bring the philosophers together once more. An opinion serves as a starting point for Strauss, an opinion that has been rendered incredible by our historical experience, i.e., the historical experience of Strauss and his readers in contrast with that of Aristotle and Machiavelli. Among the ancients there was the opinion that at periodic intervals cataclysms would occur that would destroy entire civilizations and scatter men. If the political control of the philosophers should fail, nature would thus take care to ensure that there would be no excessive development of technology and that the inventions of man would not strike against him in the long run and "become his masters and his destroyers." In light of the man-made problem of science and technology, the catastrophes of nature are the manifestation of its goodness. The prospect of the return to the beginning looks like an act of beneficence. Since Machiavelli "himself expresses" the ancient opinion about natural cataclysms, Strauss can impute to him with just as much reason what he imputes to the classical philosophers. If they relied on the view that natural necessities set limits to the misuse of the *techne* promoted by them, Machiavelli might expect that the enterprise he conceives—and every future attempt at a "conquest of nature"—would finally be subject to the same necessities. If Machiavelli, Plato, or Aristotle had believed that cataclysms controlled the excessive development of the human power of destruction, they would have been guided by an opinion "which has been rendered incredible by the experiences of the last centuries." With an eye to the centuries that separate him from Machiavelli's renewal of philosophy and connect him with it, Strauss expresses what is needful for philosophy in the present: "It would seem that the notion of the beneficence of nature or of the primacy of the Good must be restored by being rethought through a return to the fundamental experiences from which it is derived. For while 'philosophy must beware of wishing to be

---

157. IV, 87 (299); cf. IV, 10–11 (185–86); IV, 43 (231) and *Die Religionskritik des Hobbes* (1934), in *Gesammelte Schriften*, vol. 3, p. 272.—"Aristotle did not conceive of a world state because he was absolutely certain that science is essentially theoretical and that the liberation of technology from moral and political control would lead to disastrous consequences: the fusion of science and the arts together with the unlimited or uncontrolled progress of technology has made universal and perpetual tyranny a serious possibility." *Natural Right and History*, p. 23.

edifying,' it is of necessity edifying." Strauss takes into account a threefold movement: The ascent from an opinion about the world to the inner necessity of philosophy; the renewal of a traditional teaching by recourse to the genuine philosophic activity that precedes every teaching; and, uniting all three movements in one, the turn from the historical teachings and experiences that separate the philosophers to the fundamental experiences they have in common: the liberating force of knowledge, the *eros* of thought, the deepening of reflection, the happiness of understanding. The fundamental experiences that let the philosophers speak of the primacy of the good have their unifying point in the judgment that the philosophic life is good. The judgment about the life that is according to their nature finds its eloquent expression in the art of writing, which philosophers have made use of for two and a half thousand years in order to lead kindred natures to the philosophic life. The philosophic art of writing should make it possible for the true addressee to have precisely those fundamental experiences in the confrontation with the writings and books that owe their existence to that art. One of those books is *Thoughts on Machiavelli*.[158]

---

158. IV, 87 (299); cf. I, 35 (50); II, 20 (77); II, 24 (81); III, 26 (120–21); IV, 14 (193); IV, 54 (246–47); IV, 60 *in fine* (253); IV, 79 (285); IV, 81 (290). See "Farabi's *Plato*," pp. 392–93; *Natural Right and History*, p. 95; *What Is Political Philosophy?*, p. 40 and *Die Denkbewegung von Leo Strauss*, pp. 41–43 [*Leo Strauss and the Theologico-political Problem*, pp. 71–73]. Consider Niccolò Machiavelli to Francesco Vettori, Florence, December 10, 1513, in *Opere* VI *Lettere*, ed. Franco Gaeta (Milan, 1961), p. 304.—On June 6, 1959, Strauss gave a lecture in Chicago with the title "What Is Liberal Education?," in which he takes up the Hegel citation of the last sentence of *Thoughts on Machiavelli* and extends the line further (first edition, Chicago 1959, p. 12; reprinted in *Liberalism Ancient and Modern* [New York, 1968], p. 8): "Philosophy, we have learned, must be on its guard against the wish to be edifying—philosophy can only be intrinsically edifying. We cannot exert our understanding without from time to time understanding something of importance; and this act of understanding may be accompanied by the awareness of our understanding, by the understanding of understanding, by *noesis noeseos*, and this is so high, so pure, so noble an experience that Aristotle could ascribe it to his God. This experience is entirely independent of whether what we understand primarily is pleasing or displeasing, fair or ugly. It leads us to realize that all evils are in a sense necessary if there is to be understanding."

EPILOGUE

In 1972 Leo Strauss followed up *Thoughts on Machiavelli* with an essay that in a remarkable way sheds light on the book published in 1958. He took advantage of the opportunity that the second edition of *History of Political Philosophy* offered him in order to replace the Machiavelli chapter of the first edition from 1963 with his own essay and thus to treat Machiavelli once more monographically. It is not a kind of summary of the book, which would scarcely have been of greater interest to the author. Nor are we dealing with a chapter to be expected in a survey work on the history of political philosophy. If Strauss had wanted to write a contribution appropriate for the textbook edited by him and Joseph Cropsey, he would have been free to do so already in 1963. In fact, the essay, which was supposed to find its final destination as the thirteenth piece in *Studies in Platonic Political Philosophy*, appears somewhat ill suited, owing to its approach and its difficulty, to a volume about which the editors in the first sentence of the preface say, it is "intended primarily to introduce undergraduate students of political science to political philosophy." In "Niccolo Machiavelli" politics in the narrower sense remains of subordinate significance. The *Prince* is treated comparatively briefly. By far the greatest attention is given to the *Discourses*. There is no mention of Machiavelli's *enterprise* or of *spiritual warfare, propaganda,* or *obfuscation*.[159] Strauss places the emphases in such a way that the impression left by the three "last sections" from *Thoughts on Machiavelli* is in any case not reinforced. He corrects the rhetoric of the epilogue in important respects. And the surmise suggests itself that he undertakes the shift in emphasis and the corrections in light of the reception, or nonreception, that the book had found in the fourteen years since its publication. It is certain that in "Niccolo Machiavelli" Strauss presents the actual theme of *Thoughts on Machiavelli* in such a way that it can no longer be overlooked, and that he underlines for his longest book the statement he made in 1964 about all his studies: the theologico-political problem

---

159. Of the 35 paragraphs of the essay, 5 are devoted to the *Prince*, 21 to the *Discourses* (not counting overlaps), *Mandragola* and *Castruccio Castracani* each receive a single paragraph, as was the case in *Thoughts on Machiavelli*. *Istorie fiorentine*, *Arte della guerra*, and the remaining writings of Machiavelli's are not mentioned at all. Cf. the recommended readings at the end of the chapter and consider the explanation of categories A and B of recommended readings at the beginning of *History*, p. viii.—"Niccolo Machiavelli" has been published three times so far: *History of Political Philosophy*, second edition (1972), pp. 271–92; third edition (1987), pp. 296–317; *Studies in Platonic Political Philosophy* (1983), pp. 210–28. The essay is cited from the first publication with the specification of paragraphs.

is the central theme. It is no less certain that Strauss's extraordinary essay deals with difficult passages of the theologico-political treatise. In particular it serves as a supplement for the better understanding of the peak in IV, 26. I limit myself to a few indications, which for one or another of us might be useful.

Right at the beginning, the essay raises the question, what is virtue?—a question that Strauss elsewhere distinguished as "distinctly philosophic" in contrast with the political questions of citizens. Two moves suffice for Strauss to reach, via Socrates and the *Ethics* of Aristotle, the virtue of magnanimity, which figures so prominently in IV, 26, and in agreement with the *Ethics* to set it off from a *sense of shame*, which as we read in Aristotle "is not a virtue." In this way Strauss makes the reader aware that the opposition of the virtue of *magnanimity* and the vice of *humility* in IV, 26 is due to his clarifying presentation. With the next move, which calls upon the prophet Isaiah (6: 3 and 5), Strauss arrives at the explication of the central sentence of IV, 26: "When the prophet Isaiah received his vocation, he was overpowered by the sense of his unworthiness: 'I am a man of unclean lips amidst a people of unclean lips.' This amounts to an implicit condemnation of magnanimity and an implicit vindication of the sense of shame. The reason is given in the context: 'holy, holy, holy is the lord of hosts.' There is no holy god for Aristotle and the Greeks generally. Who is right, the Greeks or the Jews, Athens or Jerusalem?" Before he introduces Machiavelli into the text, Strauss formulates, for one last time in his œuvre, the alternative "Athens or Jerusalem," which he investigates in *Thoughts on Machiavelli* as in no other book of his, but without explicitly mentioning it. Likewise, for the last time he calls to mind that the right and the necessity of philosophy depend on the answer to the question whether human wisdom is sufficient to resolve with reasons the alternative "Athens or Jerusalem." If philosophy lacked such reasons, would it not rest upon an act of faith just as its opponent does? And would this not mean the complete and final defeat of "Athens"? "For a philosophy based on faith is no longer philosophy."[160]

In light of the confrontation of the prelude, it cannot be surprising that there is no mention of the Great Tradition in "Niccolo Machiavelli." Instead,

---

160. Strauss continues: "Perhaps it was this unresolved conflict which has prevented Western thought from ever coming to rest. Perhaps it is this conflict which is at the bottom of a kind of thought which is philosophic indeed but no longer Greek: modern philosophy. It is in trying to understand modern philosophy that we come across Machiavelli." "Niccolo Machiavelli" 1. Cf. "On Classical Political Philosophy," p. 90; "Preface to Spinoza's Critique of Religion" (1961), in *Liberalism Ancient and Modern*, p. 256 (next to last paragraph *in fine*). See *Das theologisch-politische Problem*, pp. 30–34 [*Leo Strauss and the Theologico-political Problem*, pp. 16–18].

Strauss speaks of Christianity as having seen itself compelled, with its takeover of the Latin language, to safeguard "to some extent" classical literature and with it its "mortal enemy" (28). Also he now explicitly opposes Machiavelli to Augustine, who does not appear in *Thoughts on Machiavelli* (9). Overall, Christianity receives a distinctly greater visibility. Strauss makes explicit reference to it in ten paragraphs, for the first time in the thirteenth paragraph. Five paragraphs in a row are devoted to the confrontation with Christianity (25–29). They form the longest section of the text.[161] Strauss chooses five pieces from the *Discourses* for more detailed commentary. In doing so he places *Discourses* III, 1 in the center, the chapter that contains the sole mention of Christ by Machiavelli in the *Discourses* and the *Prince*.[162] In contrast to *Thoughts on Machiavelli* (IV, 6), in the essay, in its twenty-sixth paragraph, Strauss translates the passage that has the death of Christ as its subject and that takes into account the political consequences of the appeal to the example of the passion. "The Christian command or counsel not to resist evil is based on the premise that the beginning or principle is love. That command or counsel can only lead to the utmost disorder or else to evasion. The premise, however, turns into its extreme opposite."[163]

In the center of the group of five paragraphs on Christianity, Strauss repeats his interpretation of *Discourses* I, 26, Machiavelli's characterization of the Biblical God as a tyrant. This time he prefaces it with a consideration of the meaning of the number 26, which connects the relevant chapter of the *Discourses* with the 26 chapters of the *Prince*. "We have seen that the number of chapters of the *Discourses* is meaningful and has been deliberately chosen. We may thus be induced to wonder whether the number of chapters of the *Prince* is not also meaningful. The *Prince* consists of 26 chapters. Twenty-six is the numerical value of the sacred name of God in Hebrew, of the Tetragrammaton. But did Machiavelli know of this? I do not

---

161. The terms "Christianity," "the Christians," and "Christian" appear in paragraphs 13, 14, 19, 20, 22 five times, in Strauss's section on Christianity (25–29) seventeen times, and altogether twenty-two times. The terms "Bible" and "biblical" appear in paragraphs 21, 22, 28 five times and three times, respectively, "anti-Bible" once in paragraph 22 and "anti-biblical" once in paragraph 28. The expression "New Testament" (twice) is restricted to paragraph 27.

162. Strauss stresses the centrality through the sequence of the selection: "a selection of the following five chapters or quasi-chapters: I proem, II proem, II 1 [*recte*: III 1], I 26 and II 5." "Niccolo Machiavelli" 17. To the single mention of Christ by Machiavelli in paragraph 26 there corresponds a single mention of Jesus by Strauss in paragraph 27. Cf. paragraph 15.

163. Note the alteration that Strauss makes in his translation of Machiavelli's passage about Christ. Cf. *What Is Political Philosophy?*, p. 44, and *Thoughts on Machiavelli* IV, 12 (186–89).

know."¹⁶⁴ Since Strauss admits that he does not know whether the numerical value of the Tetragrammaton was known to Machiavelli, the reference to this meaning of the number 26, which is immediately replaced by another meaning, and which is not mentioned in *Thoughts on Machiavelli*, seems strange. The strangeness disappears if we read the essay as a supplement to the book and keep in mind that *Strauss* knew the numerical value of the Tetragrammaton when he wrote IV, 26. Strauss continues: "Twenty-six equals 2 times 13. Thirteen is now and for quite some time has been considered an unlucky number, but in former times it was also and even primarily considered a lucky number. So 'twice 13' might mean both good luck and bad luck, and hence altogether: luck, *fortuna*. A case can be made for the view that Machiavelli's theology can be expressed by the formula *Deus sive fortuna* (as distinguished from Spinoza's *Deus sive natura*)—that is, that God as fortuna is supposed to be subject to human influence (imprecation)." For a more detailed investigation of this theology or quasi-theology, Strauss takes up a formulation from *Discourses* III, 35, which he has interpreted in paragraph 14 as Machiavelli's referring the reader to the *Prince*, and thus refers his reader to *Thoughts on Machiavelli*, which is no more mentioned in "Niccolo Machiavelli" than the *Prince* is mentioned in the *Discourses*: "But to establish this would require an argument 'too long and too exalted' for the present occasion." This is followed by the interpretation of the blasphemy of the twenty-sixth chapter of the *Discourses*.¹⁶⁵ At the end Strauss strengthens the pedagogical intention that Machiavelli pursues when he induces "his readers par excellence, whom he calls 'the young'" to think forbidden thoughts. "This is an important part of his education of the young or, to use the time-honored expression, of his corruption of the young" (27).

The explication of IV, 26, which begins with the first two mentions of "magnanimity" or "condemnation of magnanimity" in the first paragraph and continues with multiple hints and references dispersed throughout the

---

164. "Niccolo Machiavelli" 27. Strauss's "I do not know," which helps us with an explication of IV, 26, is preceded in paragraph 17 by an "I believe," which illuminates an important assertion in IV, 50 (242), and is followed by a second "I believe" in paragraph 31, which points to III, 53 (164), a paragraph in *Thoughts on Machiavelli* that stands in a certain connection to paragraphs 26 and 27 of the essay.

165. "Let us therefore see whether we cannot get some help from looking at the 26th chapter of the *Discourses* . . ." "Niccolo Machiavelli" 27. While the meaning of Machiavelli's chapter 26 is disclosed by the preceding chapter 25 of the *Discourses*, the meaning of Strauss's paragraph 26 is disclosed by the succeeding paragraph 27 of the essay.

text,[166] comes to a conclusion, as it seems, with the third and last mention of "magnanimity" in the thirty-first paragraph. Preceding this is the sole appearance of "humility" in a succinct recapitulation of the criticism Machiavelli levels against "our religion" (25). Strauss comments on the history of Camillus, which Machiavelli narrates in *Discourses* III, 23, the fall of the celebrated savior of Rome from the Gauls, who by his likening himself to a God incurs the hatred of the people. Camillus had his triumphal chariot drawn by four white horses: "therefore the people said that through pride he had wished to equal the sun-god or, as Plutarch has it, Jupiter (Livy says: Jupiter et sol). I believe that this rather shocking act of *superbia* was in Machiavelli's eyes a sign of Camillus' magnanimity" (31). What, as Strauss believes, Machiavelli considers as *magnanimitas*, the people see as punishable because blasphemous *superbia*. In the all-important case it is for Machiavelli consequently a command of political prudence to replace *magnanimitas* by *humanitas*, magnanimity by humanity.[167]

In his conclusion, Strauss readjusts the earlier presentation of the relationship of Machiavelli to Socrates (33–35). We read now that Machiavelli did not quite "forget" Socrates, as stated twice in the epilogue, but rather Socrates was "suppressed" by Machiavelli. Moreover, Strauss stresses with much greater emphasis than he did in the epilogue the dividing line that connects Machiavelli with Socrates, Aristotle, and Xenophon and distinguishes him from the Sophists.[168] Strauss's final word is the formal proclamation of a common front in which Machiavelli and Socrates stand against the "Sophists": "Xenophon, the pupil of Socrates, was under no delusion about the sternness and harshness of politics, about that ingredient of politics which

---

166. In addition to the cited passages, see for example paragraph 20 and paragraph 30, which incorporates the fifth section of chapter IV: "The substance of what Machiavelli says or suggests regarding religion is not original. As is indicated by his use of the term 'sect' for religion, he goes in the ways of Averroism, that is, of *those medieval Aristotelians who as philosophers refused to make any concessions to revealed religion*. While the substance of Machiavelli's *religious teaching* is not original, his manner of setting it forth is very ingenious. *He recognizes in fact no theology but civil theology*, theology serving the state and to be used or not used by the state as circumstances suggest. He indicates that religions can be dispensed with if there is a strong and able monarch. This implies indeed that religion is indispensable in republics." My emphasis.

167. "the central reason that Camillus became hated was . . . the suspicion that out of pride he wished to become equal to a god, namely, to the sun. Yet it was less pride or ambition than its manifestation by an overt act which made Camillus hated" III, 53 (164). See Pp. 69–70 and 83.

168. "Niccolo Machiavelli" 33; IV, 82 (291) and IV, 84 (292) in each case *in fine* concerning the "forgotten" Socrates. 34–35; IV, 83 (292) on the separation from the Sophists.—Socrates is mentioned almost as often by name in the 35 paragraphs of the essay as he is in the 224 paragraphs of the book.

transcends speech. In this important respect Machiavelli and Socrates make a common front against the Sophists." When we ask ourselves in what way the end of the essay is joined with its beginning, Strauss's determination of the "Sophists" gives us a clue: "the Sophists believed or tended to believe in the omnipotence of speech."[169] It is the sole mention of omnipotence.

---

169. "Niccolo Machiavelli" 35. Cf. Genesis 1; John 1 and 17.

CHAPTER THREE

The Right of Politics and the Knowledge of the Philosopher: On the Intention of Jean-Jacques Rousseau's *Du contrat social*

I

Du contrat social is the work of a philosopher who speaks as a citizen to citizens in order to determine anew the right and the limits of politics for all to see. Its author knows that the philosophic treatment of politics demands a political writing. Whoever undertakes to write about politics must put up with being asked and must himself be clear about the capacity in which he writes, to what end, and for whom.[1] Jean-Jacques Rousseau already answers the question "Who speaks?" on the title page, where he places *Citoyen de Genève* in apposition to his name, as he did in the case of the political writings that preceded the *Contrat social*. Adopting the language of the readers of his time, he confirms in the preface to the first book that he addresses himself to them as *citoyen* and not as *prince* or *législateur*. Stated more precisely, he addresses himself as a member of a sovereign to other contemporary or future members of a sovereign who, like himself, have the duty, arising from the right to cast a vote on public affairs, to inform themselves about the principles of political right. The self-characterization as a *membre du souverain* marks the transition to the concise conceptual apparatus of the book, which proceeds, however, by explicit appeal to the "free State," as whose citizen the author was born. His birth put him in the fortunate position, when reflecting on the civil order, of "always finding new reasons to love the government" of his own country. With the investigations whose yield he presents in *Du contrat social*, Rousseau met his duty as a citizen. The teaching that he will advocate is proof of and is protected by his patriotism.[2]

---

1. Politics is identified twice as the subject of the writing in the two central sentences of the preface of the first book: "On me demandera si je suis prince ou législateur pour écrire sur la Politique? Je réponds que non, et que c'est pour cela que j'écris sur la Politique." Jean-Jacques Rousseau, *Du contract social; ou, Principes du droit politique* (Amsterdam, 1762), I, preface, 2, p. 2 (351). I cite according to book, chapter, and paragraph. The page numbers given in parentheses are from the edition by Robert Derathé, *OCP*, III, whose wording I follow. In addition to the first edition and the posthumous edition of the *Contrat social* edited by Paul Moultou and Pierre-Alexandre Du Peyrou, *Collection complète des œuvres de J. J. Rousseau* (Geneva, 1782), I have also consulted the editions of Edmond Dreyfus-Brisac (Paris, 1896), Georges Beaulavon (Paris, 1914), C. E. Vaughan (Manchester, 1918), Maurice Halbwachs (Paris, 1943), Bertrand de Jouvenel (Geneva, 1947), Ronald Grimsley (Oxford, 1972), and Bruno Bernardi (Paris, 2012).

2. While the first word of the *Contrat social* is *Je* and the last is *moi*, the arc of the preface to the first book spans from *Je veux* to *mon pays!* The preface is the only part of the writing that ends with an exclamation point.—Rousseau already in 1755 used the space that the reference to the "government," i.e., the governmental system of his native city, opened up for him outside Geneva when he chose the *Dédicace à la République de Genève* of the *Discours sur l'origine et les fondemens de inégalité parmi les hommes* as the place to outline his political theory for the

Rousseau cannot speak as a citizen to citizens about politics without bringing its foundations into view. He can neither enlighten the citizens as to their rights nor instruct them as to their duties without laying bare the principle by which they become citizens and are bound as citizens. He cannot present to them his teaching of the well-ordered political community without making visible that such a political community needs the knowledge of the philosopher. If Rousseau appears as advocate for a "body politic" that allows the citizens to recognize themselves in a "common I," he proves himself as promoter of the cause common to the philosophers. *Du contrat social* has for its author a philosopher, whose investigations from the outset aim at knowledge of the "nature of the body politic," who thinks political life with constant regard to the philosophic life, and who, while observing the civil order, never loses sight of the natural order.[3] The gulf separating the philosopher from the citizen comes to light in the opening that Rousseau has follow immediately after the praise of the political community in which he was born as a citizen: "L'homme est né libre, et partout il est dans le fers." Rousseau begins the first chapter of the first book with a sentence whose entire import is disclosed only after the reading of all four books and forty-eight chapters. For the treatise, properly understood, presents a single commentary on the challenging beginning to which it returns over and over again, which it illuminates and deepens. "Man was born free, he is born free, and everywhere he is in chains." Thanks to the linguistic structure Rousseau uses,[4] the first half of the sentence can be read both diachronically and synchronically; thus the lost freedom can be ascribed to the species as well as to the individual, so that in the second half the chains stand for the history of socialization as well as for social conventions, which necessarily impose constraints upon nature. The prelude deals with man in society. It speaks of the fundamental dependence of political, civil, sociable existence. It concerns master and servant equally. The chains also hold for the citizen,

---

first time and to announce the principle of sovereignty of the people to "the human race." See *Discours sur l'inégalité*, Kritische Ausgabe (Paderborn, 1984), 6th edition 2008, pp. 11–12 n. 12 and p. 74; cf. p. 10 n. 10; further *Discours sur l'économie politique*, OCP III, p. 267. The praise of Geneva did not keep the government in Geneva from banning the *Contrat social* together with *Émile* on June 19, 1762, and having both books burned in public. In France, on June 11, 1762, *Émile* was burned by the executioner on the steps of the Palais de justice in Paris, whereas the *Contrat social* remained unmolested.

3. I, 7, 2 (362); I, 9, 8 (367); cf. I, 6, 1 and I, 6, 5 (360); I, 6, 7 (361); I, 8, 2 (364–65). The first book alone refers to *nature* twenty times.

4. See the later use of language in I, 2, 8 (353): "Tout homme né dans l'esclavage naît pour l'esclavage ..."; in I, 4, 5 (356): "ils naissent hommes et libres"; and in IV, 2, 5 (440): "Décider que le fils d'une esclave naît esclave, c'est décider qu'il ne naît pas homme."

who deems himself fortunate to live in a "free State." Nothing Rousseau says to the citizen holds out the prospect that the chains might be removed from him. He promises him solely and certainly an answer to the question what "can make legitimate" the transition to the civil state, how the chains can be justified. To the preceding question, namely, how the "change" from being born free to being in chains might have come to pass, Rousseau answers with a laconic "I do not know." It is the first in a series of passages in the *Contrat social* that raise or point to philosophic questions only to make it explicit that they are being disregarded. The anthropological analysis and the genealogical reconstruction that Rousseau presented in the *Discours sur l'inégalité* seven years before to a Plato or a Diogenes for their consideration go unmentioned. They stand outside the framework. This cannot conceal from the reader of Rousseau that the opening of the *Contrat social* presupposes precisely that analysis and reconstruction. And if in *Du contrat social* Rousseau sets himself the task of making vivid to the citizens how their chains can be made legitimate, he will not accomplish this task without helping the attentive reader to achieve a better understanding of the meaning of the chains themselves. The *Contrat social*, which is designed to set forth the right of politics, cannot help but show at the same time the limits of politics.

Rousseau approaches the subject of the first book, the grounding of the legitimate political community, in a remarkable trio of steps that sets the course for all that follows. In the first three sentences of the second paragraph of the first chapter, *droit* is spoken of three times. Rousseau begins with force, which can compel but cannot obligate a people to obedience, since the right it claims extends only as far as the power to compel obedience, and by the same right the people frees itself from the compulsion to obey when it has the necessary power to do so. The right of the first sentence adds nothing to force. It grounds no obligation. By contrast, the second sentence asserts from the perspective of the citizen that the social order is "a sacred right, which provides the basis for all the others." The citizen knows of rights and duties, he does not know only external compulsion and force. He lives in a thick web of engagements, ends, and tasks, which he affirms, in which he believes, and which he makes his own, a web that is anchored in the order of the political community and that receives from this order its decisive justification. In the third sentence Rousseau answers the question as to the justifying reason of the social order itself. Since the "sacred right" does not come from nature, it must be, "therefore, founded on conventions." The excluded third between the alternative natural origin or human convention is divine command. In the exclusion of divine authority as a source of right, Rousseau's trio of steps has its vanishing point. Whereas the first step treats *force* and *droit* as coextensive, the third step shows the specific strength of the *droit sacré* of the second step as the *droit fondé sur des conventions*. The right of the second step is grounded as right by convention and sanctified by the consent, the will, the belief of the people of the first step. The philosophic conclusion of the third step links together the observation of the world of natural events, to which the first step corresponds, with the insight into political life, to which the second step is due. From the trio of steps result two tasks, which Rousseau takes on in the first book, and an antagonism that is determinative for all four books. On the one hand, Rousseau must clarify, as he immediately adds, the conventions on which the sacred right of the political community, on closer inspection, rests. On the other, he must answer the question of what constitutes the people—introduced in the first sentence and without whose consent a right based on convention cannot be thought—as the subject of consent, of binding decisions and statements. Rousseau brings these two tasks together by inquiring back from conventions in the plural to the *one* convention that is able to create the people as political subject and to make it the source of all right. In substance, the fifth chapter, "That One Always Has to Go Back to a First Convention," follows the first seamlessly. In chapters 2, 3, and 4, which interrupt the argument, Rousseau confronts positions that are unable to ground the legitimate political community or are incompatible with it. In the central of the three chapters there appears for the first time a prominent variation of the doctrine that the three steps of the first chapter silently rejects and face to face with which Rousseau develops the conception of the *Contrat social*. With the title "Of the Right of the Stronger," and equipped with a biting commentary, he cites the word of Paul from the Letter to the Romans, according to which all power comes from God.[5]

---

5. "Toute puissance vient de Dieu, je l'avoüe; mais toute maladie en vient aussi. Est-ce à dire qu'il soit défendu d'appeller le médecin? Qu'un brigand me surprenne au coin d'un bois: non seulement il faut par force donner la bourse, mais quand je pourrois la soustraire suis-je en conscience obligé de la donner? car enfin le pistolet qu'il tient est aussi une puissance." I, 3, 3 (355); cf. Paul, Romans 13: 1, and Jacques-Bénigne Bossuet, *Politique tirée des propres paroles de l'Ecriture sainte* VI, 2 (De l'obéissance due au prince), ed. Jacques Le Brun (Geneva, 1967), pp. 192–93. Calvin comments on Paul's saying as follows: "Ratio cur debeamus subiecti esse magistratibus, quod Dei ordinatione sunt constituti. quod si ita placet Domino mundum gubernare, Dei ordinem invertere nititur, adeoque Deo ipsi resistit quisquis potestatem aspernatur: quando eius (qui iuris politici author est), providentiam contemnere, bellum cum eo suscipere est." *Commentarius in Epistolam Pauli ad Romanos*, ed. T. H. L. Parker (Leiden, 1981), p. 282.

The fourth and final step in the course of the grounding, the transition to the *one* convention, Rousseau undertakes in the central chapter of the first book, in which he also introduces the central concepts of *bien public* and *corps politique*. The advocate of the citizens explains that even if he were to grant everything he has refuted thus far, even if, in other words, he were to concede the opinions about the foundations of rule that contradict reason or conflict with the good of the citizens, opinions he opposed in chapters 2, 3, and 4, even then "the abettors of despotism" would still have won nothing. The rejected teachings might have shown how a despot subjugates a multitude, by what means authorities obtain obedience, what defines the relationship of a master to slaves. Thereby, they at best brought about an *aggrégation*; they did not, however, reach an *association*. Even those teachings that appealed to conventions of one kind or another came no further, no matter whether they tied the transference of the title to rule to the condition of the guarantee of peace and security,[6] or whether they claimed a covenant that sanctioned an absolute rule and an unconditional obedience.[7] Those teachings have not shown how the people, which is supposed to make a covenant, becomes a people, or what makes the people, which must transfer rights, into the bearer of these rights. If Rousseau were to grant everything that he rejected in the interest of the citizens, the citizens would thereby still not be in a state of right that could obligate them. They would not be citizens, since there would be no body politic. To ground free of contradiction a collective subject that can enter into and enact conventions that are binding, regulate public deliberation and voting, act politically, recourse to a first, unanimous convention is needed. Only in such a convention does one reach "the true foundation of society."[8]

The *one convention*, in which society has its true foundation, is the title-bestowing *contrat social*. In the eminently political act, which constitutes the people and to which the citizens owe their being citizens, resides Rousseau's answer to the initial questions, what is able to make the chains of society legitimate and what is able to ground the sacred right of the social order. The social contract can bear the burden that Rousseau puts on it only

---

6. Cf. I, 4, 2–3 (355–56) and II, 4, 10 (375).

7. "Enfin c'est une convention vaine et contradictoire de stipuler d'une part une autorité absolue et de l'autre une obéissance sans bornes. N'est-il pas clair qu'on n'est engagé à rien envers celui dont on a droit de tout éxiger, et cette seule condition, sans équivalent, sans échange n'entraîne-t-elle pas la nullité de l'acte?" I, 4, 6 (356); for this, consider *Profession de foi du Vicaire Savoyard*, par. 71, *OCP* IV, p. 589 and Paul, Romans 9: 11–23.

8. I, 5, 1–3 (359).

insofar as it rests on unanimous consent and because it rests on strict necessity. In the sixth chapter, in which Rousseau introduces the *contrat social*, he begins, as in the first chapter's three steps, with force, strength, power, beyond which the right of the state of nature does not go. Since *la force et la liberté* are the primary instruments the individual has at his disposal for his self-preservation, it would not suffice for the care the individual owes to himself if he were to delegate the power of disposal over these instruments to a higher power, if he were to accept the constraints upon himself that the state of right demands of him, if he were to agree to duties that society imposes on him, unless the individual were to see himself necessitated by compelling reason to agree to such a change or it were to appear advantageous to him regarding his own good. As a historical presupposition of the *contrat social*, which he also calls *pacte social*, *pacte fondamental*, or *traité social*, Rousseau has only to assume that the contracting individuals have reached the point at which they can no longer remain in the state of nature, since the forces over which they have command as individuals do not suffice to overcome the obstacles to their self-preservation, and they are dependent upon additional forces, which can arise for them solely from a unification, from an association that defends and protects the person and the goods of each associate with its entire common force. Although the citizens will grant him this assumption without difficulty, Rousseau is not satisfied with demonstrating the requirement of the *acte d'association*. The advocate of the social contract speaks as if the conclusion of the contract would have to be promoted in a public deliberation in order to reach unanimous consent. Thus, he offers his listeners the prospect of finding by means of the social contract a *forme d'association* "by which each, uniting with all, nevertheless obeys only himself and remains as free as before." Readers who did not pay the opening of the first book the attention it deserves may grasp later when they reach the third book the extent of the *pia fraus* that Rousseau introduces. Its political meaning will concern us further. At the place where Rousseau argues for the first time for the transition to the civil state, the pious fraud serves his purpose of giving this state a more attractive look in the eyes of the contracting individuals and of playing down rhetorically the deep incision that in the same passage he determines in its necessity with clear distinctions and sharp concepts. For the transition, of which Rousseau says, with a retrospective glance at the history of the species, that it demanded from the human race nothing less than a change in its "way of being," without which it would have perished, has such far-reaching consequences that it can be made binding only by the strict compliance with the determinations of the *contrat social*: In order that the abandonment of *liberté naturelle* in favor of a *liberté conventionelle* can be legitimate, it must take place according to the nature of the social contract. The nature of the contract fixes the structure of the body politic, and the slightest deviations from the clauses it prescribes invalidate the contract, so that the members of the body politic are no longer bound and revert to their natural freedom. How far-reaching the step is that the social contract demands is indicated by the clause to which all the others lead back. It reads: "l'aliénation totale de chaque associé avec tous ses droits à toute la communauté."[9] That each contracting individual alienates himself with all his rights to the political community, which is brought about by the act of alienation, means not that prior to or outside of the political community he had rights that would be different from his force, strength, or power, but rather that he reserves no rights to himself and thus the collective subject of which he is part becomes the sole source of right and the ultimate authority for political decision. Without an *aliénation sans réserve*, the state of nature would persist, or it would erupt again in the midst of society, since the core question of sovereignty, *Quis iudicabit?*, would remain unanswered. By means of the *aliénation totale ou sans réserve*, the *contrat social* brings to life a body politic whose members are bound only by themselves and which nevertheless as sovereign is capable of action. The nature of the social contract supplies the rule that Rousseau insisted at the beginning of the preface be both *legitimate* and *sure*.[10]

The principles of political right, which the complete title of the writing announces, go back without exception to the social contract. Stated more precisely, they present a cohesive interpretation of its nature. The sequence *Du contract social ou Principes du droit politique* is thus well grounded. In the first version of the treatise the title still read *Du contract social ou Essai sur la forme de la République*, an announcement that in its contrastive reference would have pointed to Plato and Machiavelli, with whom Rousseau in fact carries on a continuous dialogue highly significant for the understanding of the writing, and who are the sole philosophers who repeatedly come to

---

9. Rousseau continues: "Car premierement, chacun se donnant tout entier, la condition est égale pour tous, et la condition étant égale pour tous, nul n'a intérêt de la rendre onéreuse aux autres." I, 6, 6 (360–61); cf. II, 4, 3 (373).

10. "Je veux chercher si dans l'ordre civil il peut y avoir quelque regle d'administration légitime et sûre, en prenant les hommes tels qu'ils sont, et les loix telles qu'elles peuvent être: Je tâcherai d'allier toujours dans cette recherche ce que le droit permet avec ce que l'intérêt prescrit, afin que la justice et l'utilité ne se trouvent point divisées." I, preface, 1 (351).

speak or are mentioned by name in the text without being criticized.[11] Rousseau even considered replacing *Du contrat social* with *De la société civile* on the title page of the Geneva manuscript, but again rejected this change.[12] The title finally chosen by Rousseau is not only substantively compelling but also especially striking in its appeal to the political addressee. Unlike the earlier versions, it highlights the provocative thesis of the writing and connects it with the promise of its practical significance. It designates the convention that grounds society theoretically, without placing the accent on the conversation the writing enters into with the philosophers. Instead, it emphasizes the principles of right, to which citizens can appeal if they consent to the contract for which the treatise pleads. The definitive title supports and underscores Rousseau's decision to appear first and preferably in the persona of the advocate.[13] The advocate of the body politic shows what it means to be a

---

11. II, 7, 2 (381); II, 8, 1 (385); III, 6, 15 (412). II, 3, 4 note (372); II, 7, 11 note (384); III, 6, 5 (409) as well as note (ed. 1782, *OCP* III, p. 1480); III, 9, 4 note (420); III, 10, 3 note (422).—Rousseau changed the subtitle from *Essai sur la constitution de l'Etat* to *Essai sur la formation du corps politique* and *Essai sur la formation de l'Etat* to *Essai sur la forme de la République*. In his edition, Edmond Dreyfus-Brisac reproduces a facsimile (alongside p. 245) of the title page of the manuscript of the *Première version*, which is in Geneva; cf. *OCP* III, p. 1410.

12. Blaise Bachofen, Bruno Bernardi, and Gilles Olivo suggest in their edition of *Du contract social ou Essai sur la forme de la République (Manuscrit de Genève)* (Paris, 2012), pp. 11–12 and 31), that Rousseau's editing of the main title be read as occurring in the following stages: (1) *De la Société Civile*, (2) *Du Contract Social*, (3) *du Contract social*. According to their hypothesis, Rousseau had written the new version of the title (2) above the title line (1), then rejected it and crossed it out, only finally to write it below the title line (1) once again (3). Accordingly, the original title of the manuscript would have been *De la société civile* and not *Du Contract Social*. Speaking against this proposal, however, is the handwriting of the manuscript, both the size of the script and the arrangement of the topmost line *Du Contract Social*, which corresponds to the size and the arrangement of the original subtitle, *Essai sur la constitution de l'Etat*, and the matching distances that both lines maintain to the *ou*, which occupies a line of its own between the main title and subtitle. With the arrangement originally chosen by Rousseau, he could write the title *De la société civile* that he later considered and the final version only below the main title, *Du Contract Social*.

13. A number of changes to the structure and rhetorical orientation that Rousseau sets out to make to the *Première version* are in harmony with the new accentuation of the title. Among these is the preface to the definitive version, which emphasizes that the author speaks as a citizen. The critique of "Fausses notions du lien social," which he reserved for chapter I, 5 of the *Première version* and which there followed the presentation of his conception in chapters I, 3 "Du pacte fondamental," and I, 4 "En quoi consiste la souveraineté, et ce qui la rend inaliénable," now in the revised form and divided into three chapters (I, 2–4) precedes his own answer in I, 6 and the advocative introduction to it in I, 5. But, most importantly, Rousseau deletes the long discussion in chapter I, 2, "De la société générale du genre humain," with which, after only a few lines composing chapter I, 1 "Sujet de cet ouvrage," the *Première version* actually began. In this discussion, Rousseau confronted in particular Diderot's article *Droit naturel* (*Encyclopédie*, volume V, 1755) without mentioning him by name, and the heading of the chapter alluded to article II *De la société générale du genre humain naît la société civile, c'est-à-dire celle des Etats*,

citizen in the demanding sense. The advocate of the citizens explains how the right of the sovereign is to be defended against all attacks that claim a higher right, whether it be historical, natural, or divine. For the presentation of the principles of political right, Rousseau deploys ten consecutive chapters, beginning with chapter I, 6 "Du pacte social" and ending with chapter II, 6 "De la loi." The arc extends from the contract by which the sovereign emerges to the law through which the sovereign expresses its will, and the sovereign is determined by Rousseau essentially as will. In fact will, which characterizes the sovereign, is spoken of before the first mention of the sovereign as one of a number of correlations of the body politic. Rousseau's interpretation of the nature of the social contract commences with the formulation of the contract itself, which introduces the key concept of the principles, the *volonté générale*: "Each of us puts his person and his full power in common under the supreme direction of the general will; and we as a body receive each member as an indivisible part of the whole." The *volonté générale* forms the hinge linking both halves of the formula of the contract, which, divided by a semicolon, expresses the fundamental change of subject, which is brought about by the unreserved transfer of power by the associates. With the evocation of the *volonté générale*, the binding of individuals to a We, the transformation of the person into the integral component of a new whole is accomplished. The formula of the contract identifies the *volonté générale* as the central determination of the body politic long before Rousseau designates the legislative power as the heart of the State.[14] The collective body that the contract produces "is made up of as many members as the assembly has voices/votes"; at the same time, the collective body receives through the contract, as Rousseau confirms at the beginning of the interpretation, "its unity, its common *I*, its life and its will." To leave no doubt as to what he has grounded with the *contrat social*, Rousseau adds that the "public person," which emerges from "the union of all the others," once bore the name *Cité*, i.e., *polis* or *civitas*, and is now called *République* or *corps politique*.[15]

---

des peuples et des nations in book I of *Politique tirée des propres paroles de l'Ecriture sainte* by Bossuet (ed. Jacques Le Brun, p. 11), who likewise goes without mention. The philosophic critique of Diderot, who related the *volonté générale* to the human species, and of other theoreticians who raised the "general society of the human race" to the bearer of natural rights, appears to Rousseau to be dispensable for the unfolding of the *Principes du droit politique*: It would have diverted attention away from the direct address to the citizens. Finally, Rousseau turns the sentence "L'homme est né libre, et cependant partout il est dans les fers," with which chapter I, 3 "Du pacte fondamental" began (*OCP* III, p. 289), in its final, polished version, into the opening of the book and thus puts it right up at the front of his political teaching.

14. I, 6, 9 (361), consider the formulation of the *Première version* I, 3, 3 (p. 290). III, 11, 3 (424).
15. I, 6, 10 (361–62).

Rousseau introduces the body politic as a complex unity of reciprocal relations and twofold characterizations. Its members call it *Etat* when it is passive, *Souverain* when it is active, and *Puissance* when compared with bodies of its kind. The body politic is, in other words, the sovereign insofar as it exercises the supreme authority, the State insofar as it receives its order from the laws that as sovereign it gives, and it is a consolidated power, effective externally as well as internally, insofar as it encounters other bodies politic from which it distinguishes itself, with which it cooperates, against which it asserts itself. The *Citoyens* are as *Sujets* subordinate to the laws of the State, which they *in corpore* have enacted as *Souverain*.[16] The twofold obligation that each associate enters into with himself through the *acte d'association* finds its expression in the twofold characterization of the citizen. As a member of the sovereign the associate is obligated in relation to the individual, and as a member of the State the associate is obligated in relation to the sovereign. By contrast, the sovereign remains unbound by any obligation in relation to itself, for "it is contrary to the nature of the body politic for the sovereign to impose on itself a law that it cannot break." To that extent, the sovereign is in the position of the individual who contracts with himself: Unlike those he enters into with others, the individual can annul such a contract on his own warrant. That there cannot be "any kind of fundamental law that is obligatory," "not even the social contract," for the sovereign, for the people in exercising the supreme power as warranted by the contract, follows from the *contrat social* and marks the founding of a collective subject that knows how to claim to be the sole source of right.[17] The founding of the body politic is simply not compatible with a state in which *the individual* would obey only himself and thus remain as free as he would be without his political belonging. When the advocate of the contract emphasizes that the *associate* enters into a twofold obligation *with himself*, the philosopher leaves no doubt that *the citizen* has entered into this obligation with himself *as sovereign* and *as subject*, in functions defined by the body politic. But the citizen stands not only in the reciprocal relation of sovereign and subject. As part of the sovereign, he bears in addition, as we have seen, the twofold characterization of being a *membre*, a part of an assembly, and a *membre*, a part of a body, of an assembly that comprises all citizens and counts according to votes, and of a body that incorporates them in a common I, leads a life of its own, and has a particular will. While Rousseau

---

16. I, 6, 10 (362); cf. the more precise formulation in III, 13, 5 (427).
17. I, 7, 2 (362–63); cf. II, 12, 2 (393–94); III, 18, 9 (436).

makes explicit the twofold characterization of the citizen as sovereign and subject, he neglects to do so with the twofold characterization that lies in belonging to an assembly and to a body. Through the ambiguous talk of *membre*, he even keeps the twofold characterization concealed or undetermined to a certain degree. For the adequate interpretation of his teaching of the principles of political right and especially of the *volonté générale*, however, the second twofold characterization of the citizen is of decisive importance. The "individualistic" reading, which appeals to belonging to an assembly, testifies to this in its own way, as does the "holistic" reading, which argues for belonging to a body. If the twofold characterization is not thought, Rousseau's often invoked "paradoxes" remain unsolved. If it is thought, the conjuring of mystical traditions in order to grasp the conception of the *volonté générale* is also made superfluous.

Citizens are sovereign only *in corpore*, not as individuals. For this reason, in one of the two twofold characterizations the *souverain* in the singular stands in contrast to the *sujets* in the plural. In order that the will of the sovereign can manifest itself, the assembly of the citizens is needed. But the will of the sovereign becomes manifest only if the citizens in the assembly vote *as citizens*, not as private persons but as members of the *corps politique*. The other of the two twofold characterizations points to this. According to the principles of political right the assembly of the people is the highest organ of the body politic. It can rightfully be put at the disposition of nothing or no one. Nevertheless, it can do justice to the task the social contract assigns to it only to the extent that its members identify with the *moi commun* to which they belong, and understand as their cause the cause of the whole of which they are a part. The advocate, who solicits the consent of actually existing citizens, does not in every case emphasize the fundamental "change" that the contract demands.[18] The sovereign of the *Contrat social* presupposes the citizen in the eminent sense, who for his part presupposes a series of political, institutional, economic conditions. Only in light of this presupposition is the normative meaning of the famous statement of chapter 7 disclosed, which identifies the Is and Ought of the sovereign: "The

---

18. For instance, when he says: "Or le Souverain n'étant formé que des particuliers qui le composent n'a ni ne peut avoir d'intérêt contraire au leur; par conséquent la puissance Souveraine n'a nul besoin de garant envers les sujets, parce qu'il est impossible que le corps veuille nuire à tous ses membres, et nous verrons ci-après qu'il ne peut nuire à aucun en particulier. Le Souverain, par cela seul qu'il est, est toujours tout ce qu'il doit être." I, 7, 5 (363); cf. I, 9, 6 (367); II, 1, 1 (368) and II, 3, 2 (371); consider II, 3, 2 note (371) and IV, 1, 4–6 (438).

sovereign, by the mere fact that it is, is always everything it ought to be." For the sovereign *is* only if the general will speaks and exercises its directing power. The problem of the sovereign, that the will of the citizen and the will of the individual are not congruent, Rousseau tellingly treats on the basis of the engagements that the *sujets* have to fulfill in relation to the *souverain*, in regard to the duties that the subjects have to fulfill within the body politic. In the second passage in the book in which Rousseau speaks about the *volonté générale*, and with the first mention after he has introduced the concept in the formula of the contract, he states that "each individual as a human being can have a particular will contrary to or different from the general will he has as a citizen." The citizen is *comme citoyen* the bearer of the *volonté générale*, but he is not completely absorbed in being a member of the body politic; instead, he remains an independent, a physical, a natural being, whose interest might very well conflict with the common interest and the duties that the *corps moral et collectif* that is based upon convention asks of him. If he wanted to enjoy the rights of the citizen without fulfilling the duties of the subject, this would be an injustice, whose pervasiveness would have as its consequence the ruin of the body politic. The individual can be misled to such injustice—it is the only time Rousseau speaks of injustice in book I—if, in contrast to the evidence of his "absolute and by nature independent existence," he considers the artificial body of the State, "since it is not a human being," as an *être de raison*, an imaginary being born from reason alone. The problem of the subjects, of their injustice or their lack of law-abidingness, is met with by the force, strength, power that the contract transfers to the State, by which the contract gives it a real presence. For the social contract contains tacitly, i.e., necessarily, the obligation "that whoever refuses to obey the general will, shall be constrained to do so by the entire body." Elucidating, the advocate continues: "which means nothing other than that he shall be forced to be free." Civil freedom, as distinguished from natural freedom, rests on convention and on coercion. That the body politic when necessary forces obedience to the *volonté générale* is the condition of the freedom of its members, which consists in being obligated to obey no authority other than that held by the sovereign, the assembly of citizens. It is in addition the condition of the freedom the citizens enjoy among one another, "for it is this condition which, by giving each citizen to the fatherland, guarantees him against all personal dependence." Thus, Rousseau can finally say about the force that guarantees the obedience or subordination of the *volonté particulière* of the subject to the *volonté générale* of the sovereign that "it alone renders legitimate civil engagements that without it would be absurd, tyrannical, and liable to the most enormous abuses." We have arrived once more at the chains with which the book begins.[19]

The problem of the sovereign has not yet been solved with the problem of the subjects. The answer that the principles of political right provide for the one case evidently is of no use for the other. The institution of a legitimate coercive power can defend against the injustice of the subjects; it cannot ensure the justice of the members of the sovereign. Since the sovereign possesses supreme power, there is no guarantor who could guarantee that the citizen in the people's assembly is determined by the *volonté générale* and subordinates his *volonté particulière* to it. The sanction to which the sovereign is subject is the death of the body politic or the dissolution of the social contract. The advocate of the contract refers to the assurance implied by the double generality of the sovereign: Since the sovereign is general insofar as it encompasses all citizens, and since it declares its will exclusively in general laws to which all the members of the sovereign are subordinate as subjects, the sovereign cannot want to privilege or disadvantage any citizen, burden one more or relieve another less.[20] That the *volonté générale* of the citizen and the *volonté particulière* of the individual are not congruent seems, accordingly, to remain without consequences in the case of the members of the people's assembly. It certainly would remain without consequences only if (1) the laws were not only valid for all, but also concerned all in equal measure, or if (2) the general will were exhausted in being the intersection of the diverging particular wills. The first assumption would presuppose that the conventional equality that the contract establishes would render natural inequality insignificant, that the citizens would not be different with regard to their capability and their neediness, or that differences of force or of genius, for instance, would be irrelevant to the body politic.[21] The second assumption would permit an association of individuals to come into being on the basis of particular interests that can be generalized, but would not permit its coming to be a polis or republic, in which citizens lead a political life and can understand themselves in relation to a whole they affirm as meaningful. Therefore, Rousseau makes the *volonté générale* the hinge of a contract that obligates individuals to become citizens, and the central determination of a body politic that receives each member as an indivisible part of the whole. The philosopher has the reader understand that the figure of double

---

19. I, 7, 6–8 (363–64); cf. II, 4, 8 (375); II, 5, 2 (376) and consider II, 12, 3 (394).
20. I, 7, 5 (363); II, 4, 5–8 (373–75); II, 6, 5 (379).
21. Cf. I, 9, 8 (367); II, 4, 10 (375); II, 5, 2 (376). Consider II, 6, 6 (379); III, 5, 4–7 (406–7).

generality does not suffice to put the body politic under the direction of the *volonté générale* and to make the Is and the Ought of the sovereign congruent. The double generality of the sovereign, that both the subject of the will and the matter over which it decides are general, is a necessary principle of political right. But if the *volonté générale* is to be able to express itself, it is requisite in addition that the members of the sovereign vote *comme citoyens*, that they pose the question whether their decision is "advantageous to the State," that they direct their will to the *bien public*, to the *bien commun*, to the *bien général*.²² For the general will is general not only according to subject and matter, but first and foremost according to its goal: It always aims at the general good of the body politic. The conception of the *volonté générale* is based upon both the interest *and* the justice of the citizen. It is the attempt to intertwine a strict postulate of right with a substantial orientation of politics. The fact that Rousseau pursues both strands explains the detachment of the *volonté générale* from the empirical will of the assembly, his insistence upon "characteristics" that allow him to say that the *volonté générale* is "missed" in the vote, that the members of the sovereign "elude" it and that in the end it grows "mute," although it would never be "annihilated" or "corrupted" as long as the body politic preserves itself in life, that it is "always constant, unalterable, and pure," yet nevertheless be made "subordinate" to others that "prevail over it."²³ Rousseau's assertion that the *volonté générale* is *toujours droite*, which has caused so much offense and was designed to do so, does not refer to any mystical entity fitted with infallibility.²⁴ It also does not rely on a quality that would put man as man

---

22. I, 5, 1 (359); I, 7, 7 (363); II, 1, 1 (368); II, 4, 8 (375); IV, 1, 5–6 (438).
23. IV, 1, 5–6 (438); IV, 2, 4 (440); IV, 2, 8–9 (440–41).
24. To clarify a related misinterpretation, it should be noted that the *volonté générale* is just as little a self-subsisting entity, standing in conflict with another entity, called the *volonté de tous*. In the conception of the *Contrat social*, the *volonté générale* is a governing *concept* that designates the will of the *corps politique*. The will of the *corps politique* aims at the *bien public*. It is exercised by the *corps politique* in its highest activity as *souverain* (I, 5, 1; I, 6, 9; I, 6, 10). For its manifestation, it needs an *assemblée*, in which it can express itself as the *volonté du corps du peuple* (I, 6, 10; II, 2, 1). Its bearers are the members of the sovereign, when they *comme citoyens* orient their will toward the *bien public*, to the good of the body politic (I, 7, 7; IV, 1, 5; IV, 1, 6). Rousseau uses the concept in the headings of two chapters: "Si la volonté générale peut errer" (II, 3) and "Que la volonté générale est indestructible" (IV, 1). The *volonté générale* does not have a counterconcept in the "volonté de tous." Rousseau speaks twice in the entire treatise of "volonté de tous." In the one passage, he stresses the determination of the general will as being directed only to the common interest, whereas the will of all, as individuals, is directed to private interest and is only the sum of particular wills. To the extent that the common interest coincides with private interest, the general will can agree with the will of all (II, 3, 2). In the other passage,

in a position to hit unerringly upon what is right, whether by means of his capacity for generalization, which would prescribe to him what is right, or by means of his conscience, which would prompt him to what is right.[25] The statement is meant to highlight the necessary directedness of the body politic to its own good, which is general in relation to the citizens, while particular in relation to the political community itself. It follows the Platonic proposition that each always wants what is good for himself, which does not imply that he always knows what is good for himself.[26] In Rousseau's statement the result of the hermeneutics of political life finds expression, that the citizens as citizens are united by the will to increase the utility for the political community and to ward off what is harmful to it. This is why Rousseau can establish with certainty that the *volonté générale* is not in doubt when in the moment of the greatest danger the existence of the political community is at stake. The dire emergency shows with the greatest clarity the aim of the *volonté générale* and what its standard is.[27]

Rousseau speaks of the situation in which the social bond begins to loosen and the State begins to lose its strength, so that particular interests gain in influence. In this situation, unanimity no longer rules in the vote in the people's assembly, and the general will is no longer the will of all (IV, 1, 4). Cf. the use of language in the *Première version* I, 7, 3, p. 310 and in the *Lettres écrites de la montagne* VI, 19, *OCP* III, p. 807.

25. Rousseau's political conception of the *volonté générale* contradicts Diderot, who raised humanity to the level of the subject of a general will in order to obtain from the *volonté générale de l'espèce* a moral principle, which would obligate man as man: "C'est à la volonté générale que l'individu doit s'adresser pour savoir jusqu'où il doit être homme, citoyen, sujet, père, enfant, et quand il lui convient de vivre ou de mourir. C'est à elle à fixer les limites de tous les devoirs. Vous avez le *droit naturel* le plus sacré à tout ce qui ne vous est point contesté par l'espèce entière. C'est elle qui vous éclairera sur la nature de vos pensées et de vos désirs. Tout ce que vous concevrez, tout ce que vous méditerez, sera bon, grand, élevé, sublime, s'il est de l'intérêt général et commun." Diderot held "que la volonté générale est dans chaque individu un acte pur de l'entendement qui raisonne dans le silence des passions sur ce que l'homme peut exiger de son semblable, et sur ce que son semblable est en droit d'exiger de lui." And he made a claim for the certainty of the principle of generalization when he asserted that "des deux volontés, l'une générale, et l'autre particulière, la volonté générale n'erre jamais." *Droit naturel* VII and IX, in Denis Diderot, *Œuvres complètes* (*OC*) (Paris, 1975–), VII, pp. 28–29.

26. "Il s'ensuit de ce qui précede que la volonté générale est toujours droite et tend toujours à l'utilité publique: mais il ne s'ensuit pas que les délibérations du peuple aient toujours la même rectitude. On veut toujours son bien, mais on ne le voit pas toujours." II, 3, 1 (371). Rousseau already argued earlier: "il ne dépend d'aucune volonté de consentir à rien de contraire au bien de l'être qui veut" II, 1, 3 (369). Cf. II, 4, 5 (373) and II, 6, 10 (380).

27. "en pareil cas la volonté générale n'est pas douteuse, et il est évident que la premiere intention du peuple est que l'Etat ne périsse pas." IV, 6, 4 (456). This is the penultimate passage in which Rousseau speaks in the *Contrat social* about the *volonté générale*.

In order to put the body politic under the direction of the general will, citizens are necessary who as subjects obey the laws and who as members of the sovereign give priority to the common good. Since the sovereign is not subordinate to any power, the gap between the demand of the *volonté générale* and the claims of the *volonté particulière* can be closed only by the citizen seeing his good in the good of the body politic or by his hoping to achieve it through service to the common good. What is necessary, consequently, is the love, the virtue, or the belief of the citizen: The *amour de la patrie*, the love of the fatherland, which Rousseau conceives as an extension of *amour de soi*, love of oneself. The strength or effort of fulfilling his duty, and the self-admiration or the satisfaction that *amour-propre*, self-love, gains from the elevation to virtue. The conviction of being part of a greater whole that is worthy of devotion and in light of which one's own worthiness is measured, a belief that has its resonance in *amour de soi* and in *amour-propre*. To provide form, nourishment, support for the citizen's love, virtue, and belief, good laws, a public education, and political institutions are necessary that solidify the social bond, counteract social inequalities, work against economic dislocations, and anchor the "sacred right" of the order of the political community in the experience of active life. Since *souverain* and *sujet* designate "identical correlatives" of the citizen, who, even if considered in different respects, remains *one*,[28] the presuppositions to which the problem of the sovereign refers concern the subjects no less. In fact, Rousseau is far from being satisfied with the guarantee of coercive power that the principles of political right provide for the solution to the problem of the subjects. Later, in the draft constitution for Poland, he will put the political task into the formula that "the law rule the hearts of the citizens."[29] If the subordination of the *volonté particulière* to the *volonté générale* were secured only by force in the case of the citizen in his capacity as subject, little would speak in favor of the claim that the subordination would come about without force in the case of the same citizen in his capacity as a member of the sovereign. What is necessary in order to place the body politic under the direction of the general will is, in other words, a well-ordered political community or what in the immediate sequel to his

---

28. "l'essence du corps politique est dans l'accord de l'obéissance et de la liberté, et . . . ces mots de *sujet* et de *souverain* sont des corrélations identiques dont l'idée se réunit sous le seul mot de Citoyen." III, 13, 5 (427).

29. "Il n'y aura jamais de bonne et solide constitution que celle où la loi régnera sur les cœurs des citoyens. Tant que la force législative n'ira pas jusques là, les loix seront toujours éludées." *Considérations sur le gouvernement de Pologne* I, 6, OCP III, p. 955. Cf. *Projet de constitution pour la Corse*, OCP III, p. 950.

exposition of the principles of political right Rousseau treats as wise *institution*, institution or founding, constitution, but also instruction. It belongs to the wisdom of Rousseau's *institution* that it leaves it to the citizens to consent to it with an awareness of their freedom and, supported by their pride, to obey only themselves, to make service to the republic into their cause.

II

The philosopher, who develops the principles of political right from the nature of the social contract, demonstrates *ad oculos* the necessity of his knowledge for the legitimate political community. But the knowledge of the philosopher also has a special place and prominent placeholder in the structure of the *Contrat social* itself. The questions that arise once the concept of the *volonté générale* is thought and its political presuppositions are investigated—the question about where the good laws come from that are needed in order to have citizens give good laws, the question of who will educate the educators, the question of who will institute the institutions that make the citizens into citizens according to the understanding of the principles, in summa, the question of how the well-ordered political community can be created that is the condition for the *volonté générale* to reach its goal and that cannot be well ordered if it is not subject to the direction of the *volonté générale*—all these questions lead to the seventh chapter of the second book, "Du Législateur." There, wisdom steps onto the political stage, to counter the perplexity to which the teaching of the principles of political right has led the reader. Rousseau prepares this turn in the tenth and final paragraph of the tenth and final chapter of the part about the principles. At the end of chapter II, 6, "De la loi," in which he defines the law formally as the act of the general will, he comes to speak once again of the people always wanting the good for itself. He calls to mind the Platonic premise of the doctrine of the general will and moves without delay straight to the political problem par excellence, which consists in orienting the will toward knowledge of the good, making the will see, giving it eyes, helping it to judge, and bringing the enlightenment the will needs for its purpose. "How will a blind multitude, which often does not know what it wills because it rarely knows what is good for it, carry out by itself an undertaking as great, as difficult as a system of legislation? By itself the people always wills the good, but by itself it does not always see it. The general will is always right, but the judgment that guides it is not always enlightened. It must be made to see objects as they are, sometimes as they should appear to it." The body politic is dependent upon the linkage between understanding and will. It needs the guidance of insight. "Individuals see the good they reject; the public wills the good it does not see. All are equally in need of guides: The first must be obligated to conform their wills to their reason; the other must be taught to know what it wills." The presentation of the principles of political right in chapters I, 6–II, 6 ends with an undisguised plea for knowledge to lead the political community, and it closes with the sentence: "Hence arises the necessity of a lawgiver."[30]

"Du Législateur" is the philosophically most substantial chapter of the writing. It breaks the political problem down into seven problems, which so interpenetrate that the last link in the chain is joined to the first. The chain as a whole concerns the relation of the philosopher to politics.[31] At the beginning, Rousseau places the problem of the benevolent or caring God (I). In order to discover the best rules suited to the nations, i.e., the various particular political societies, *une intelligence supérieur* would be necessary. A superior insight would be needed, which Rousseau puts beyond human reach with the three following determinations and has appear as the insight of a God: A higher intelligence (1) "who saw all of men's passions and experienced none of them," (2) "who had no relation to our nature and knew it thoroughly," (3) "whose happiness was independent of us and who was nevertheless willing to attend to ours." The criteria that identify the sought-after lawgiver as a God[32] set out clearly the problem of the divine lawgiver. He is supposed to act for the good of men without sharing with them a common good. In order to bridge the gap, Rousseau, following the example of Machiavelli, introduces the reward of glory, a glory, however, that, as Rousseau explains, shines visibly for the lawgiver only from afar, when the legislation is already in decline or belongs to the past. Thus, the final determination characterizing the higher intelligence under discussion reads as follows: (4) "finally, one who, preparing his distant glory in the progress of

---

30. II, 6, 10 (380). See also II, 3, 4 (372).

31. In the *Contrat social* as well as in his other writings, Rousseau exercises reserve when speaking affirmatively about the philosopher, using instead *le sage* or *le génie* in order to prevent any confusion with the philosophers à la mode. In II, 7, 11 (384), he explicitly distances himself from the "orgueilleuse philosophie" of the philosophes. This is the sole use of *philosophie* in the *Contrat social*. In addition, *philosophique*, *philosophe*, and *philosopher* each appear once in, respectively: I, 8, 3 (365), IV, 8, 13 (463), and IV, 8, 32 note (468). For this, see my *Über das Glück des philosophischen Lebens*, pp. 123–30 with n. 62 [*On the Happiness of the Philosophic Life*, pp. 89–94].

32. Consider III, 6, 16 (413) and cf. *Über das Glück des philosophischen Lebens*, pp. 91–101 and 335 [*On the Happiness of the Philosophic Life*, pp. 63–72 and 256].—While Rousseau speaks in II, 7, 1 (381) of *une intelligence supérieure* in the singular, he shifts to the plural in the last sentence of the paragraph: "Il faudroit des Dieux pour donner des loix aux hommes." In the *Première version*, by contrast, he kept to the singular: "En un mot, il faudroit un Dieu pour donner de bonnes loix au genre humain" II, 2, 1, pp. 312–13. The shift to the plural "Dieux" in II, 7, 1 establishes the connection to the important mentions of "Dieux" in I, 2, 6 (353) and IV, 8, 1 (460), which are without precedent in the *Première version*.

times, could work in one century and enjoy the reward in another."³³ But would the prospect of a *gloire éloignée* for the superior insight of a God or of a philosopher be a sufficient reason to engage in the work of legislation?³⁴ If a higher intelligence is needed for the institution of a people, the problem of origin is designated (II). The legitimate institution that rests on the social contract presupposes a wise founding, whose extraordinary rarity Rousseau emphasizes, or a historical preparation that makes possible in the first place an order in harmony with the principles of political right. The "mechanic who invents the machine" is not subject to its shaping force, and the insight of the founder, to which it falls to create citizens out of men, is not brought about by convention.³⁵ The transformation of the individual into a member of the body politic, which the social contract has for its object, demands a more comprehensive change than the interpretation of the *Contrat social* first indicates. The problem of the anthropological transformation of the citizen (III) is nowhere expressed more clearly than in the description of the task with which the *Législateur* sees himself confronted. "Anyone who dares to institute a people must feel capable of, so to speak, changing human nature; of transforming each individual who by himself is a perfect and solitary whole into a part of a larger whole from which this individual, as it were, receives his life and his being; of altering man's constitution in order to strengthen it; of substituting a partial and moral existence for the physical and independent existence we have all received from nature. In a word, he must take from man his own forces, in order to give him forces which are foreign to him and of which he cannot make use without the help of others."³⁶ The *aliénation totale*, the determination to which Rousseau, in the chapter "Du pacte social," traces back all the other determinations of the social contract, is not exhausted in the act of alienating all the claims

---

33. The fourth determination is not yet present in the *Première version*, while each of the first three determinations has a predecessor in that text: II, 2, 1, p. 312.—When in 1764 the Corsican Mathieu Buttafoco urges Rousseau, as *Législateur*, to give Corsica a constitution, in order to win Rousseau over for the task he takes up word for word three of the four determinations that Rousseau invokes for the characterization of the *intelligence supérieure*, and applies them to Rousseau, with the appropriate adaptations. Captain Mathieu Buttafoco to Rousseau, August 31, 1764, *Correspondance complète de Jean Jacques Rousseau*, ed. R. A. Leigh (Geneva–Banbury–Oxford, 1965–98), 52 volumes (*CC*), XXI, pp. 85–86.

34. Consider Leo Strauss, *The Argument and the Action of Plato's "Laws"* (Chicago, 1975), II, 12, p. 29 and see *Über das Glück des philosophischen Lebens*, pp. 231–35 [*On the Happiness of the Philosophic Life*, pp. 173–76].

35. II, 7, 2 (381).

36. II, 7, 3 (381–82); cf. I, 6, 6 (360); II, 4, 5 (373); III, 2, 7 (401); further *Émile ou de l'éducation* I, *OCP* IV, pp. 248–49.

to right and reserved rights in favor of the body politic, but instead refers to the demand for a still deeper intervention into the constitution of man.[37] Problem III underlies problem II and explains the priority of problem I. The institution of a people needs a benevolent lawgiver who has sufficient knowledge of the nature of man and of the nature of the body politic. A founder who begins his work with knowledge of the necessities to which it is subject. A wise man who does not succumb to the illusion that the tension between society resting on convention and nature might ever be resolved or permanently mastered by the art of the lawgiver.

The principles of political right ground the necessity of a *Législateur* who has no support in them, of a superior insight that has no constitutional place in the legitimate order. "The lawgiver is in every respect an extraordinary man in the State. If he must be so by his genius, he is no less so by his office." For his position or his activity should not be confused with either *magistrature* or *souveraineté*. It "constitutes the republic," but it "does not enter into its constitution." The *Législateur* explicitly has at his disposal the authority neither of the sovereign nor of the magistrate, i.e., of the government. The wise lawgiver is not part of the institution, but the institution is not well ordered without him. Rousseau shows the insuperable tension between politics and philosophy by nothing more clearly than by the problem of the extraconstitutional position of the *Législateur* (IV), than by the outside and above in which he keeps and leaves wisdom. At the same time, he once again illuminates an aspect of the problem of the divine lawgiver (I), by emphasizing that "he who has command over the laws" is not allowed to have command over men, since otherwise the lawgiver would be exposed to the corrupting effect of personal rule and "could never avoid having particular views vitiate the sanctity of his work." Lycurgus represents the deistic model. "When Lycurgus," Rousseau reports, "gave his fatherland laws, he began by abdicating the kingship." One also reads in Plutarch that Lycurgus left the polis he had instituted never to return; he did so, however, only after he had the citizens swear an oath that they would remain committed to the work of his legislation without making any changes until he had returned to them.[38] Certainly it cannot be said that the *Législateur* of the *Contrat social* "has command over the laws." Rousseau insists instead that

---

37. Concerning the formulation "d'altérer la constitution de l'homme" in II, 7, 3, it should be noted that throughout his writings Rousseau uses *altérer* in the sense of "to change for the worse," "spoil," or "distort," and not in the neutral sense of "change." In the *Première version* he even wrote: "qu'il mutile en quelque sorte la constitution de l'homme pour la renforcer" II, 2, 3, p. 313.

38. II, 7, 4–5 (382). Plutarch, *Lycurgus* 29; cf. 3–5.

"he who drafts the laws" does not or should not have any *droit législatif* and that "the people itself cannot, even if it wanted to, divest itself of this nontransferable right." For, according to the contract, only the *volonté générale* is capable of obligating individuals, and the conformity of a *volonté particulière* to the *volonté générale* can be established with assurance or in a binding way only "once it has been submitted to the free suffrage of the people." Rousseau adds: "I have said this already, but it is not useless to repeat it." Thus, in the middle of the chapter "Du Législateur," he reminds the reader once more of the nonnegotiable core of the principles and the fundamental problem of politics, namely, that insight cannot dispense with the consent of the people (V).[39] The discrepancy between the superhuman task (problems I, II, and III), on the one hand, and the authority of the *Législateur*, grounded in his wisdom alone, not supported by the constitution, and dependent upon the approval of the many (problems IV and V), on the other,[40] is finally so intensified by the problem of the communication of the wise with the unwise (VI) that it appears unbridgeable: "The wise who want to speak to the vulgar in their own language rather than in the language of the vulgar would not be understood by the vulgar. Yet there are a thousand kinds of ideas that it is impossible to translate into the language of the people." The problem of the communication with the people rests, on the one hand, on natural inequality: "Views that are too general and objects that are too remote are equally beyond its grasp." On the other hand, it is historically conditioned: The individuals would have to be decisively shaped by the giving of the constitution, they would already have to be citizens in order to evaluate the political order not only according to the standard of their particular interests, and to be prepared to take upon themselves willingly the privations that good laws demand from them (problem III). In short: the people would have to be the work of wise institution in order to be able to appreciate the institution of the wise (problem II).[41]

Since the *Législateur* neither has command over the means of coercion in order to enforce his insight with the sovereign, nor is able to communicate his wisdom to the people in language appropriate to wisdom, since, for

---

39. II, 7, 6–7 (382–83); cf. II, 1, 3 (368–69).

40. "Ainsi l'on trouve à la fois dans l'ouvrage de la législation deux choses qui semblent incompatibles: une entreprise au dessus de la force humaine, et pour l'éxécuter, une autorité qui n'est rien." II, 7, 8, (383).

41. "Pour qu'un peuple naissant put goûter les saines maximes de la politique et suivre les regles fondamentales de la raison d'Etat, il faudroit que l'effet put devenir la cause, que l'esprit social qui doit être l'ouvrage de l'institution présidât à l'institution même, et que les hommes fussent avant les loix ce qu'ils doivent devenir par elles." II, 7, 9 (383).

his task of "instituting" the people so that the *volonté générale* expresses itself and reaches its goal, he can find support neither from *la force* nor from *le raisonnement* alone, he must "of necessity have recourse to an authority of a different order" and make use of a rhetoric with which he can successfully persuade, if not convince. Thus, we arrive at the problem of uplifting speech or of the noble lie (VII), which comes in response to the six previous problems. The necessity of conferring upon legislation the authority of a higher superhuman origin "at all times forced the fathers of nations to resort to the intervention of heaven and to honor the Gods with their own wisdom."[42] The noble lie, which Rousseau speaks of without referring to it by name, not only retrospectively concerns the divine authority that the mythic lawgivers claimed for themselves (from which its answer to problems II, IV, and VI comes to light); it concerns likewise the beliefs that peoples could ever be subject to the laws of the State as they are subject to the laws of nature, and that in the formation of the political community the same power would be discerned that is at work in the development of man, opinions that peoples should take to be true so that they can "freely obey," i.e., so that they do not refuse to give their consent to insight and "bear with docility the yoke of public felicity" (in which the answer to problems III and V appears).[43] With the "yoke of public felicity" Rousseau has once again invoked the "chains" from the beginning of the first book. And the compulsion that forced the great lawgivers to conceal their wisdom by attributing it to the Gods leads us back to the *gloire éloignée* from the beginning of the chapter (problem I), whose significance now emerges in full clarity: the prospect of glory far in the distance is fulfilled for the *grand Législateur* only by the insight that knows wisdom in the concealment of his wisdom. The highest recognition that can be granted to the lawgiver lies enclosed in the knowledge of the philosopher, who comprehends the political problem in its necessary articulation, beginning with the problem of the caring God and ending with the problem of uplifting speech.

Immediately following the exposition of the seven problems, in the eleventh and longest paragraph of the chapter, Rousseau praises the lawgiver as no philosopher since Machiavelli did. Since the *raison sublime* needed for the institution and maintenance of the well-ordered political community

---

42. The first use of *sagesse* in the *Contrat social* coincides with the treatment of the noble lie, with the transformation of human wisdom into divine authority. Rousseau introduces the appeal to the wisdom of the Gods in the tenth of the twelve paragraphs that make up the chapter, just as Plato has the Athenian Stranger introduce the appeal to the cosmic Gods in the tenth book of the twelve books that make up the *Nomoi*.

43. II, 7, 10 (383); consider *Projet de constitution pour la Corse*, OCP III, p. 950 (last fragment).

goes beyond the grasp of *les hommes vulgaires*, the *Législateur* places the decisions of sublime reason, which are his own, "in the mouth of the immortals in order to rally by divine authority those whom human prudence could not move."[44] Sublime reason requires uplifting speech. Yet it is not exhausted by such speech. And it in no way proves to be mere cleverness or ingenuity. As little as legislation is a work of the Gods whom the lawgivers make speak for them, just as little does its permanence rest upon miracles of which the lawgivers avail themselves, for "empty tricks" can perhaps bring about a passing bond, but "only wisdom makes it durable." The *Législateur* needs wisdom in order to find belief among those whom he addresses as well as to create an institution that justifies that belief. "The great soul of the lawgiver is the true miracle, which must prove his mission." The work of the *Législateur* has its basis in the *raison sublime*, the *sagesse*, the *grande âme* that distinguish him, and thus in his nature: it is the truth of the noble lie, if truth is proper to it.[45] As examples of founders who honored the Gods with their own wisdom, Rousseau draws upon neither Minos nor Numa. Instead, he refers to the oldest and most recent prophets of the three revealed religions. For he speaks only of the law of Judaism and of the law of Islam, each of which appeals to the *one* God of faith in revelation as its author and of which Rousseau says that they "still bear witness today to the great men who dictated them." Rousseau cushions this assertion, with which he dares to go quite far, by a sharp separation from the philosophes, who carried out their struggle against revealed religions in the name of enlightenment and under the banner of the treatise *De tribus impostoribus*, which

---

44. Rousseau adds to this statement a footnote that quotes a relevant passage from *Discorsi* I, 11. Machiavelli supports Rousseau's argument (problems VI and VII). After the sentence cited by Rousseau, he continues: "Però gli uomini savi che vogliono tôrre questa difficultà ricorrono a Dio. Cosí fece Ligurgo, cosí Solone, cosí molti altri che hanno avuto il medesimo fine di loro." *Discorsi sopra la prima deca di Tito Livio* I, 11, ed. Francesco Bausi, *Opere di Niccolò Machiavelli* (Rome, 2001), I/2, p. 80.—Chapter II, 7 contains three footnotes. The first refers to the legislation of Lycurgus, which brought about "the Spartans' happiness" (381). The second speaks about the merit that Calvin earned as political founder rather than as theologian, and contains the only quasi-explicit reference to Christianity, which is mentioned in II, 7 as little as is Jesus: "Quelque révolution que le tems puisse amener dans *notre culte*, tant que l'amour de la patrie et de la liberté ne sera pas éteint parmi nous, jamais la mémoire de ce grand homme ne cessera d'y être en bénédiction" (382, my emphasis). While Rousseau speaks in the previous footnotes about Lycurgus and Calvin, in the third footnote he allows Machiavelli to speak for himself.

45. "Tout homme peut graver des tables de pierre, ou acheter un oracle, ou feindre un secret commerce avec quelque divinité, ou dresser un oiseau pour lui parler à l'oreille, ou trouver d'autres moyens grossiers d'en imposer au peuple. Celui qui ne saura que cela pourra même assembler par hazard une troupe d'insensés, mais il ne fondera jamais un empire, et son extravagant ouvrage périra bientôt avec lui." II, 7, 11 (384).

had become a slogan. Where "prideful philosophy or blind party spirit" sees only imposters who were lucky, *le vrai politique,* the true statesman in the Platonic sense or the true political theorist, admires the "great and powerful genius" that animates and dominates the institutions created by the lawgiver-prophets, institutions that last for centuries.[46]

Rousseau redeems the "great soul" of the lawgiver-prophet for the glory that it deserves by recognizing it as the true author of the divine law. At the same time, he unavoidably offers a sketch of the political genealogy of revealed religion. The conclusion is marked by the laconic rejection of the opinion "that among us, politics and religion have a common object," an opinion he attributes to Bishop William Warburton. Against the Christian political theologian, Rousseau contends that "at the origin of nations" religion serves instead as the instrument of politics. From the very beginning primacy is given to politics.[47]

The wisdom of the *Législateur* remains determinative for the entire second half of the second book. The five chapters that follow II, 7 deal with the necessity of the knowledge of the wise for the well-ordered political community, which is not limited to the founding, and which Rousseau no longer expounds using the example of the lawgiver-prophet. The three chapters "Du peuple" (II, 8–10) begin with the *sage instituteur* and end with the *homme sage.* In the chapter "Des divers sistêmes de législation" (II, 11), the *Législateur* asserts his dominant presence. And the last chapter of the book, "Division des loix" (II, 12), concludes with the *grand Législateur,* who there, after having been invoked in II, 7, makes his second, most important, and final appearance.[48] The three successive chapters "Of the People," to which correspond the three successive chapters in the third book, "How Sovereign Authority Is Maintained" (III, 12–14), focus on the matter with which the *Législateur* is concerned, in order to show the fundamental insights, the kinds of particular knowledge, and the judgment about how to combine and apply them that he needs for the "institution" of a people. For an institution

---

46. II, 7, 11 (384). *Le politique* in the *Contrat social* can mean both "statesman" and "political theorist." The Platonic ambiguity of the term stands in the background: in addition to II, 7, 11 see II, 9, 5 (388) and II, 12, 5 (394). However, the meaning "political theorist" or "political author" (sometimes in the sense of "political ideologue") predominates: II, 2, 2 (369); II, 2, 2 (370); III, 6, 14 (412); III, 7, 3 (413). *Le vrai politique* is mentioned only in II, 7, 11.

47. II, 7, 12 (384). For the use Rousseau makes of Warburton, cf. *Über das Glück des philosophischen Lebens,* pp. 431–32 [*On the Happiness of the Philosophic Life,* pp. 335–36].

48. II, 8, 1 (384); II, 10, 5 (391); cf. II, 10, 2 (389); II, 10, 4 (390). II, 11 4 (393); II 11, 5 (393). II, 12, 5 (394). *Sagesse* appears four times in the *Contrat social.* The only two uses that refer to individuals are to be found in II, 7, 10 and 11 (383–84) and concern the *Législateur.* The two other uses of the term refer to the aristocratic institution of the senate: III, 5, 5 note (407) and III, 6, 13 (412).

can count as good only if it is good for the particular people to which it is supposed to be given. Laws that are in themselves good must coincide with a people "that is suited to bear them." The knowledge that the good institution in a given case, as in the vast majority of cases, cannot be actualized belongs explicitly to the insight of the wise, and is not its least part. In fact, the emphasis on the rarity of success is the leitmotif of Rousseau's discussion. The first of the three chapters delves in detail into the historical presuppositions of legislation, the second concentrates on the knowledge appropriate to the nature of the subject matter, the third refers to natural conditions in the narrower sense. In all three chapters Rousseau makes explicit the decisive importance of adequate knowledge: in II, 8 it concerns the stage of development of a people, and in particular its maturity for legislation; in II, 9 the determination of the size of a State; in II, 10 the relation between population and territory that allows the political community a maximum of strength and self-sufficiency.[49] Moreover, Rousseau shows by his action that the wise must know how to use not only uplifting speech but also admonishing speech. In the history chapter he addresses peoples in order to explain to them that revolutions, like crises in the life of individuals, can bring about a fundamental turn for the better, quickly adding, however, that they are *événements rares*, and furthermore events that cannot be repeated in the life of a people. "Free peoples, remember this maxim: Freedom can be gained; but it can never be recovered." In the center of the triad is a warning against losing sight, amidst the purposes of internal order, of the requirements of external security, the dictate of the self-preservation of the political community. Finally, the third chapter culminates in a tableau that brings together the historical presuppositions and the natural conditions of good legislation so concisely that it will hardly fuel readers'

---

49. II, 8, 5 (386); II, 9,5 (388); II, 10, 1–2 (388–89).—As an example of a fateful, flawed judgment about the state of development of a people, Rousseau cites the judgment of Czar Peter I: "Il a vu que son peuple étoit barbare, il n'a point vu qu'il n'étoit pas mûr pour la police; il l'a voulu civiliser quand il ne faloit que l'agguerrir. Il a d'abord voulu faire des Allemands, des Anglois, quand il faloit commencer par faire des Russes." When Rousseau attributes to Peter merely "le génie imitatif" and denies him "le vrai génie," he aims his critique at Voltaire, who had presented the Czar as the model statesman and lawgiver. In the preface to his *Histoire de l'Empire de Russie sous Pierre le Grand*, Voltaire calls the Czar in 1759 "peut-être de tous les princes celui dont les faits méritent le plus d'être transmis à la postérité," and four years later in the second part of the work, Voltaire refers to Peter as the "vrai politique" (II, 8). In 1759 Voltaire contrasts Peter as *législateur* with Lycurgus and Solon, in order to praise Peter I as the one who, by his laws, "a formé les hommes et les femmes à la société, qui a créé la discipline militaire sur terre et sur mer, et qui a ouvert à son pays la carrière de tous les arts." *Œuvres historiques*, ed. René Pomeau (Paris, 1957), pp. 532, 1687, 1688–89.

expectations that the solution to the political problem might be within their immediate reach.[50]

The final orientation for the undertaking of the *Législateur* and the proper domain of his effectiveness are discussed in the two concluding chapters of book II. "If one inquires," Rousseau begins the chapter "Of the Various Systems of Legislation," "into precisely what the greatest good of all consists in, which ought to be the end of every system of legislation, one will find that it comes down to these two principal objects: *freedom* and *equality*. Freedom, because any individual dependence is that much force taken away from the body of the State; equality, because freedom cannot subsist without it." The lawgiver considers, in regard to the body politic as a whole, the two "principal objects" that all legislation has to handle. He adopts the perspective of the citizen who understands himself as a member of this body and conceives his freedom as essentially civil freedom, as freedom to be a citizen. No less political is his interest in equality which, seen up close, proves to be the concern that the concentration of social power and the accumulation of economic wealth conflict with the authority of the laws and undermine the sovereignty of the people. "No citizen should be so rich that he can buy another, and none so poor that he is compelled to sell himself." The outbreaks of social and economic inequality, the extreme deviations from the Aristotelian mean, favor tyranny and endanger the political order of the republic.[51] The "general objects of every good institution" must be adapted according to the particular conditions, so that each people receives "a particular system of institution." Just as important as the point of view on adaptation is the outlook on distinctiveness. Each people is supposed to receive an unmistakable imprint, which strengthens its cohesion, and a task, which establishes the pride of the citizens. If, however, the *Législateur*

---

50. II, 8, 3-4 (385); II, 9, 4 (388); II, 10, 5 (390-91): "Quel peuple est donc propre à la législation? Celui qui, se trouvant déjà lié par quelque union d'origine, d'intérêt ou de convention, n'a point encore porté le vrai joug des loix; celui qui n'a ni coutumes ni superstitions bien enracinées; celui qui ne craint pas d'être accablé par une invasion subite, qui, sans entrer dans les querelles de ses voisins, peut résister seul à chacun d'eux, ou s'aider de l'un pour repousser l'autre; celui dont chaque membre peut être connu de tous, et où l'on n'est point forcé de charger un homme d'un plus grand fardeau qu'un homme ne peut porter; celui qui peut se passer des autres peuples et dont tout autre peuple peut se passer; celui qui n'est ni riche ni pauvre et peut se suffire à lui-même; enfin celui qui réunit la consistance d'un ancien peuple avec la docilité d'un peuple nouveau."

51. "Voulez-vous donc donner à l'Etat de la consistance? rapprochez les degrés extrêmes autant qu'il est possible: ne souffrez ni des gens opulens ni des gueux. Ces deux états, naturellement inséparables, sont également funestes au bien commun; de l'un sortent les fauteurs de la tirannie et de l'autre les tirans; c'est toujours entre eux que se fait le trafic de la liberté publique; l'un l'achette et l'autre la vend." II, 11, 2 note (392).

is mistaken and chooses a principle for the institution that is not in harmony with the *nature des choses*, his undertaking will fail, and ultimately the State will be destroyed. The allusion to Horace's saying *Naturam expelles furca tamen usque recurret*, with which Rousseau ends the chapter, refers to the standard against which the art of the lawgiver has to prove itself. The chapter "Classification of the Laws" discloses where this art reaches its ownmost possibilities. To the three kinds of laws the reader can expect according to the presentation of the principles of political right—namely, the *loix politiques*, which concern the sovereign, the government, and the order of the State, as well as the *loix civiles* and the *loix criminelles*, which regulate civil and criminal law— Rousseau there adds a fourth kind of laws, which he calls "the most important of all" and to which he devotes the longest paragraph of the chapter. It "is graven neither in marble nor in bronze," but is inscribed "in the hearts of the citizens," and it makes up "the true constitution of the State": Rousseau speaks "of morals, of customs, and above all of opinion" and says about them that they are the part to which "the great lawgiver attends in secret." The reader of the later draft constitutions for Corsica and Poland can follow in detail which institutions Rousseau the lawgiver uses in order to shape the way of life of the people, to stabilize the political system, to achieve the autarky of Corsica, or to preserve Poland's integrity; how he orchestrates public education by means of economic measures, national tasks, festivals and honors, rewards and punishment; which ways he chooses to try to implant new valuations in the political class, to put *amour-propre* in the service of the political community, and to make possible the citizens' identification with the *moi commun*. The draft constitutions show what the *grand Législateur* attends to *en secret*, and they shed light on why chapter II, 12 of the *Contrat social* proclaims that *mœurs, coutumes,* and *opinion* are the most important kind of laws, although according to the principles of political right they are precisely not this: laws.[52]

The introduction of wisdom is tantamount to the disillusionment of political idealism in the *Contrat social*. In the economy of the work, the six chapters on *l'art du Législateur* form the counterweight to the preceding ten chapters on the *principes du droit politique*. The principles of right, which are not marked with a historical index because they rest exclusively on a coherent interpretation of the nature of the social contract, are thus politi-

---

52. II, 12, 5 (394). Six chapters earlier, in the last chapter of the part dealing with principles, Rousseau determined the law as the act of the general will and, therefore, as the act simply of the sovereignty of the people: II, 6, 5 and 7 (379).

cally situated, and in anticipation of the movement of books III and IV, are brought into contact with historical reality. If the principles ground the revolutionary claim always to be able to establish the illegitimacy of the existing order and bring about its removal, the art of the lawgiver highlights the improbability of a well-ordered political community.[53] The moderation of the section II, 7-12 is expressed emblematically by Rousseau's statement that there is "one country left in Europe" capable of receiving "legislation," i.e., suited to an institution in accord with the *Contrat social*, namely, the island of Corsica. This statement comes at the end of the three chapters "Du peuple."[54] The moderation that results from the consideration of political *realia* accords with the disillusionment that the lawgiver himself represents. For the figure of the *Législateur* serves Rousseau not so much to solve the political problem as instead to lay it bare, to characterize it, to embody it. The *Législateur* is no deus ex machina removing the difficulties that emerge when the principles of right are going to be implemented. And the *Contrat social* leaves no doubt that a "wise institution," which is not possible everywhere and always, will be of limited duration even if it is successful. For due to the insuperable tension between its own nature, conventional or moral, and the nature of its members, the body politic is subject to necessities that prevent it from preserving itself in being permanently.[55] The *Législateur* indicates that in a well-ordered political community wisdom must lead. But Rousseau does not derive from the need of the body politic a duty of the wise to subject his wisdom to the service of the general will, nor does he ascribe to the wise the right to suspend the general will and assume the position of sovereign in order by means of his insight to rule for the general good. On the contrary, at the end of the part about the art of the lawgiver, he emphasizes the indispensable principle of right of the sovereignty of the people in words more clear than in any other place: "a people is always master to change its laws, even the best of them; for if it pleases it to harm itself, who has the

---

53. "Ce qui rend pénible l'ouvrage de la législation, est moins ce qu'il faut établir que ce qu'il faut détruire; et ce qui rend le succès si rare, c'est l'impossibilité de trouver la simplicité de la nature jointe aux besoins de la société. Toutes ces conditions, il est vrai, se trouvent difficilement rassemblées. Aussi voit-on peu d'Etats bien constitués." II, 10, 5 (391).

54. The last paragraph of the three chapters, II, 10, 6 (391), reads: "Il est encore en Europe un pays capable de législation; c'est l'Isle de Corse. La valeur et la constance avec laquelle ce brave peuple a su recouvrer et défendre sa liberté, mériteroit bien que quelque homme sage lui apprit à la conserver. J'ai quelque pressentiment qu'un jour cette petite Isle étonnera l'Europe." The follower of the Corsican national hero, Pasquale Paoli, who writes to Rousseau on August 31, 1764 (see Footnote 33), will refer to Rousseau's "eulogy" and urge him to be "cet homme sage."

55. Cf. I, 6, 6 (360); I, 7, 7 (363); I, 9, 8 (367); II, 7, 3 (381-82); III, 2, 5-7 (400-401); III, 11, 1-3 (424).

right to prevent it from doing so?"[56] The wise needs the consent of the people in order to obtain legal force for his insight. Also subject to this reservation is the only law that Rousseau himself proposes in the *Contrat social*, whose articles he formulates precisely, whose acceptance by the sovereign he advocates, and with which he has the treatise culminate politically: the law concerning a civil profession of faith.[57] About Plato, the one other philosopher who appears in the *Contrat social* as a possible *Législateur*, Rousseau reports that he refused to give laws to the Arcadians and Cyrenians, because he knew that a wise institution could not be realized in their case: Both peoples were too rich to allow for the introduction of civil equality.[58]

Rousseau's confirmation of the principles of political right in the most philosophic part of the *Contrat social* gives us the occasion to ask why Rousseau, in contrast to all his predecessors, makes the sovereignty of the people *and* the supremacy of wisdom or insight into the supporting pillars of his political teaching, thus building up a tension that his successors will tear down all too quickly. Since the most philosophic part of the work is obviously at the same time the most Platonic, it makes sense to follow a trail that Rousseau lays by making explicit references to Plato, and that begins in this part. Rousseau refers to Plato three times by name, twice in book II, chapters 7 and 8 and once in book III, chapter 6. In the center stands the lawgiver Plato, *le sage instituteur*, whose wisdom is proven by his rejecting the demand to become a lawgiver. The lawgiver is flanked by two mentions of the author Plato, both of which pertain to a single dialogue, the *Politikos*. The second is found in the politically most important chapter of the third book, "Of Monarchy." There Rousseau offers Plato's "king by nature," whose knowledge, whose insight, and whose judgment identify him as a true statesman, in contrast with the monarchs with whom one has to reckon in the historical reality of *Gouvernement royal*. Rousseau appeals to Plato's emphasis on the rarity of the statesman in the philosophically demanding sense. The first mention in the chapter "Du Législateur" likewise points out the rarity of the statesman. Here the appeal to the *Politikos* serves to underline the exceptional case of the founder, the still greater rarity of a

---

56. II, 12, 2 (394); cf. I, 7, 2 (362); III, 18, 3 (435); III, 18, 9 (436).

57. IV, 8, 31–35 (467–69).

58. II, 8, 1 (385); cf. Plutarch, "Qu'il est requis qu'un Prince soit savant," in *Les œuvres morales de Plutarque* (Geneva: Iacob Stoer, 1621) (translation by Amyot), I, p. 425 [*Moralia* 50, 779D]. Plutarch offers another interpretation, less succinct and less political, of why, in Plato's view, their wealth rendered the Cyrenians unfit to receive good laws and an order for their State from him: "car il n'est rien si haut à la main, si farouche, ne si mal-aisé à donter et manier, qu'un personnage qui s'est persuadé d'estre heureux."

grand Législateur by comparison with a *grand Prince*. But Rousseau begins the reference to the *Politikos* with another comparison, which harbors an explosive potential. When Plato determined the statesman in his book, he made use of the same reasoning that Caligula employed, with the difference that Caligula reasoned as to fact, whereas Plato reasoned as to right.[59] Rousseau presupposes that the reader remembers the place where he first spoke about Caligula's reasoning. He speaks of Caligula's *raisonnement* in fact three times in the *Contrat social*, as often as he speaks of Plato. In chapter II, 7 the two series converge. If we want to understand what Rousseau is saying with the first mention of Plato, we have to go back to the first mention of Caligula's *raisonnement*. In chapter I, 2 Rousseau explains that according to a report of Philo, Emperor Caligula argued that, just as a shepherd, *un pâtre*, is of a higher nature than his flock, so the shepherds of men, *les pasteurs d'hommes*, who are their chiefs, are likewise of a higher nature than their peoples. From this Caligula inferred that either kings are Gods or peoples are beasts.[60] The difference between Caligula's reasoning and Plato's chain of thought, therefore, consists in this, that Caligula derived the *nature supérieure* of kings from the fact of the rule of kings, while Plato grounded the king's right to rule in his *nature supérieure*, i.e., he tied it to the presupposition that the "king by nature" would be as different from the people by virtue of his superior insight as a shepherd is from the flock he tends and over which he has command. The first mention of Plato indicates to the reader that among the titles to rule that Rousseau rejects in book I before beginning the part dealing with the principles, he leaves one title undiscussed: the rule that rests upon superior insight.[61] To speak in the language of the first book: of the two manifestations of natural inequality that Rousseau refers to by

---

59. "Le meme raisonnement que faisoit Caligula quant au fait, Platon le faisoit quant au droit pour définir l'homme civil ou royal qu'il cherche dans son livre du regne; mais s'il est vrai qu'un grand Prince est un homme rare, que sera-ce d'un grand Législateur?" II, 7, 2 (381).

60. I, 2, 6–7 (353). Rousseau read Philo's *De legatione ad Caium* [11, 76] in the translation by Arnauld d'Andilly, *Relation faite par Philon de l'Ambassade dont il estoit le chef, envoyée par les Juifs d'Alexandrie vers l'Empereur Caïus Caligula*, which d'Andilly had added as an appendix to his edition of Flavius Josephus's *Histoire des Juifs*. There Caligula's *raisonnement* reads: "Comme ceux qui conduisent des troupeaux de bœufs, de moutons et de chevres, ne sont ni bœufs, ni beliers, ni boucs; mais sont des hommes d'une nature infiniment plus excellente que celle de ces animaux: De mesme ceux qui commandent à tout ce qu'il y a de creatures dans le monde meritent d'estre considerez comme estant beaucoup plus que des hommes, et doivent estre tenu pour des Dieux." Paris, Louis Roulland, 1696, vol. 5, p. 490.

61. As Rousseau indicates with his statement about Plato in II, 7, 2 (381), one cannot raise the objection against Plato that he raises against Grotius shortly before the passage about Caligula: "Sa plus constante maniere de raisonner est d'établir toujours le droit par le fait. On pourroit employer une méthode plus conséquente, mais non pas plus favorable aux Tirans." I, 2, 4 (353).

name, the claim that appeals to *la force* is not only treated several times, but also becomes the subject of a chapter of its own, the central chapter I, 3 of the discussion; by contrast, *le génie* is not mentioned by name until the last sentence of book I, to return later as the genius of the lawgiver of II, 7 and to show its paramount importance.[62]

Rousseau could have said about the insight that brings about the order what he does say about the force that provides protection: the transference of a right to rule presupposes the constitution of a collective subject as the source of right and, consequently, the social contract; no title, no claim, no capability becomes a right without the legitimating decision of the sovereign. These are, however, not two symmetrical cases, so that the discussion of the one claim would render discussion of the other superfluous because the reader could simply transfer the answer. Rousseau's nondiscussion draws attention precisely to this fact. While *la force* explicitly finds its place in the body politic's legal structure, *le génie* is just as explicitly denied such a place. Rousseau negates and preserves force in the force of the sovereign. Insight, on the contrary, on which the principles of right depend, he keeps outside the order that is determined by those principles, which is why the work that is owing to the *intelligence supérieure* of the lawgiver achieves the force of law only through the consent of the sovereign. That Rousseau preserves the exceptional status of insight, and at the same time insists on the sovereignty of the people, is due to political prudence. Rousseau is familiar with the arguments that the *Politikos*, properly understood, makes available. He knows that the commandment of knowledge is incommensurable with the demands and needs of the political community; that the introduction of insight as a title to rule would shatter the social order; that the exception cannot be made normal; that the wise would have to be compelled to the exercise of rule; that the philosopher's "statesman" would most probably be imitated by the sophist; that the people would not be able to distinguish the one from the other; that the "king by nature" plays all too easily into the hands of the despot, who seeks to take control of his claim and reputation, just as Caligula appropriated the allegory from the *Politikos* in order to invert it into its opposite for his own purposes. But Rousseau's political prudence is not exhausted by this, as it were, transhistorical prudence, which

---

62. In the *Contrat social*, *génie* appears seven times. Following the passage concerning natural inequality ("inégaux en force ou en génie") in I, 9, 8 (367), the next five uses concern the *Législateur*, either directly or by contrast ("génie imitatif" versus "vrai génie"): II, 7, 4 (382); II, 7, 5 note (382); II, 7, 11 (384); II, 8, 5 (386). The seventh use refers to a modern philosopher whose error Rousseau corrects: III, 4, 6 (405).

he shares with most of his predecessors, and which moved none of them to raise the sovereignty of the people to the principle of right to which he raises it. It is clear to Rousseau that recommending the rule of the philosophers prepared the way for the rule of the priests, which it was supposed to protect against, and that the appeal to the authority of insight runs the risk of being surpassed and nullified by the appeal to the authority of an insight that claims to be superior to all reason.

Rousseau develops the conception of the *Contrat social* conscious of the caesura that revealed religion means for politics and for philosophy. The challenge of Christianity in particular determines the rhetoric and the strategy of the treatise. Rousseau avoids every appearance that could bring philosophy into proximity with religion. He also renounces any public exhortation to philosophize. He relies on leading the reader who is fit for philosophy to philosophy by the pointed treatment of the political alternative. The writing that depicts the political life in the most demanding sense does everything to reinforce the primacy of politics over religion. And it promotes as much as it can the pact with the strongest political power, the alliance with the people, which other philosophers, above all Machiavelli, already had conceived of in view of the same caesura. In the chapter "De la Monarchie," in which Plato is mentioned for the last time, Machiavelli is given his appearance as the teacher of peoples, and *Il Principe* is recommended to the attention of the reader as "the book of republicans." Rousseau's chapter has, as little as does Machiavelli's book, only the monarch or the prince in the ordinary sense for its subject.[63] Rousseau makes common front with Machiavelli against theocracy, which both take to be the most tyrannical rule,[64] since it seeks to control its subjects all the way into their innermost realm and leaves them exposed to the most extreme persecution. Rousseau

---

63. III, 6, 5 (409). For the posthumous edition of the treatise, Rousseau added a footnote to the sentence "Le Prince de Machiavel est le livre des républicains" that underlines the esoteric dimension of the *Principe* just as it indicates the far-reaching thrust of the opposition between republic and monarchy. The footnote, which the edition of the *OCP* places in the apparatus, has the following wording in the edition of 1782 : "Machiavel étoit un honnête-homme et un bon citoyen: mais attaché à la maison de Médicis, il étoit forcé dans l'oppression de sa Patrie de déguiser son amour pour la liberté. *Le choix seul de son exécrable Héros manifeste assez son intention secrete*, et l'opposition des maximes de son livre du Prince à celle[s] de ses discours sur Tite-Live et de son histoire de Florence, démontre que ce profond Politique *n'a eu jusqu'ici que des Lecteurs superficiels ou corrompus*. La Cour de Rome a sévérement défendu son livre, je le crois bien; c'est elle qu'il dépeint le plus clairement." My emphasis; consider Leo Strauss, *Thoughts on Machiavelli* (Glencoe, IL, 1958), p. 332 note 54.

64. Or, according to a distinction in the *Contrat social*, which, however, Rousseau makes obligatory neither for the *Contrat social* nor for his other writings: the *most despotic* rule; see III, 10, 10 (423), cf. I, 2, 4 (353) and IV, 8, 28 (467).

names the counterposition to the conception of the *Contrat social* only in chapter IV, 8. Three times—in the first sentence of the first, in the second sentence of the central, and in the third sentence of the last paragraph of "De la Religion civile"—we encounter, respectively, *le Gouvernement Théocratique, la Théocratie,* and again *le Gouvernement Théocratique.* Rousseau introduces the concept in the third and final passage in which he speaks of Caligula's *raisonnement,* just as he introduced the Gods in the *Contrat social* in the first Caligula passage, and, with them, the allegory of God as shepherd who has command over his flock. The Caligula passages leave no doubt that Rousseau applies the concept in the comprehensive sense of the rule of God, the sense in which the term was coined by Flavius Josephus, and that he does not limit it to the rule of the priests.[65] The *Contrat social* is the counterproject to theocracy in all of its manifestations. It opposes the sovereignty of the people to the sovereignty of God. Just as various forms of government are compatible with the republic, i.e., with the sovereignty of the people, theocracy, the appeal to the sovereignty of God, can also lead to various regimes. The *Contrat social* stands in opposition to each of them, from the monarchy of the divine right of kings to the hierocracy of the religion of the priest, by grounding society on a convention of natural beings, and by insisting upon the right of politics over against the authority of revelation. The intention of Rousseau's *Du contrat social* remains misunderstood as long as the treatise is not understood as a response to the challenge of theocracy.

---

65. None of the editors of and commentators on *Du contrat social* have, as far as I can tell, drawn upon the locus classicus of the concept *theocracy.* Georges Beaulavon explains *Gouvernement Théocratique* in IV, 8, 1 as "Gouvernement où la puissance appartient aux prêtres"; Maurice Halbwachs writes: "Gouvernement par des personnages sacrés, ayant un caractère surnaturel, prêtres ou plutôt rois-prêtres." No one has taken up the thread that Rousseau offered with the passages about Caligula. For in the same volume of d'Andilly's translation of the *Histoire des Juifs* that includes the translation of Philo's *Relation* that Rousseau cites, one also finds, in d'Andilly's translation of *Contra Apionem* II, 165, the first use of the term *theokratía* in Greek literature: "Les diverses nations qui sont dans le monde se conduisent en des manieres differentes. Les unes embrassent la Monarchie: les autres l'Aristocratie; et les autres la Democratie. Mais nostre divin Legislateur n'a étably aucune de ces sortes de gouvernement. Celuy qu'il a choisi a esté une Republique à qui l'on peut donner *le nom de Theocratie, puis qu'il l'a renduë entierement dépendante de Dieu*; que nous n'y regardons que luy seul comme l'auteur de tous les biens et qui pourvoit aux besoins generalement de tous les hommes; que nous n'avons recours qu'à luy dans nos afflictions, et que nous sommes persuadez *que non seulement toutes nos actions luy sont connuës, mais qu'il penetre nos pensées.*" *Response à Appion* [II, 164–66], in *Histoire des Juifs,* vol. 5, p. 410; my emphasis.

III

The right of politics proves itself in the historical concreteness of politics. Rousseau arrives at the reality determinative for the political life of the citizen in the second half of *Du contrat social*, after the anticipatory consideration from the perspective of the founder. Books III and IV, which focus on the *loix politiques* or on what is commonly called the constitution of the State, include within the course of the argument what up to this point the presentation of the principles of *droit politique* has deliberately ignored: executive power, the form of government, the organs and authorities within the *corps politique*, which are certainly subordinate to or derived from the sovereign, but which do not for that reason have less importance for the articulation of politics.[66] In fact, the advocate of the social contract could from the outset have removed all plausibility from the prospect that by entering the contract an association would be founded in which each, "uniting with all, nevertheless obeys only himself and remains as free as before," if he had not only put before his audience the reciprocal correlation between lawgivers and those subject to the law, but at the same time introduced government as a *corps intermédiaire*, to whose decisions the members of the association would owe obedience. A duty of obedience not limited to the government insofar as it enforces the laws of the sovereign, but rather explicitly extended to the ordinances, measures, decrees of the executive power as such. The government's authority to compel obedience resists translation into the "identical correlatives" of sovereign and subject, which designate aspects of one and the same citizen. The introduction of government as a separate body marks a caesura in the *Contrat social*. In the first half of the treatise, *le gouvernement* or *le magistrat* is merely announced as the object of investigation, and the particular meaning of the terms as Rousseau uses them is hinted at without being clarified. The reader learns no more about *magistrature* than that it is the act of a particular will and is concerned with particular matters and that neither *magistrature* nor *souveraineté* pertains to the *Législateur*.[67] Rousseau underlines the caesura that his treatment of the government implies by the peculiarities of the beginning of book III. At

---

66. Rousseau makes the cohesion of the two books explicit already in the table of contents, in which he characterizes their subjects as follows: "Livre III. Où il est traité des loix politiques, c'est-à-dire de la forme du Gouvernement" and "Livre IV. Où continuant de traiter des loix politiques on expose les moyens d'affermir la constitution de l'Etat." (The edition of the *OCP* does not reproduce Rousseau's table of contents.)

67. II, 4, 6 (374); II, 6, 9 and note (380); cf. II, 6, 6 (379). II, 2, 1 (369); II, 6, 8 (379); II, 7, 4 (382).

the head of the part of the treatise that with eighteen chapters is by far the longest, he places a one-paragraph preface, which emphasizes that the "precise meaning" of the concept of *gouvernement* has "not yet been very well explained," i.e., has not been adequately determined by Rousseau in books I and II as well as by his predecessors. The third book shares the peculiarity of the preface with the first book whose nine chapters are prefaced by three paragraphs. This distinguishes the two books of the *Contrat social* whose conception and terminology—in regard first to the sovereign and then to government—most clearly deviate from the tradition. Moreover, Rousseau opens chapter III, 1 "Of Government in General" with the explicit demand for careful and attentive reading. A demand that is without parallel in the *Contrat social* and presents the final link in a tripartite preparation for the innovation that awaits the reader.[68] After Rousseau has confirmed that the legislative power belongs exclusively to the people, and that "all acts" of the people as sovereign "can only be laws," he introduces government as the institution and the function that serves as "the means of communication between State and sovereign" and exercises public power by order of the sovereign. The first definition of *gouvernement* determines government as a *corps intermédiaire*, a body as means and mediator between the subjects and the sovereign. "The members of this body are called magistrates or *kings*, that is to say, *governors*, and the body as a whole bears the name *prince*." Rousseau's provocative nomenclature adopts terms familiar from political reality in order to give them a new meaning. "Prince" designates the totality of the government which, far from being sovereign, is "merely the minister" of the sovereign. The prince acts according to and under the supervision of the sovereign. "Kings" refers to the members of government, whom the people can install and also again remove. They are "mere officers of the sovereign" and "trustees" of the power vested in them for a limited time. The second definition of *gouvernement* in III, 1 determines government "or the supreme administration" as "the legitimate exercise of the executive power." Decisions about particular matters belong to its responsibility. Thus, Rousseau calls by the name *gouvernement* both the body and the authority of government. In the first case, he uses *prince* or *magistrat* as

---

68. "J'averti le lecteur que ce chapitre doit être lû posément, et que je ne sais pas l'art d'être clair pour qui ne veut pas être attentif." III, 1, 1 (395). The paragraph that opens the first chapter is preceded by the paragraph of the preface, and this in turn is preceded by the final paragraph of book II announcing the theme of the following book (II, 12, 6), which is not the case for any other book. Each of the three paragraphs consists of a single sentence.

a synonym for *gouvernement* and *les magistrats* when speaking about the individual governors. In the second case, the synonym is *magistrature*, and both, *gouvernement* as well as *magistrature*, are sharply distinguished from their counterconcept, *souveraineté*.[69]

The determination of the "precise meaning" of *gouvernement* has several implications that come to have a bearing in books III and IV. (1) The definition of government as a specific function, authority, or capacity allows for a differentiated consideration of the body politic and first and foremost of the sovereign. For it is actually a complement to and specification of the doctrine of sovereignty. When the sovereign declares its will in general form about a general matter, it is an act of sovereignty. When the sovereign makes a decision about a particular matter or issues a particular order, it is on the contrary an act of government or of magistracy. Whereas the sovereign cannot delegate the acts of sovereignty to another body without violating the social contract and putting the body politic into question, the sovereign can and must entrust a particular body with acts of government if the body politic is going to be capable of action. This does not mean that the sovereign would have to or even could delegate all acts of government to this body. To give an example that is more than an example: The people's assembly, which establishes the form of government for the political community, carries out this establishment, which is the subject matter of a "political law," by an act of sovereignty. If the same people's assembly subsequently decides by vote which persons should be entrusted with the government, such a decision is itself an act of government: The people's assembly chooses the trustees of executive power in its capacity as government.[70] (2) The distinction between the functions of sovereignty and government puts Rousseau in the position to make the doctrine of the sovereignty of the people compatible with the most diverse forms of government and to handle with great flexibility democratic, aristocratic, monarchical, or mixed government depending on the historical circumstances and concrete conditions. Thus, he can show that each is a legitimate form of government according to the principles of political right— democracy, in which government lies in the hands of the whole people or of the great majority, aristocracy, in which it is exercised by a small number or by an elite, and monarchy, in which it devolves upon one or, as in Sparta,

---

69. III, 2–3 (395–96); cf. II, 6, 5 (379). III, 4–7 (396); cf. III, 2, 1–4 (400).

70. III, 17, 1–5 and 7 (433–34). Likewise, the sovereign who by law reserves for itself the right of pardon exercises this right in a concrete case in its capacity as government. Cf. I, 5, 5 and 7 (377).

two kings—and nevertheless insist without restriction that the republic, in which sovereignty remains the preserve of the citizens in their totality, is the only legitimate form of political community.[71] (3) The distinction between the functions of sovereignty and government puts Rousseau in the position to formulate sharply the subordination of the government as an institution, body, or organ to the sovereign, and nonetheless highlight the intrinsic right of the *corps intermédiaire*. The subordination of government is succinctly expressed by the fact that the institution of government is traced back not to a contract between the people and the government, but rather to the will and disposal of the sovereign. The right of government rests on a law, and the governors acquire their office on the basis of a decision by the sovereign. A contract of government or of rule is incompatible with the social contract, which permits no division of sovereignty.[72] That the sovereign delegates executive warrants to a particular body by way of a commission is in harmony with three insights: First, the body politic needs an effective coercive power that enforces the laws and thus secures the foundation of the freedom of the citizens.[73] Second, the political community is in need of an institution that deals continuously with ongoing domestic and foreign affairs, and that in the best case combines experience and expertise, judgment and resoluteness in order to guide it. Finally, the delegation of executive responsibilities serves to protect the sole source of right, the sovereign in its ownmost function: The body in which the *volonté générale* is supposed to express itself about general matters is not subject to the danger of being disturbed or corrupted by constant decision-making about particular matters. Laws are not assimilated to orders and remain institutionally separate from specific measures.[74] (4) The definition of government as a body mediating between the citizens as subjects and the citizens as sovereign is the starting point for a consideration of the strength or weakness of government depending upon the contraction or expansion of the body: The government's power of enforcement decreases with the number of governors, so that it is weakest in the "democratic" and strongest in the "monarchical" government. Underlying this maxim, which enables Rousseau to correlate different forms of government with political communities according to the size of the territory and population—a State with a large territory needs a concentrated government, a small city-state allows an expanded government—is in turn an analysis of the forces

---

71. III, 3, 1–5 (402–3).
72. III, 1, 6 (396); III, 16, 1–7 (432–33). See above P. 123.
73. See Pp. 128–29.
74. Cf. III, 4, 1–3 (404).

operating within the *corps intermédiaire*, or more precisely: the wills that are at work in its members. Rousseau distinguishes three wills in the person of the magistrate, which are "essentially different": (I) The *volonté propre de l'individu*, which is directed toward the individual's own advantage; (II) the *volonté commune des magistrats* or *volonté de corps*, which is exclusively concerned with the advantage of the government as a body; and (III) the *volonté du peuple* or *volonté souveraine*, which determines the governor as citizen and pursues the good of the body politic. In a "perfect legislation" the first will would have to be "null," the second would have to be "very subordinate," and consequently the third, the *volonté générale ou souveraine*, "always dominant and the sole rule of all the others." "According to the *natural order*, on the contrary, the more concentrated these different wills are, the more active they become," i.e., the more they are concerned with the individual as the natural center. Therefore, the *volonté générale* is "always the weakest," the *volonté de corps* has the second place, and the *volonté particulière*, "the first place of all": "so that in the government each member is first of all himself, and then magistrate, and then citizen. A gradation that is the direct opposite of that required by the *social order*." The diagnosis of the conflict between the natural and the social order, which Rousseau provides in regard to the *corps intermédiaire* of the government, is obviously of considerable significance not only for the investigation of the forms of government and their correlation with different political communities, but also for the consideration of the body politic as a whole.[75]

Rousseau's explanation of the twofold sense of *gouvernement* deserves special attention not only owing to the far-reaching implications it has for the consideration of the body politic. It also demands special attention owing to the two peculiarities that are tied to it in the rhetoric of the third book. For one thing, Rousseau subjects the speech of the tradition about the "best government" to persistent critique. For another, he explicates his teaching of the legitimate "forms of government" by reference to governments that are illegitimate according to the principles of political right. The critique of the "best government" underlines Rousseau's orientation to political reality and expresses his maxim that "not only can different governments be good for different peoples, but they can also be good for the same people at different times," an orientation and a maxim that in turn correspond to his effort to secure as much room as possible for the "art of the lawgiver": The determination of the form or strength of the government that is fitting in

---

75. III, 2, 5–7 (400–401), my emphasis. Cf. III, 1, 17 and 20 (398, 399); III, 10, 1 *in princ.* (421); III, 10, 9 note *in fine* (423).

light of the natural requirements and historical circumstances, i.e., the appropriate contraction or expansion of the *corps intermédiaire*, is left to the judgment of the *Législateur*.[76] The critique, which begins in the first chapter and intensifies up to the ninth chapter,[77] culminates at the end of the first half of book III in an ironic answer to the question concerning the best government and in the no less ironic invitation to calculate the quality of regime by means of the quantity of the population, according to its increase or decrease.[78] The political realism highlighted by Rousseau's attacks on the doctrine of the best regime should not obscure from the reader the fact that the *Contrat social* has already answered the normative question that the tradition discusses as the question of the best regime. Rousseau can show such great flexibility with his doctrine of the "forms of government" in book III because what is most important, the sovereignty of the people and the extraconstitutional place of wisdom, has been firmly established since books I and II. The republic as the only legitimate form of political community is presupposed from the very beginning in Rousseau's investigation of "governments." That he adduces as examples governments to which he can ascribe no legitimacy brings the discussion into contact with the political reality of the readers. That he shifts back and forth between his own and the traditional nomenclature has the same critical function as his challenging practice of using the designations *Rois* and *Prince* for the governors and government that his predecessors used for the sovereign. With reason, Rousseau prefaces the treatment of government with a warning.

---

76. III, 1, 9 (397). III, 2, 13 (402): "l'art du Législateur est de savoir fixer le point où la force et la volonté du Gouvernement, toujours en proportion réciproque, se combinent dans le rapport le plus avantageux à l'Etat."

77. "On a de tous tems beaucoup disputé sur la meilleure forme de Gouvernement, sans considérer que chacune d'elles est la meilleure en certains cas, et la pire en d'autres." III, 3, 7 (403); cf. III, 7, 3 (413). "Quand donc on demande absolument quel est le meilleur Gouvernement, on fait une question insoluble comme indéterminée; ou si l'on veut, elle a autant de bonnes solutions qu'il y a de combinaisons possibles dans les positions absolues et relatives des peuples." III, 9, 1 (419).

78. "*Toute chose d'ailleurs égale*, le Gouvernement sous lequel, sans moyens étrangers, sans naturalisations, sans colonies les Citoyens peuplent et multiplient davantage, est infailliblement le meilleur: celui sous lequel un peuple diminue et dépérit est le pire. Calculateurs, c'est maintenant votre affaire; comptez, mesurez, comparez." III, 9, 4 (420), my emphasis.—The dispute about the characteristic sign of a good government as between "the subjects," who praise public peace, and "the citizens," who praise the freedom of individuals, which Rousseau does not decide in the text of III, 9, he does decide, with explicit appeal to Machiavelli, at the end of a long note that he appends to the chapter: "A little agitation gives vigor to souls, and what causes the species truly to prosper is not so much peace as freedom." III, 9, 4 note (420).

Aristocracy is the form of government to which Rousseau devotes the central chapter of his discussion of governments. It has in common with monarchy that Rousseau conjoins only these two governments with wisdom. In the case of aristocracy the conjunction is positive, in the case of monarchy it is negative. Aristocracy and monarchy designate the actual poles of the confrontation.[79] Rousseau distinguishes three kinds of aristocracy, one natural, one elective, and one hereditary. With "natural" aristocracy, about which he says that it is "suitable only to simple peoples," it is not a government in Rousseau's technical sense, but a regime in which authority is granted on the basis of experience or of age, which means that the good is identified with the ancient.[80] Hereditary aristocracy, in which political authority is bequeathed to the children along with the goods of the father, without the sovereign's being asked or intervening, Rousseau calls "the worst" of all legitimate governments; "the best," by contrast, is that based upon election: it is "aristocracy properly so-called." Aristocracy has three important advantages over democracy: (1) Legislative and executive power do not lie in the same hands, so that the exercise of sovereign power is not confused with ordinary orders and individual decisions. (2) Unlike government in democracy, where all citizens are born to be magistrates, government in aristocracy is limited to a small number, and magistrates acquire their office only through election. (3) The council assemblies, which deal with governmental business, can convene more easily, pending affairs are better discussed and more efficiently settled, and "the State's prestige is better upheld abroad by venerable senators than by an unknown or despised multitude." The central advantage, the election of the governors, makes the awarding of public offices depend on the public esteem of persons, their capabilities and virtues, and creates the possibility for the *Législateur* to have directing influence, since the *estime publique* in turn depends upon the citizens' *opinion*, to which the *Législateur* "attends in secret." If probity,

---

79. "De l'Aristocratie" is the fifth of the nine chapters of the first half of book III that are directly concerned with government, and the third of the five chapters that are concerned with the forms of government in particular. III, 3: "Division des Gouvernemens"; III, 4: "De la Démocratie"; III, 5: "De l'Aristocratie"; III, 6: "De la Monarchie"; III, 7: "Des Gouvernemens mixtes." For wisdom (*sagement gouverné, les plus sages, l'extrême sagesse*) see III, 5, 5; III, 5, 7; III, 5, 5 note (407) and (*sage, sagesse* in each case used contrastively) III, 6, 11 (411); III, 6, 13 (412).

80. "Les premieres sociétés se gouvernèrent aristocratiquement. Les chefs des familles délibéroient entre eux des affaires publiques; Les jeunes gens cédoient sans peine à l'autorité de l'expérience. Delà les noms de *Prêtres*, d'*anciens*, de *sénat*, de *Gérontes*. Les sauvages de l'Amérique septentrionale se gouvernent encore ainsi de nos jours, et sont très bien gouvernés." III, 5, 2 (406).

insight and enlightenment, and experience are the decisive factors in the election of the governors, these qualities are "so many further guarantees of being wisely governed." The *lumières* among the *magistrats* in III, 5 have more than a hidden interconnection with the *sagesse* of the *grand Législateur*, which Rousseau introduced into the argument of the treatise ten chapters earlier. Next to the emphasis on the art of the lawgiver, the singling out of aristocracy among the forms of government marks the greatest approximation of Rousseau's political teaching to that of the ancients.[81] Rousseau points out that aristocracy demands "somewhat fewer virtues" than democracy, but requires others "that are proper to it." As an example he mentions moderation among the rich and contentment among the poor, "for it seems that a strict equality would be out of place in aristocracy; it was not even observed in Sparta." That aristocracy would demand moderation especially from the wise he does not emphasize.[82]

At first glance, monarchy seems to be treated by Rousseau as a form of government like all the others. Its peculiarity, according to the nomenclature used in chapter III, 1–5, is that the artificial person of the "prince" coincides with the natural person of the monarch, that the collective "kings" is reduced to a single king, or that the body of the government has the appearance of *one* physical body. Since in monarchy the *volonté de corps* of the *prince* and the *volonté particulière* of the *magistrat* are *one*, the government achieves a maximum of force. If the *volonté particulière* of the monarch, which can have command of executive power without loss through friction with other magistrates, also dominates the *volonté du peuple*, "everything proceeds toward the same goal." But this is the end of the consideration of monarchy as a legitimate government. Rousseau immediately adds that the goal toward which the monarch orients the machinery of State so efficiently is not "public felicity." "Kings want to be absolute." They do not want to be "kings" in Rousseau's sense, they do not want to be "ministers" of the sovereign, they want to be the sovereign themselves. The monarch, the king, the prince who is treated in chapter III, 6 negates the sovereign of the *Contrat social*. Therefore, in the chapter "Of Monarchy" the *souverain* has

---

81. "En un mot, c'est l'ordre le meilleur et le plus naturel que les plus sages gouvernent la multitude, quand on est sûr qu'ils la gouverneront pour son profit et non pour le leur." III, 5, 7 (407). Compare the list of advantages needed by the governors so that the citizens "be ruled wisely," *la probité, les lumières, l'experience*, in III, 5, 5 (407) with the list of qualities "that all citizens have in common in a well-constituted State," *le bon-sens, la justice, l'intégrité*, in IV, 3, 8 (443).

82. III, 5, 4 (406); consider III, 10, 3 note (422). III, 5, 5–6 (406–7); cf. Pp. 134 and 144–46. III, 5, 9 (407); cf. Footnote 81 and Pp. 135–36 as well as 147–49.

no place; therefore, Rousseau there distinguishes between *gouvernement monarchique* and *gouvernement républicain;* therefore, deviating from the technical language of the treatise, he opposes monarchy to republic.[83] At the beginning of the critique of the prince, who is the actual subject of the discussion, Rousseau explains why kings who want to rule absolutely do not follow the maxim that gaining the love of their peoples is the best means of securing their rule: The absolute prince will not rely on the power that can accrue to him from the love of the subjects, since for him this power remains precarious and falls to him only conditionally, i.e., he is unable to manage or compel it by what is within his control. In contrast to the power that accrues to him from the fear of the subjects, since it is up to him to spread terror and obtain obedience through punishments. Rousseau does not spell out the argument that Machiavelli presented in a famous chapter of the *Principe*. But he emphatically refers the reader to "the book of republicans." At the conclusion of his critique he comments that the reality of monarchy he has illuminated has not escaped the notice of "our authors," yet they have not been disturbed by it.[84] "The remedy, they say, is to obey without a murmur. God in his wrath sends bad kings, and they must be endured as punishments from heaven." Just as at the conclusion of his critique of the right of the stronger in chapter I, 3 Rousseau brought into play Paul's saying "There is no power but from God," so he now calls to mind the political meaning of that saying, the theological legitimation of illegitimate rule. And as in the first passage, he limits himself once again to a brief ironic rejection of the theological position. Among its most prominent proponents was Jean Calvin.[85]

---

83. Hilail Gildin has pointed out that the word *souverain*, which appears in all the other chapters in which Rousseau discusses the forms of government, goes without mention solely in the chapter on monarchy: *Rousseau's "Social Contract": The Design of the Argument* (Chicago, 1983), p. 114. For the distinction between monarchy and republic see III, 6, 5 (409); III, 6, 8 (410); III, 6, 13 (412); consider further III, 8, 6 (415); III, 8, 7–8 (416). Cf. II, 6, 9 note (380).

84. Earlier Rousseau objected to the *politiques royaux* that they endow the prince with all the virtues that he would need and always assume that "the prince is what he should be." III, 6, 14 (412); cf. I, 7, 5 (363).

85. III, 6, 16 (413); see P. 120 and Pp. 148–50 as well as Footnote 63. "la parolle de Dieu ... nous rendra obéissans non seulement à la domination des Princes qui iustement font leur office, et s'acquittent loyallement de leur devoir, mais à tous ceux qui sont aucunement en prééminence, combien qu'ils ne facent rien moins que ce qui appartient à leur estat. Car combien que nostre Seigneur testifie que le Magistrat soit un don singulier de sa libéralité, donné pour la conservation du salut des hommes, et qu'il ordonne aux Magistrats ce qu'ils ont à faire, néantmoins semblablement il déclare que quels qu'ils soyent ne comment qu'ils se gouvernent, qu'ils n'ont la domination que de luy. Tellement que ceux qui n'ont esgard en leur domination qu'au bien publique sont vrais miroirs et comme exemplaires de sa bonté; d'autre part, *ceux qui s'y portent*

The usurpation of sovereignty by the "prince" is the overarching theme of the second half of book III. It is characterized by Rousseau as the constant danger the body politic faces. Not only kings want to be absolute. Government works ceaselessly against sovereignty. The executive expands its power at the expense of the legislative. And since in the body politic there is no *volonté de corps* that would be equal to that of the prince, it "must sooner or later come to pass that the prince ends up oppressing the sovereign and breaking the social contract." The tendency to the usurpation of sovereignty is no less than the "inherent and inevitable vice" or the fundamental flaw that "relentlessly from the moment of the birth of the body politic" works toward its destruction, "just as old age and death destroy a man's body." Rousseau's recourse to old age and death is by no means incidental. He not only speaks of the "natural inclination" of the government to contract or concentrate, i.e., to pass from democracy over into aristocracy and from aristocracy over into kingship. He also calls the dissolution of the State resulting from the usurpation of sovereign power by the government (whether by the prince as a whole or by individual members), or the "degeneration" into ochlocracy, oligarchy, and tyranny, the "natural and inevitable tendency of the best constituted governments." The "death of the body politic" receives a chapter of its own in the *Contrat social*, since in the long run no "work of art" is able to assert itself against nature, and politics cannot deny its anthropological conditions. "If Sparta and Rome perished, what State can hope to last forever?" Knowledge of the principles of political right puts the philosopher in the position to show the citizen what can "make legitimate" the chains of the civil condition. But bound up with precisely this knowledge is the insight that nothing and no one will "make eternal" the legitimate political community.[86] The change of human nature by the *Législateur*, who sets out to transform individuals into citizens, has its limits. Even his art does not know how to prevent the "ceaseless" action

---

iniustement et violentement sont eslevez de luy pour punir l'iniquité du peuple. Mais les uns et les autres semblablement tiennent la dignité et maiesté laquelle il a donnée aux supérieurs légitimes." Jean Calvin, *Institution de la Religion Chrestienne* (1560) IV, 20, 25, ed. Jean-Daniel Benoit (Paris, 1961), p. 530, my emphasis.

86. I, 1, 1 (351) and III, 11, 1 (424): "ne songeons donc point à le rendre éternel." Cf. Thomas Hobbes, *Leviathan* II, 30: "so, long time after men have begun to constitute commonwealths, imperfect, and apt to relapse into disorder, there may principles of reason be found out, by industrious meditation, to make their constitution, excepting by external violence, everlasting. And such are those which I have in this discourse set forth: which whether they come not into the sight of those that have power to make use of them, or be neglected by them, or not, concerneth my particular interests, at this day, very little." Ed. Michael Oakeshott (Oxford, 1946), p. 220.

of the *volonté particulière* against the *volonté générale*, and this is true, as is shown by Rousseau's investigation of the *corps intermédiaire* with a constant eye to the *corps politique* as a whole, both for the *magistrats* and for the *citoyens* or *sujets*. The fundamental flaw inherent in the body politic cannot be eliminated by the *Législateur*, it can only be identified in all clarity, so that the citizens endeavor with the force they have to counteract the usurpation of sovereignty. The three chapters "How the Sovereign Authority Is Maintained" (III, 12–14), which follow "Of the Death of the Body Politic" and form the counterpart to the three chapters "Of the People" (II, 8–10) in the treatment of the art of the lawgiver of the preceding book, are a single exhortation addressing the citizens to preserve sovereign authority, to defend it resolutely against every encroachment, and to protect it vigilantly against insidious erosion. The emphasis that Rousseau places on the danger of the usurpation of sovereignty has its deepest reason in his locating "the principle of political life" in sovereign authority. Being a citizen stands or falls with the exercise of this authority. Subjects prove themselves as citizens in the defense and protection of the sovereignty of the people. The three chapters that deal with the necessity and possibility of the people's assembly (III, 12), the institutional provisions for its regular convocation (III, 13), and its orderly procedure (III, 14) steer straight to the core of political life.[87]

Just as the body politic has its center in the sovereign authority of the citizens, the political life of the citizen has its core in his engagement for the republic. Participation in sovereignty and service to the State give political life the content that makes it possible to understand itself within the horizon of the body politic, determining itself from it and projecting itself toward it. For the citizen who identifies himself with the *moi commun*, the orientation toward the *corps politique* or, stated more precisely, toward the *corps politique* in view of its best possibilities, becomes the center of gravity of life. His identification and his participation are two sides of the same public cause that moves and fulfills him. Political life and the body politic are thus threatened with two dangers. On the one hand, through the usurpation of the supreme power, which destroys participation. On the other through the atrophy of the engagement of the citizens, which allows the identification

---

87. III, 10, 1–3 (421); III, 10, 5–8 (422–23); III, 11, 1–2 (424). "Le principe de la vie politique est dans l'autorité Souveraine. La puissance législative est le cœur de l'Etat, la puissance exécutive en est le cerveau, qui donne le mouvement à toutes les parties. Le cerveau peut tomber en paralysie et l'individu vivre encore. Un homme reste imbécille et vit: mais sitôt que le cœur a cessé ses fonctions, l'animal est mort." III, 11, 3 (424).

with the republic to corrode. Since the two dangers are intertwined with one another, Rousseau appeals to the sense of citizenship with the warning against the usurpation of sovereign authority, in order to subject to criticism, immediately following the chapter on the maintenance of sovereignty, the decline of political life, which plays into the hands of usurpation. "As soon as public service ceases to be the citizens' principal business," Rousseau begins III, 15, "and they prefer to serve with their purse rather than with their person, the State is already close to ruin. Is there a call to battle? They pay troops and stay home. Is there a summons to council? They name deputies and stay home. Finally, by dint of laziness and money, they have soldiers who enslave the fatherland and representatives who sell it." The chapter "Of Deputies or Representatives" is from the outset designed as a provocation. The statements that sovereignty cannot be represented and that in the future it will be possible for the sovereign to preserve its rights only if the political community is "very small" have achieved fame.[88] The first statement merely repeats, however, what the part dealing with the principles left in no unclarity: either sovereignty, the *volonté générale*, is present or it is not. And in the case of the second statement, it is not a definitive article but rather the formulation of an expectation that lends validity to a maxim of political prudence.[89] The true provocation of the chapter lies not in the critique of representation in itself, but rather in the critique of the valuations of the modern world and in the image of political life delineated by means of this critique. The critique of the deputies or the representatives is, as the opening of the chapter shows, above all a critique of the citizens who let themselves be represented, who do not exercise their rights as members of the *corps politique* and want to buy their way out of their duties. It holds for the opinion that the dissolution of public tasks, services, activities are for the citizen tantamount

---

88. "La Souveraineté ne peut être réprésentée, par la même raison qu'elle ne peut être aliénée; elle consiste essentiellement dans la volonté générale, et *la volonté ne se réprésente point*: elle est la même, ou elle est autre; il n'y a point de milieu. Les députés du peuple ne sont donc ni ne peuvent être ses réprésentans, *ils ne sont que ses commissaires; ils ne peuvent rien conclurre définitivement*. Toute loi que le Peuple en personne n'a pas ratifiée est nulle; ce n'est point une loi." III, 15, 5 (429–30), my emphasis. "Tout bien examiné, je ne vois pas qu'il soit désormais possible au Souverain de conserver parmi nous l'exercice de ses droits si la Cité n'est très petite." III, 15, 12 (431).

89. Consider the emphatic reference to the assemblies of the Roman people and the detailed discussion of them in chapters III, 12 and IV, 4 as well as Pp. 144–45. In the *Considérations sur le gouvernement de Pologne*, Rousseau will explicate a decade later how the reform of the largest territorial State in Europe could be brought about in accordance with the principles of political right.

to a gain in freedom. It takes aim at the thinning out and the diminishment, the parceling and cropping of his existence. Emblematically, Rousseau's challenge gets expressed in his praise of the *corvées*, which are less opposed to freedom than taxes, and in his attack on the modern esteem for commerce, money, and finance. "The word *finance* is a slave's word; it is unknown in the polis. In a truly free State the citizens do everything with their hands and nothing with money. Far from paying to be exempted from their duties, they would pay to fulfill them themselves." The citizen in the eminent sense, the *citoyen* in contrast to the *bourgeois*,[90] makes the cause of the political community into his cause. He does not withdraw from public affairs but actively seeks them. The "common happiness" is an essential part of his own happiness. He finds himself, he actualizes his *amour de soi* and his *amour-propre*, in engagement for the republic.[91] The provocation that lies in the presentation of political life is outdone only by the provocation that implies putting political idealism into question by having recourse to nature. For the chapter culminates in a dramatically staged moment, in which Rousseau's philosophic reservation toward political life comes to light. Rousseau refers to the Greeks, in whose case the people was "constantly" assembled in the agora in order to do everything itself that had to be done. Their cause was freedom. Yet their freedom had a favorable climate, i.e., conditions, that escaped their power to shape matters, and it had for its presupposition the unfreedom of the slaves, who performed the labor. Following upon the example of the Greeks comes the exclamation: "What! Freedom can only be maintained with the help of servitude? Perhaps. The two extremes meet. Everything that is not in nature has its inconveniences, and civil society more than all the rest." Addressing modern peoples, Rousseau adds: "You have no slaves, but you are slaves; you pay for their freedom with your own. Well may you boast of this preference; I find in it more cowardice than humanity."[92]

---

90. Rousseau introduced the politico-philosophic distinction between *citoyen* and *bourgeois* in *Émile*, which he published in parallel with the *Contrat social*: I, pp. 249–50.

91. "Mieux l'Etat est constitué, plus les affaires publiques l'emportent sur les privées dans l'esprit des Citoyens. Il y a même beaucoup moins d'affaires privées, parce que la somme du bonheur commun fournissant une portion plus considérable à celui de chaque individu, il lui en reste moins à chercher dans les soins particuliers . . . Sitôt que quelqu'un dit des affaires de l'Etat, *que m'importe!* on doit compter que l'Etat est perdu." III, 15, 3 (429). See Pp. 132–33 and cf. *Über das Glück des philosophischen Lebens*, pp. 161–63 [*On the Happiness of the Philosophic Life*, pp. 118–20].

92. III, 15, 1 (428–29). III, 15, 2 (429); cf. also for the praise of the *corvées*, *Projet de constitution pour la Corse*, pp. 930 and 932 as well as *Considérations sur le gouvernement de Pologne*

What slaves due to cowardice means more exactly and what in the end is the source of the spirit of servitude among the moderns, Rousseau will address only in the penultimate chapter of the fourth book. The third book in contrast highlights clearly the limits set to political life. The analysis of the *corps intermédiaire* and the image of the *citoyen* in the demanding sense disclose the coercion of conventions, to which political life is subject, and the power of the illusions inherent in it. However, the book not only exposes the chains that cannot be removed from the civil state, since this state "is not in nature."[93] In addition, resuming and advancing the discussion of the second half of book II, the third book explicitly maintains that the chains can by no means be "made legitimate" everywhere and always: Political freedom "is not within the reach of every people." The body politic remains tied to natural conditions and historical presuppositions that are not to be found everywhere and cannot be made effective at all times. If the reader is told in book II that at present there is practically no country in Europe that could receive an institution in the sense of the *Contrat social*, he learns in book III that only "very few nations" have laws and that where there are laws, i.e., where there has been success in bringing a body politic into being, it carries within itself the seeds of its death from the moment of its birth. There are laws in accord with the principles of political right solely in a body politic in which sovereign authority is intact or, what amounts to the same, in which the people is able to exercise such authority. For laws are acts of the *volonté générale* not only insofar as the *volonté générale* has expressed itself in them, but insofar as it constantly expresses itself in them. They are *valid* because the *volonté générale* does not alter or eliminate them, although it *could* alter or eliminate them.[94] The usurpation

---

XI, 5 and 10, pp. 1006, 1009. III, 15, 9–10 (430–31); cf. *Lettres écrites de la montagne* IX, 45, p. 881: "Les anciens Peuples ne sont plus un modele pour les modernes; ils leur sont trop étrangers à tous égards. Vous surtout, Génevois, gardez votre place . . . Vous êtes des Marchands, des Artisans, des Bourgeois, toujours occupés de leurs intérêts privés, de leur travail, de leur trafic, de leur gain; des gens pour qui la liberté même n'est qu'un moyen d'acquérir sans obstacle et de posséder en sûreté."

93. The dramatic peak of III, 15, Rousseau's statement about *société civile*, puts into perspective the praise the advocate of the social contract presented in Chapter I, 8 "De l'état civil." A praise formulated in such a way that the reader might be all too ready to ignore the decisive qualification to which it is linked: "que *si les abus de cette nouvelle condition* [sc. l'état civil] *ne le dégradoient souvent au dessous de celle* [sc. la condition ou l'état de nature] *dont il est sorti*, il [sc. l'homme] devroit bénir sans cesse l'instant heureux qui l'en arracha pour jamais . . ." I, 8, 1 (364), my emphasis.

94. III, 8, 1 (414); III, 15, 8 (430); cf. II, 10, 5 (391) and II, 10, 6 (391). III, 11, 3–5 (424–25).

of sovereignty, therefore, strikes at the very heart of the legitimate political community. And since Rousseau traces the fundamental flaw of the body politic in the final analysis back to a necessary contradiction between the natural order and the social order, the longest book of the *Contrat social* stands more than any other book under Horace's saying according to which ultimately nature is victorious over the work of art.

IV

The limits of politics, which books II and III of the *Contrat social* determine transpolitically and politically, book IV takes into account historically. To the recourse to nature, which precedes and reaches beyond the body politic, and to the investigation of the necessities that are at work in its inner structure, is added at the end of the treatise the treatment of the power that in history conflicts most with the body politic. Like the plea for the right of politics, the consideration of the limits of politics also has its vanishing point in the chapter on religion, in which all important lines of argument and strands of action of the *Contrat social* converge. Yet even before Rousseau refers to theocracy and Christianity by name for the first time in the penultimate chapter, the fourth book is directed to history in a particular way. The main part is made up of four chapters, which are concerned with Roman institutions, with the comitia (IV, 4), the tribunate (IV, 5), dictatorship (IV, 6), and the censorship (IV, 7). Rousseau has two reasons for putting so much weight on them. First, they have the task of making vivid the political order of a pre-Christian political community and thus of preparing the presentation of the historical caesura Christianity signifies (IV, 8). Second, the discussion of the institutions of the "freest and most powerful people on earth" serves to show the reader how the principles of political right can be interpreted and must be applied so that a body politic may preserve itself in life for some time.[95] With chapters IV, 4–8, Rousseau draws a line back to the chapters of the second half of book II, which had as its theme the art of the lawgiver and focused attention first on the presuppositions under which the principles of political right can or cannot be realized. This is true for the fourth book almost in its entirety, for chapters IV, 1–3 are also concerned with the historical conditions to which the embodiment of the principles is tied, and with the maxims that deserve attention regarding their implementation. The fourth is linked with the second book, but the emphasis lies no longer with the problem of founding, but rather with the difficulties of the preservation of the legitimate political community, which achieved its capacity

---

95. IV, 4, 2 (444). The commentators who hold that chapters IV, 4–7 can be more or less neglected, or believe that Rousseau used them as filler in order to have a fourth book that corresponds approximately to the length of the three previous books, fail to recognize the two crucial functions that the four chapters fulfill. If, for reasons of the economy of this essay, I treat Rousseau's discussion of the Roman institutions briefly—like much else—I am aware of the great interest that it has for Rousseau's political teaching in the narrower sense: Here it stands alongside the in-depth analyses Rousseau submitted of the political communities of Geneva, Corsica, and Poland.

for action only with the introduction of the government in book III. The composition and the decomposition of the body politic stand between books II and IV, the description of its life and its death, the dissection and diagnosis of the usurpation of sovereign power as its constant danger. It is only consistent that the first chapters of the last book highlight once more the central concept of the part dealing with the principles (IV, 1–3). Rousseau clarifies *ex negativo*, he illuminates from historical loss, he underscores by the prospect of its ultimate "becoming mute" the presuppositions that are needed so that the *volonté générale* can express itself and exhibits "all characteristics." Now, since with the triad of *Souverain, Législateur, Gouvernement* the image of the political community is complete and the danger of its destruction has been named, it clearly emerges as the *conditio sine qua non* of the legitimate order that the citizens in the people's assembly vote *comme citoyens* and that as members of the *corps politique* their action is oriented toward the *bien publique*.[96] The question how the will of the citizens can be oriented toward the good of the body politic in such a way that it achieves its goal brought the *Législateur* onto the scene at the end of the part dealing with the principles (II, 6). At the beginning of book IV Rousseau draws attention to the fact that simplicity of the conditions, of the morals, and of the citizens themselves might bring about what in other historical circumstances the wisdom of the lawgiver has to put into effect: the connection between will and judgment. As long as the "social bond in the hearts" is intact, the political requirements remain manageable and "the common good is everywhere fully evident," there is need for "very few laws," and legislation occurs with broad unanimity. *Simplicité* obviously stands in for *sagesse*.[97] But because the state of simplicity is fragile and simplicity does not know how to help itself, the reader will do well to see in the praise of simplicity that opens the concluding book of the *Contrat social* the hint at the secondary simplicity that is grounded in the art of the lawgiver, the knowledge of the statesman, the insight of the philosopher and made possible by institutions, supported by faith, achieved by means of education.

The maxims of political prudence, which stand with the principles of political right in the *Contrat social*, take up more space in the fourth book than in any before. In contrast to the principles claiming universal validity, the maxims focus on particular circumstances. Saturated with experience, they take into consideration the concrete situation and practical expediency. They are first spoken about after the advocate of the citizens has explicated

---

96. IV, 1, 4–6 (438); IV, 2, 9 (441); IV, 3, 8 (443). See Pp. 129–31.
97. IV, 1, 1–3 (436–37).

the principles of political right and wisdom becomes the theme in II, 7. Rousseau refers to the "sound maxims of politics" in one breath along with the "foundational rules of raison d'état," without thereby discussing either any further. In the chapters on legislation (II, 7–12), it is nevertheless not difficult to discern, for example, that the right of the people, founded upon the principles, to change its laws, "even the best," at any point encounters the maxim that the laws should be changed as little as possible so that the laws do not suffer a loss of their force. In fact, Rousseau exemplifies the difference between a guaranteed right and a political maxim in the book that immediately follows using the most prominent case of a change of law: In III, 18 he confirms once again that the sovereign can change the form of government, i.e., the relevant political law, whenever it pleases the sovereign, only to add that changes of this sort are always dangerous and that one "should never touch the established government unless it becomes incompatible with the public good; but this circumspection is a maxim of politics and not a rule of right." The primary addressee of the maxims is the potential statesman. For him Rousseau suffuses book IV with rich illustrative material providing orientation about the institutions of a well-ordered political community. As the most important example for the communication of his viewpoints, he, like Machiavelli, draws upon the Roman republic. Rousseau prefixes the chapter "Of the Roman Comitia," the first about Rome and, in terms of paragraphs, the most extensive of the whole treatise, with the remark that the historical consideration that follows "will perhaps explain more concretely all the maxims" he could establish regarding how votes in the people's assembly should be cast and collected. In other words, he leaves it to the reader to establish for himself the maxims for the sovereign organ. And he does not neglect especially to maintain that the historical discussion of the people's assembly addresses a *lecteur judicieux*, just as he stated at the beginning of the theoretical discussion of the government that it required a *lecteur attentif*.[98] The judicious reader will learn from the complex discussion of the comitia by curia, by centuries, and by tribes, the broad latitude Rousseau allows for the statesman's practical reason to implement the principles. In particular, he will take from this discussion that Rousseau ties the legitimacy of the political order not to the equal weight of the votes, but certainly to the inclusion of all the citizens in the vote of the people's assembly. He will attend to the praise of "mixed government"

---

98. II, 7, 9 (383); III, 18, 3 (435); IV, 3, 10 (443) and III, 1, 1 (395). Cf. further for the maxims of politics II, 8, 4 (385); II, 9, 2 (387); II, 11, 4 (393); III, 6, 5 (409); III, 6, 13 (412); IV, 1, 1 (437); IV, 2, 4, (440); IV, 2, 11 (441); IV, 3, 7 (443); IV, 4, 2 (444); IV, 4, 10 (446); IV, 4, 36 (453).

and to the advice for balancing between political actors and social forces. In addition, the plea for adaptation of the institutions to the state of the body politic, for instance the recommendation of secret ballots in the face of advanced corruption, will not be lost on him.[99] The attentive reader will also take note of a series of points that the historical discussion gives him to consider as it were in passing: From the role that is attributed to force, to war, and to the military with the emergence of Rome's political order, to the point that the institution of the freest and most powerful people goes back not only to a *sage instituteur* but to at least two or more founders, and the emphasis, in the center of the chapter, on the superiority of the morals of the ancients in comparison with those of the moderns, all the way to the challenge to the "authority of Cicero," the criticism of the most famous philosopher of Rome, which Rousseau has followed by a sharp criticism of the politician two chapters later.[100] Common to the three institutions Rousseau treats immediately after the comitia is that they are not required by the principles of political right, but are instead motivated by the maxims of political prudence. Unlike the *Souverain* and *Gouvernement*, they are not constitutive of the *corps politique*, but in contrast to the *Législateur* they do not remain extraconstitutional. They are instead part of the institution, i.e., their position is subject to legal regulation by the sovereign. Unlike the people's assembly, they have no legislative authority, yet in contrast to the *Législateur* they fulfill their function by acts of a kind of magistracy. What unites the *Tribunat*, *Dictature*, and *Censure* is that they are supposed to provide solutions to the problem that the *Législateur* embodies. They are as many attempts to take into account institutionally the indispensability of insight for the political community, which cannot be covered by norms. They offer second-best solutions to partial aspects of the task that book II ascribed to wisdom. The tribunate should mediate as an independent agency between government and people and act as a moderating influence on both.

---

99. IV, 4, 21 (449); IV, 4, 25 (450) and IV, 4, 32 (451–52); IV, 4, 35–36 (452–53).

100. IV, 4, 3–4 (444–45), IV, 4, 5–8 (445–46), IV, 4, 14 (447); IV, 4, 19 (448); IV, 4, 36 (452–53), cf. IV, 6, 10 (457–58). In the first note of chapter IV, 4 (444) Rousseau refers to the duality of force, strength, power and convention, which characterizes the origins of Rome: "Le nom de *Rome* qu'on prétend venir de *Romulus* est Grec, et signifie *force*; le nom de *Numa* est grec aussi, et signifie *Loi*. Quelle apparence que les deux premiers Rois de cette ville aient porté d'avance des noms si bien rélatifs à ce qu'ils ont fait?" (Cf. *Considérations sur le gouvernement de Pologne* II, 6, pp. 957–58.) The epigraph Rousseau chose for the *Contrat social* calls attention to this same duality of force and convention, if the reader looks up the quote from Virgil's *Aeneid*—*foederis aequas / Dicamus leges* (let us declare the equitable stipulations / laws of a contract)—and considers the context of the exhortation to enter into the contract and who expresses it. *Aeneid* XI, 321–22; cf. Roger D. Masters, *The Political Philosophy of Rousseau* (Princeton, 1968), p. 302.

As the highest guardian of the laws, it is incumbent upon the tribunate to preserve the political order. Its charge is to stop the usurpation of sovereign power by the government and to prevent the sovereign from making too hasty changes to the laws. The dictatorship responds to the inflexibility of the laws, the impossibility of regulating the state of exception generally, and the necessarily limited foresight of the lawgiver as concerns extraordinary events and circumstances. It serves as a strictly commissioned instrument to be able to defend public safety and the integrity of the fatherland in moments of the greatest danger. It has the warrant to "silence" the laws for a brief period and to suspend sovereign authority if the defense against an immediate threat to the existence of the State demands it, since "in such a case the general will is not in doubt." Censorship is supposed to give voice to the *jugement publique* and precisely by this means guide this judgment. It is designed to maintain morals, nurture customs, strengthen the authority of public opinion. It guards the life element of the political community, the valuations of the citizens, the concepts of honor, worth, and recognition, the ideas of the beautiful and the noble.[101] The three institutions evidently provide an inadequate substitute for the insight actually present of a "superior intelligence." The warrants with which they are equipped are executed by magistrates whose capacity for judgment, like their other capabilities and qualities, vary considerably. To limit the power of the tribunate, Rousseau suggests intervals during which its function is suspended. In the case of the dictatorship he insists on a commission of a very short measure that never permits extension. And he explicitly refuses the censors any use of coercion.[102] Conceived as partial substitutes, *Tribunat, Dictature, Censure* point back to the *Législateur*. Indeed, no chapter calls the *Législateur* to mind more emphatically than the chapter on censorship, which concludes the discussion of the Roman institutions and immediately precedes the investigation of the *Religion civile*.[103]

---

101. IV, 5, 1–3 (451–54); IV, 6, 1–4 (455–56); IV, 7, 1–6 (458–59).
102. IV, 5, 7 (455); IV, 6, 10 (458); IV, 7, 7–8 (459).
103. "l'opinion publique est l'espece de loi dont le Censeur est le Ministre ..." "Redressez les opinions des hommes et leurs mœurs s'épureront d'elles mêmes. On aime toujours ce qui est beau ou ce qu'on trouve tel, mais c'est sur ce jugement qu'on se trompe; c'est donc ce jugement qu'il s'agit de regler. Qui juge des mœurs juge de l'honneur, et qui juge de l'honneur prend sa loi de l'opinion." "Les opinions d'un peuple naissent de sa constitution; quoique la loi ne regle pas les mœurs, c'est la législation qui les fait naitre; quand la législation s'affoiblit les mœurs dégénerent, mais alors le jugement des Censeurs ne fera pas ce que la force des loix n'aura pas fait." IV, 7, 1, 3 and 4 (458–59). Consider II, 6, 10 (380) and II, 12, 5 (394) and see Pp. 132, 134–35, 143–44.

"De la Religion civile," the longest and next to "Du Législateur" the most elaborate chapter of the *Contrat social*, brings to a conclusion not only the confrontation of the principles of political right and the maxims of politics with historical reality. Since with theocracy it introduces the counterconcept that profiles politically and determines philosophically the meaning of the conception of the sovereignty of the people, it tacitly contains the invitation to reflect on the treatise as a whole from the vantage point of the end.[104] If what had mattered to Rousseau were solely the classification of religion according to the principles of political right, the last five paragraphs or the third section of the chapter would have sufficed. Moreover, such a classification could already have taken place in the second half of book I or in the first half of book II, in any case prior to chapter II, 7. Chapter IV, 8 is, however, not concerned solely with the legal regulation (part III, paragraphs 31–35), but in addition with the typology (part II, paragraphs 15–30), and first and foremost with the genealogy of the relationship between politics and religion (part I A, paragraphs 1–7: before Christianity; part I B, paragraphs 8–14: since Christianity), whereby in the center of each of the three sections stands the confrontation with Christianity, which up to that point Rousseau did not mention by name. "De la Religion civile" extends, as does no other chapter, from the beginnings of political societies all the way to the problem that Christianity implies for the body politic in the present. It places the social contract within the widest historical perspective. The renewed treatment of politics and religion joins with the political genealogy of revealed religion outlined in II, 7.[105] The opening goes back prior to revealed religion and with the original appeal to the rule of the Gods closes a gap that Rousseau left open seven years before in his anthropological reconstruction of the development of humanity: "Men at first had no other kings than the Gods, nor any other government than the theocratic one." The Gods, whom the *Discours sur l'inégalité* passed over in almost total silence, now from the outset come into view in their political usefulness: The Gods promoted the sociability of men by the order they sanctioned. They helped to bring about the origin of peoples, who united under their rule, recognized themselves in it, and were distinguished from other peoples by it. And they put men in the position of appearing as *masters* owing to the authority they derived from the Gods, of demanding

---

104. See Pp. 148–50.
105. See II, 7, 10–12 (383–84) and Pp. 140–41. Rousseau wrote the first draft of the later chapter IV, 8 in the *Première version* on the reverse side of the manuscript pages that contain the chapter *Du Législateur* (Edition Bachofen, Bernardi and Olivo, pp. 93–107).

obedience, and of finding belief.[106] Thus, in regard to the social contract the Gods show a Janus face: They create the historical presuppositions of the convention that provides the basis for the body politic; and they empower an illegitimate rule that is in opposition to the body politic.[107]

The unity of politics and religion remains preserved until the irruption of Christianity. Since "one placed God at the head of every political society," there were "as many Gods as peoples." Polytheism was based in politics. It originated from the necessity of the collection and the division of political society. The Gods were created by poets and codified by lawgivers. Their being was coextensive with the laws, which determined it by prescribing their cult. The unity of politics and religion made war among the Gods into war among peoples. War was simultaneously political and theological. Rousseau emphasizes that in war men did not fight for the Gods, but rather "it was, as in Homer, the Gods who fought for men; each asked his own for victory and paid for it with new altars." The power of the Gods, *Etres chimériques*, who in themselves had no common cause, extended as far as the boundaries of the nations that revered them. "The God of one people had no right over the other peoples. The Gods of the pagans were not jealous Gods; they divided the empire of the world among themselves." Against the background of this description, the innovation emerges that Moses' legislation introduced. Certainly, "even Moses and the Hebrew people *sometimes*" countenanced the idea of a coexistence of the Gods based on division. But the God of Israel is a jealous God. Moses founded the political identity of the people on a religious law that as the law of the *one* God would resist the law of every other God and would preserve the people as a people even in defeat, in captivity, or in diaspora.[108] Rousseau does not overlook the fact that the Greeks in their own way deviated from the original account of theologico-political congruence since, in order to assert their sovereignty over against the barbarians, they claimed to rediscover in other peoples the Gods common to the Greeks, who overarched the political differences among the diverse poleis. And he

---

106. "Ils firent le raisonnement de Caligula, et alors ils raisonnoient juste. Il faut une longue altération de sentimens et d'idées pour qu'on puisse se résoudre à prendre son semblable pour maitre, et se flater qu'on s'en trouvera bien." IV, 8, 1 (460). Cf. *Émile* IV, p. 646: "Toutes les conventions se passoient avec solemnité pour les rendre plus inviolables; avant que la force fut établie les Dieux étoient les magistrats du genre humain."

107. Cf. *Discours sur l'inégalité*, Seconde partie, p. 246 and "Einführender Essay," pp. xliv–xlvii as well as the *Profession de foi du Vicaire Savoyard* note 18, 8, p. 634 and *Über das Glück des philosophischen Lebens*, p. 422 [*On the Happiness of the Philosophic Life*, p. 327].

108. IV, 8, 2–6 (460–61), my emphasis. Cf. II, 7, 11 (384) and the discussion of Moses the lawgiver in *Considérations sur le gouvernement de Pologne* II, 2–4, pp. 956–57.

points out that with the establishment of their empire, the Romans were satisfied with the supremacy of their Gods, let conquered peoples keep their Gods, and often included them within the circle of their own Gods. The expansion of their rule thus had as its result that a multitude of Gods and cults were under Roman leadership consolidated in "paganism" to become eventually "one and the same religion" of the known world. What connects the original with the later polytheism is the primacy of politics.[109] The peculiarities of the Greeks and Romans, like the innovation that separates the Jews from both, serve Rousseau to set Christianity off sharply in the middle of the genealogical part from what was common to the Greeks, Jews, and Romans: Under the conditions of the *imperium romanum*, Jesus—whose name is used in only this one instance in the *Contrat social*—erected a "Spiritual Kingdom" on earth. The establishment of his empire "led, since it separated the theological from the political system, to the State's ceasing to be one, and caused the intestine divisions that have never ceased to convulse Christian peoples." The "new idea of a kingdom of the other world" not only destroyed the unity of the political community, which the Greeks and Romans had achieved politically, the Jews religiously. As the idea materialized and the institution that embodied it gained control over the requisite means, "this supposedly other-worldly kingdom was seen to become under a visible chief the most violent despotism in this world." No rule is characterized as harshly in the *Contrat social* as the rule of the Church under its head, the Vicar of Christ on earth, which bases its right and its power on the authority of God.[110] The further discussion of the historical development is characterized entirely by the dualism of spiritual and political rule. From this double rule there resulted "a perpetual conflict of jurisdiction, which has made any good polity impossible in Christian States." Rousseau adds that one could never know whether one was obligated to obey the *maître* or the *prêtre*. With extreme brevity he thus specifies the reason why for the moderns in contrast to the ancients the question of sovereignty became the central political question. At the same time, with his precise choice of words, his substitution of *prince* by *maître*, he points out that Christianity empowered a doubly illegitimate rule. The *respublica christiana*, which he will designate

---

109. IV, 8, 3 and 6 (460, 461–62). That religion in Rome served not only as an instrument of the expansion of power externally, but likewise as a means of preserving power domestically, Rousseau noted in the discussion of the comitia and of the politics of the senate: IV, 4, 22–23 (449); cf. IV, 4, 38 (453).

110. IV, 8, 8–9 (462). *Despotisme* appears eight times in the *Contrat social*. The only other correlation with a concrete institution or person concerns Emperor Tiberius: III, 10, 3 note (422). *Le plus violent despotisme* is mentioned only in IV, 8, 9.

in the typology as a *contradictio in adjecto*, was in *both* of its arms, in the monarchy of the divine right of kings as well as in the Church of the papacy, part of the despotism and incompatible with the legitimate body politic. All attempts to restore "the ancient system," i.e., to secure permanently the primacy of politics in relationship to religion, have remained until now unsuccessful: *l'esprit du christianisme a tout gagné*.[111] The kings of England and the czars, who declared themselves the heads of national churches, were not able to break the crucial power of the clergy.[112] And even "the philosopher Hobbes," who "saw clearly the evil and the remedy and dared to propose reuniting the two heads of the eagle and returning everything to political unity," had to acknowledge "that the domineering spirit of Christianity was inconsistent with his system and that the interest of the priest would always be stronger than that of the State." Rousseau concludes the historical retrospective with an arbitration award of the dispute between Pierre Bayle and William Warburton. He asserts against the modern philosopher that a State has never been founded for which religion did not serve as a base. But against the Anglican bishop he holds that in the end the Christian law is more harmful than useful to a strong constitution of the State.[113] Christianity is the problem in the politics of modernity.

To clarify the problem Rousseau introduces into the discussion three kinds of religion, on the basis of which he makes typological distinctions of the relationship between politics and religion. The *Religion de l'homme* is characterized by Rousseau as "without temples, without altars, without rites, limited to the purely internal cult of the supreme God and to the eternal duties of morality," and is called "the pure and simple religion of the Gospel," or "the true theism." The *Religion du Citoyen* by contrast holds

---

111. IV, 8, 11 (462). Among the eventually failed attempts at restoration, Rousseau names in the first place that of Mohammed. He returned to Moses' innovation and set out to found political unity on divine law, i.e., on the *one* law of the *one* God which, affecting all spheres of life, encompasses politics, religion, morality. But following the example of Christianity he made a universal claim for the law. Religion was decoupled from the people for whom the law had been given and developed a momentum of its own—"without the necessary tie to the body of the State"—on the way to the rise and fall of the empire.

112. "La communion et l'excommunication sont le pacte social du clergé, pacte avec lequel il sera toujours le maitre des peuples et des Rois. Tous les prêtres qui communiquent ensemble sont concitoyens, fussent-ils des deux bouts du monde. Cette invention est un chef-d'œuvre en politique. Il n'y avoit rien de semblable parmi les Prêtres payens; aussi n'ont-ils jamais fait un corps de Clergé." IV, 8, 12 note (463). Cf. IV, 8, 34 note (469).

113. IV, 8, 13 and 14 (463–64). See Footnote 47. In the *Première version* the opening of the chapter on religion reads: "Sitôt que les h[ommes] vivent en société il leur faut une Religion qui les y maintienne. Jamais peuple n'a subsisté ni ne subsistera sans Religion et si on ne lui en donnoit point, de lui-même il s'en feroit une ou seroit bientôt détruit" (p. 336). Cf. Footnote 105.

ideal-typically "for a single country, to which it gives its Gods, its own titular patrons"; it has "its dogmas, its rites, its external cult prescribed by the laws, and extends the duties and rights of man only as far as its altars." The *religion du Prêtre*, finally, "more bizarre" than the two other kinds, subjects men to "contradictory duties," since it gives them "two legislations, two chiefs, two fatherlands," and so prevents them from "being able to be at the same time both devout men and citizens." The third type, for which he cites the religion of the Lamas, that of the Japanese, and "Roman Christianity," Rousseau ranks, "politically considered," as "so evidently bad" that a proof is superfluous. In truth, he has already used the second half of the genealogical part for this proof, and the judgment with which he concludes the treatment of the "religion of the priest" by no means targets merely "Roman Christianity," but also actually existing Christianity altogether or Christianity tout court, which opposes the life of obedience of faith to the political life: "Everything that destroys social unity is worthless. All institutions that put man in contradiction with himself are worthless."[114] The "religion of the citizen" does not put man in contradiction with himself insofar as it makes him wholly into a citizen. It links together cult with love for the laws; it orients to the fatherland the readiness of the citizens for devotion; it teaches them to conceive service to the State as service to its tutelary God. Rousseau speaks of "a kind of theocracy" in which there ought to be "no other pontiff than the prince" and "no other priests than the magistrates," which thus presents the exact counterimage to true theocracy. But since the "religion of the citizen" is based upon error and lie, it deceives men, it makes them superstitious, and it exhausts the cult of the divinity in vain ceremonial. Designed for exclusivity, it also makes the people become "bloodthirsty and intolerant," "so that it breathes only murder and massacre, and believes it does a holy deed in killing whoever does not accept its Gods." Consequently, it proves to be "very harmful" to the security of such a people, since it puts the people "in a natural state of war with all others." Rousseau draws upon all rhetorical registers in order to allow no doubt to arise that the way back to the congruence between politics and theology, to belief in the Gods who watch over the weal and woe of the political community, who fight for it and are revered by it, is blocked.[115] The

---

114. IV, 8, 15–17 (464).

115. The reader who compares the statements of the *typology* in IV, 8, 18–19 (464–65) with the description of "all religions of the first peoples," and in particular of the religion of the Greeks and the religion of the Romans in the *genealogy*, will recognize the hyperbolic characterization of the *Religion du Citoyen* without any difficulty. This is true first and foremost for the spectacular statement about its work of devastation, which stands in conspicuous contrast to the declaration

Gods of the polis in their particularity and this-worldly anchorage were not able to withstand the other-worldly God of Christianity, nor could they persist in the face of its universal claim to truth. They were defeated and surpassed. They died because they were no longer credible. The *Religion du Citoyen* perished with them. It was based upon a lie which, recognized as a lie, lost its force.

The *Religion de l'homme* seems to be a religion within the boundaries of mere morality. The determinations with which Rousseau introduces it could make one expect a *Religion naturelle*, like the one the Savoyard Vicar presents for post-Christian man. In fact, however, Rousseau in his discussion of the first type treats Christianity once more.[116] Thus, he uses the largest part of the chapter by far for the political critique of Christianity, now beginning radically: not with the "Christianity of today" but with "that of the Gospel, which is altogether different." He goes back to the "saintly, sublime, genuine religion," in which "men, as children of the same God, all recognize one another as brothers." More precisely, he abstracts from the actuality of the *religion du Prêtre* in order to consider the idea of the "kingdom of the other world," before it entered into its historical *status corruptionis*. Christianity in no way supports the identification of the citizen with the *moi commun* of the body politic. Since Christianity, in anxious tension about the beyond, is "preoccupied solely with the things of heaven"—"the fatherland of the Christian is not of this world"—and since it has a cosmopolitan orientation, it does not encourage the political virtue par excellence, but rather works against it. Without a particular relation to the body politic, which necessarily is particular, the "religion of man" leaves to the laws "only the force" they derive from themselves, i.e., it leaves to the laws the force that is proper to external coercion, without anchoring the laws in the heart of the citizens. "What is more: far from attaching the hearts of the citizens to the State, it detaches them from it as from all earthly things." Rousseau adds emphatically: "I know of nothing more contrary to the social spirit." The Christian religion

---

"Les Dieux des Payens n'étoient point des Dieux jaloux; ils partageoient entre eux l'empire du monde," and finds its resonance within the *genealogy* solely in the interpolated remark about Moses and his people: "Ils regardoient, il est vrai, comme nuls les Dieux des Cananéens, peuples proscrits, voués à la destruction, et dont ils devoient occuper la place." IV, 8, 4 (461); cf. IV, 8, 5 (461).

116. IV, 8, 20–30 (465–67). The term *Religion naturelle* is used nowhere in the *Contrat social*. For the *Profession de foi du Vicaire Savoyard* see the Second Book of my writing *Über das Glück des philosophischen Lebens*, "Rousseau und das Glaubensbekenntnis des Savoyischen Vikars" pp. 291–438 [*On the Happiness of the Philosophic Life*, "Rousseau and the Profession of Faith of the Savoyard Vicar," pp. 221–340.]

inspires the believer with a "profound indifference" toward the this-worldly success or failure of his action and weakens his love of the fatherland. "If the State prospers, he hardly dares to enjoy the public felicity, he fears taking pride in his country's glory; if the State declines, he blesses the hand of God that weighs down on his people."[117] The confrontation with Christianity reaches its peak when Rousseau repeats, combines, and pursues all the way to conscience the critique of the legitimation of illegitimate rule by Christian theology, from Paul to Augustine, Luther and Calvin up to Bossuet, which was distributed over books I, II, and III of the *Contrat social*. The conscience of the Christian, who believes that all power comes from God, that the justice of the sovereign authority of God prevails in everything and that the bad king is a scourge of God, becomes the obstacle for the legitimate political community, the opponent of political freedom.[118] A Christian republic is a round square, since Christianity "preaches nothing but servitude and dependence." From the very beginning it supports, it promotes, it breathes despotism.[119] "True Christians are made to be slaves."[120]

In the concluding section of the chapter, Rousseau has the three kinds of the typology *Religion de l'homme*, *Religion du Citoyen*, and *religion du Prêtre* followed by the *Religion civile*. Rousseau does not introduce the *Religion civile* as a fourth kind. He does not characterize it as he has characterized the three types before. He provides no historical example for it. The term appears only once, in the framework of a law that Rousseau the *Législateur* proposes to the sovereign at the end of the treatise.[121] The legislative proposal responds to the antagonism between politics and religion, whose genealogy the first section traced, and it does justice to the problems of the three types, which the second section investigated. In contrast to the *Religion de l'homme* the *Religion civile* is indissolubly related to the particularity of the republic.

---

117. IV, 8, 21–25 (465–66). Cf. *Lettres écrites de la montagne* I, 65, 67, 71 and 71 note 2, pp. 704–6 and consider *Considérations sur le gouvernement de Pologne* I, 5–7, p. 959; III, 4, p. 961; XII, 12, p. 1019.

118. IV, 8, 26 (466). Consider I, 3, 3 (355); II, 6, 2 (378); III, 6, 16 (413) and see Pp. 120, 159. In the chapter "De la Religion civile" *conscience* is used only this one time in the 26th paragraph. The only other use of the term in the *Contrat social* can be found in the chapter "Du droit du plus fort," I, 3, 3 (335). For Rousseau's position in regard to conscience consider *Über das Glück des philosophischen Lebens*, pp. 191–93, 282–83, 355–56, 429 [*On the Happiness of the Philosophic Life*, pp. 140–42, 213–14, 272–73, 333].

119. Cf. Pp. 149–50 with Footnote 63.

120. IV, 8, 28 (467). The provocative statement about the *vrais Chrétiens* in IV, 8, 28 corresponds to the no less provocative statement about the *peuples modernes* in III, 15, 10 (431). See P. 163.

121. With the exception of the title of chapter IV, 8, *Religion civile* appears in the *Contrat social* only in the center of the third part of the chapter, in paragraph 33 (468).

Unlike the *Religion du Citoyen* it does not assign to the political community a God peculiar to it. In opposition to the *religion du Prêtre* it denies every claim to rule by a spiritual power. It ought to (1) ensure the supremacy of politics over religion, (2) underpin morality through religion, (3) contribute to anchoring the laws in the hearts of the citizens, and (4) guarantee social peace and individual freedom in matters of faith. The conception of the *Religion civile* starts from the double premise that it is important for the body politic "that each citizen have a religion, which makes him love his duties"; but the dogmas of religion are of interest to the body politic and its members only insofar as they "bear on morality and on the duties which anyone who professes it is bound to fulfill toward others."[122] At the basis of the political conception of the *Religion civile* lies, in substance, the distinction between profession and belief or thought, which Hobbes among the moderns made prominent, but which was available to philosophers at all times. Rousseau ascribes to the sovereign the right to fix by laws "a purely civil profession of faith," whose articles claim to be obligatory "not precisely" as dogmas of a religion, but instead as *sentimens de sociabilité*, as views needed for sociability, as opinions "without which it is impossible to be a good citizen or a faithful subject."[123] The sovereign can obligate no one to believe the dogmas of the legal *profession de foi*, but it may expel from the country him who does not profess those dogmas, not because he is considered "impious," but rather because he is found "unsociable." He who has publicly acknowledged the dogmas and then by his behavior indicates that he does not believe in them is threatened with capital punishment: "he has committed the greatest crime, he has lied before the laws."[124] The new valuations that the *Législateur* seeks to establish in public opinion emerge clearly from the explanations he conveys concerning the right and the requirement of a *profession de foi pure-*

---

122. "Chacun peut avoir au surplus telles opinions qu'il lui plait, sans qu'il appartienne au Souverain d'en connoitre: Car comme il n'a point de compétence dans l'autre monde, quel que soit le sort des sujets dans la vie à venir ce n'est pas son affaire, pourvu qu'ils soient bons citoyens dans celle-ci." IV, 8, 31 (468). Cf. *Lettres écrites de la montagne* V, 81, p. 787: "La Religion ne peut jamais faire partie de la Législation qu'en ce qui concerne les actions des hommes. La Loi ordonne de faire ou de s'abstenir, mais elle ne peut ordonner de croire."

123. Cf. Pp. 132–33. The right that Rousseau ascribes to the sovereign comes in response to the right that modern princes claimed for themselves, by virtue of the *ius reformandi*, to set down the Christian profession of their subjects.

124. IV, 8, 32 (468). Cf. II, 5, 6–7 (377). C. E. Vaughan (p. xl) refers to a statement that Rousseau made in 1761 in a footnote in the *Nouvelle Héloïse*: "Si j'étois magistrat, et que la loi portât peine de mort contre les athées, je commencerois par faire bruler comme tel quiconque en viendroit dénoncer un autre." V, 5, *OCP* II, p. 589 note.

ment civile. About the dogmas of the *Religion civile* themselves, he says that they ought to be "stated with precision, without explications or commentaries." Moreover, they must be "simple" and "few in number." Rousseau does not leave it at directives, but rather immediately formulates the ten dogmas that compose the "civil religion": "The existence of the [1] powerful, [2] intelligent, [3] beneficent, [4] prescient, and [5] provident Deity, [6] the life to come, [7] the happiness of the just, [8] the punishment of the wicked, [9] the sanctity of the Social Contract and of the Laws; these are the positive dogmas. As for the negative dogmas, I restrict them to a single one, [10] intolerance: it belongs to the cults we have excluded."[125] Obviously, the first half, dogmas 1–5, serves as the foundation for the second half, dogmas 6–10, and in the second half dogmas 6–8 belong together, whereas dogmas 9 and 10 each have a distinct status. Rousseau places power at the head of the attributes of the deity, in the middle beneficence, and at the end providence or care. The three pillars are designed, in unity with the intelligence and prescience that bind the structure of the attributes into a whole, to provide support for the citizen's belief in a moral world order, a meaningful order in which the citizen and the body politic, as whose member the citizen can understand himself by means "of the Social Contract and of the Laws," are assigned a distinctive place. This distinction is imparted to him by the last dogma of the first half, which stands in for the justice of the deity and forms the bridge to the second half. With belief in a caring deity who—whether through general provisions or through particular attention—takes an interest in his action, dogmas 6–9 open up for the citizen the prospect of deserved reward for the moral or political virtues and vices, if not in this life, then in a life to come. The character of the life to come is left just as much to his imagination as are the kind and duration of the happiness of the just and the punishment of the wicked. Dogmas 6–8 do not decide the dispute over the immortality of the soul, nor does dogma 5 make a commitment in favor of general or of

---

125. IV, 8, 33 (468–69). Rousseau himself carries out in 1762 what he requested from Voltaire in the *Lettre à Voltaire* of August 18, 1756. And he carries it out differently from the way he first proposed it, namely, conceived as terse articles of a law: "Je voudrais donc qu'on eut dans chaque Etat un Code moral, ou une espèce de profession de foi civile qui contint positivement les maximes sociales que chacun seroit tenu d'admettre, et négativement les maximes fanatiques qu'on seroit tenu de rejetter non comme impies, mais comme Séditieuses. Ainsi toute Religion qui pourait s'accorder avec le Code serait admise, toute Religion qui ne s'y accorderait pas serait proscrite, et chacun serait libre de n'en avoir point d'autre que le Code même. Cet ouvrage, fait avec soin, serait, ce me semble, le livre le plus utile qui jamais ait été composé, et peut être le seul nécessaire aux hommes. Voilà, Monsieur un sujet digne de vous . . ." Par. 34, *CC* IV, p. 49.

particular providence. That wisdom is not admitted among the attributes of the deity is in accord with the subphilosophic tailoring of the "purely civil profession of faith." With respect to the all-important determination of the God of the revealed religions, on the contrary, Rousseau lets no unclarity arise: Since the first dogma attests that the *Divinité* is *puissante* and not *toute-puissante*, it bars the entry of omnipotence, which would negate the possibility of philosophy, into the legal credo.[126]

The "sanctity of the Social Contract and of the Laws" anchors the particularity of the body politic in the profession of faith. For it is the body politic that is brought into being by the act of the *contrat social*, and according to the *Contrat social* it is necessarily a particular body politic: It receives a "common I" through the citizens who recognize themselves in it as its members and a determinate shape through the laws they give it.[127] The ninth dogma is constitutive of the *Religion civile*. It is what distinguishes the *Religion civile* from *Religion naturelle*. It formulates the truly political article of faith and through the formulation of the article itself expresses that the *Religion civile* is supposed to reach the citizen in the double aspect in which the *Contrat social* views him. The dogma sanctions the right of the *Citoyen*, which has its sole source in the social contract, and it sanctions at the same time—therefore, it is one article and not two—the duty of the *Sujet*, which is measured solely by the laws. With "sanctity," of which the ninth dogma speaks, Rousseau returns to the faith of the citizen, with which he began in book I, that the social order is "a sacred right, which provides the basis for all the others." In between lies the entire argument of the *Contrat social*, in the unfolding of which Rousseau once spoke of the "sanctity" of the contract and once of the "sanctity" of the work of the lawgiver and in other passages called "sacred" the power of the sovereign, the institution of the tribunate,

---

126. Cf. *Über das Glück des philosophischen Lebens*, pp. 100–101, 327–29 (on the denial of omnipotence); pp. 171, 335, 347–49, 357–63 (on the problem of wisdom and justice); pp. 87–90, 343–46 (on the question of immortality). [*On the Happiness of the Philosophic Life*, pp. 70–72, 250–52; 126, 256, 266–68, 274–79; 60–62, 263–66.]

127. In the ninth dogma, *Contract social* is capitalized. In the other seven passages in which *contract social* appears in the text, the term is written in lowercase, and there can be no doubt as to whether reference is made to the contract or to the book: I, 6, 4 (360); I, 7, 2 (362); I, 8, 2 (364); I, 9, 1 (365); II, 4, 8 (375); II, 4, 10 (375); III, 16, 2 (432). The meaning of the sanctity of the *contrat social* in the ninth dogma is determined by Rousseau's *Contrat social*. That the book of a philosopher that has as its subject the work of legislation is integrated into the work of legislation is not without precedent: *Nomoi* VII, 811 c–e. Cf. Seth Benardete, *Plato's "Laws": The Discovery of Being* (Chicago, 2000), pp. 151, 209, 215.

and the power of the laws.[128] After he destroyed the sacred right of the citizen at the beginning of the treatise, by tracing it back to a convention and basing it upon the wills of natural beings, he endeavors at the end of the treatise to restore faith in a sacred right by a convention. For the fact that the ninth dogma proclaims *la sainteté du Contract social et des Loix*, cannot conceal that the dogma is in no way derived from the eight previous dogmas, but rather, like the *Religion civile* altogether, rests on a political act, a positing, a convention. If the sanctity of the source of right and of the laws becomes part of the legal profession, it is the expression of the *volonté générale*. In other words: The *Religion civile* does not legitimize the *contrat social*, but rather the *contrat social* legitimizes the *Religion civile*. The construction at the end amounts to the same meaning as the destruction at the beginning. The "sanctity of the Social Contract and of the Laws" has its *fundamentum in re* in the nature of the contract, which the *Contrat social* explicates.[129]

The special status of the tenth article of the *Religion civile* is marked by Rousseau in three ways. Not only does he explicitly set off the prohibition against "intolerance" from the nine "positive dogmas" that precede it. In addition, since he declares it to be the single "negative dogma" and ends with it, he delegates to it the task of designating the critical thrust of the profession. And finally, this dogma alone is followed by an explanatory addition, with which he makes clear that the prohibition does not concern "intolerance" in general, but rather has in view a particular "cult." In fact, the final article of the *Religion civile* can so little dispense with "explications or commentaries" that Rousseau spends the remainder of the chapter on its explanation. The classification of "intolerance" under "the cults we have excluded" refers the reader back to the *religion du Prêtre*, about which Rousseau said in the section on typology that it is "so evidently bad" that it would be a "waste of time" even to want to prove it. The *religion du Prêtre*, or more precisely "Roman Christianity," is the immediate target of the "negative dogma" of the *Religion civile*. In the *Contrat social* Rousseau makes good on what he originally envisaged in the *Discours sur l'inégalité*: He has the book culminate in

---

128. I, 1, 2 (352); see Pp. 154-55. I, 7, 3 (363); II, 7, 4 (382). II, 4, 9 (375); IV, 5, 3 (454); IV, 6, 3 (456).

129. Cf. I, 7, 5 (363); II, 6, 5 (379); II, 7, 7 (383); II, 12, 2 (394); III, 18, 9 (436). See Pp. 126-29, 132-33, 138-39. Consider Rousseau's treatment of the sanctity of the contract in *Les rêveries du Promeneur Solitaire* VI, 9, OCP I, pp. 1053-54 and see *Über das Glück des philosophischen Lebens*, pp. 193-96 [*On the Happiness of the Philosophic Life*, pp. 142-44].

an attack on the claim to rule by spiritual power.[130] The prohibition against "theological intolerance" has the political consequences in view: "It is impossible to live in peace with people one believes to be damned; to love them would be to hate God who punishes them; one must absolutely bring them back or torment them." "Theological intolerance" necessarily produces a "civil effect." It ends up that "the sovereign is no longer sovereign" and "the priests are the true masters." The intolerance against which the tenth article of faith is directed stands in for the more deeply rooted teaching that owing to their wrong or lacking faith men must be considered as damned and, as Rousseau states more precisely in a Note of the *Profession de foi du Vicaire Savoyard*, as "enemies of God," an enmity that surpasses all other enmities and that, if believed in, must penetrate all other enmities. The identification of the believer with God's distinction between friend and enemy or with what he attributes to God as enmity harbors a political explosiveness. Therefore, Rousseau digs all the way down to that faith that is supposed to decide about salvation and damnation and is the basis for the separation into the friends and enemies of God. The critique of intolerance is an integral component of his critique of political theology. The "negative dogma" is the only one of the ten dogmas for which there is no doubt that Rousseau agreed with it, independent of the decision of the sovereign about the legislative proposal.[131] In his explanation of the prohibition against intolerance Rousseau mentions neither the "religion of the priest" nor "Roman Christianity" by name. Instead, he connects the doctrine *extra ecclesiam nulla salus* with *Gouvernement Théocratique*, in order to evoke in the penultimate sentence of "De la Religion civile" for a third and last time the conception that the *Contrat social* most fundamentally contradicts with its principles of political right. After the preparatory reference at the beginning and the characterization through its mirror image in the center of the chapter, the concluding usage points

---

130. Rousseau intended to present the critique of the spiritual power of the priests and of the inequality founded by it ("the least rational and the most dangerous of all") in the penultimate paragraph of the *Discours*. In the final editing, this critique fell victim to Rousseau's self-censorship. The evidence, among which the relevant pages Rousseau carefully preserved of a clean copy of the manuscript, lost apart from these pages, as well as an exact reconstruction, can be found in my edition of the *Discours sur l'inégalité*, pp. 386–403 and xli–xlvii. Cf. in addition the critique of "intolerance" in the *Lettre à Voltaire*, par. 33, *CC* IV, p. 49.

131. IV, 8, 34–35 (469); *Profession de foi du Vicaire Savoyard* note 17, p. 628. Rousseau's critique of "intolerance" is not restricted to the historical excesses of fanaticism or to the political aberrations of the church authorities such as the St. Bartholomew's Day Massacre or the burning of Michel Servet in Calvin's Geneva, which Rousseau cites in the later apologetic writings. See *Lettre à Christophe de Beaumont*, *OCP* IV, p. 161; *Lettres écrites de la montagne* II, 53 note, p. 726; cf. III, 50 note and 89, pp. 742, 752.

to the core of the matter designated by *theocracy*: tracing all rule and all salvation back to the sovereign authority of the *one* God, a sovereign authority that has its proxy representatives and appointed interpreters in the world and whose demand for obedience reaches all the way into the thought of the individual and binds him in his conscience.[132] As much as the political and the philosophic intention of the *Contrat social* are in agreement regarding the "negative dogma," just as little do they seem to converge regarding the "positive dogmas" of the *Religion civile*. That the sacralization of what is politically particular, which the ninth dogma lays down in general terms, promotes the identification of the citizen with the "common I" is doubtful; that taken by itself it inspires his love of the fatherland is hardly to be expected. In addition, Rousseau cannot lack clarity about the fact that dogmas 6–8 in their laconic character do not supply a sufficient answer to the question he directed at the philosopher and held up as an objection to the Savoyard Vicar, namely, what is supposed to replace the otherworldly court of the Persians' Bridge of Hell, "Poul-Serrho," in order to lend weight to the commands of morality. The *grand Législateur* might in a few hundred years find means to give the *Religion civile* a particular shape and an effective character. Rousseau himself exercises the greatest restraint. To step forward as the founder of a new cult is not his cause.[133] This is also confirmed by the later draft constitutions for Corsica and Poland. His cause is to point out the problem. He shows

---

132. Cf. the locus classicus of the concept, reproduced in Footnote 65 in the French translation in which Rousseau read Flavius Josephus. Folker Siegert has published an excellent critical edition with German translation: *Über die Ursprünglichkeit des Judentums (Contra Apionem)* (Göttingen, 2008), 2 volumes, I, p. 189. Josephus's concept of theocracy received a broad reception among the moderns from Spinoza via Vico to Voltaire. An early reference can be found in Petrus Cunaeus, *De Republica Hebraeorum libri tres* (Amsterdam, 1666), Book I, 1, p. 4 (originally Leiden, 1617).—Only in the definitive version of the chapter "De la Religion civile" did Rousseau decide on the threefold presence of theocracy, in the first sentence of the first paragraph, in the second sentence of the central paragraph, and in the third sentence of the last paragraph. In the *Première version* the terms *Théocratie* and *gouvernement Théocratique* each appear once, in paragraphs 5 and 25, respectively, of the chapter comprising 25 paragraphs (pp. 337, 342). The third and final mention of the *raisonnement de Caligula* in IV, 8, 1, which leads the attentive reader to Flavius Josephus, is also missing in the *Première version*. In it, Caligula appears not three times, but only a single time, in the second paragraph of the chapter "Du Législateur" (p. 312).

133. *Profession de foi du Vicaire Savoyard* note 18, 9–12, pp. 634–35. Rousseau deletes from the final version of "De la Religion civile" every reference to a publicly shaped cult. In the *Première version* he first wrote: "Cette profession de foi une fois établie, qu'elle se renouvelle tous les ans avec solennité et que cette solennité soit accompagnée d'un culte auguste et simple dont les magistrats soient seuls les ministres et qui réchauffe dans les cœurs l'amour de la patrie. Voilà tout ce qu'il est permis au souverain de prescrire quant à la religion." Par. 24, p. 342; cf. par. 8, p. 338.

lawgivers of the future a way, which in the present he neither can nor wants to go. The present is subject to the reservation he expresses in *Émile*. There he places in front of his outline of a life that is capable of being in agreement with itself in the midst of a depraved society the verdict: "The two words *fatherland* and *citizen* have to be stricken from modern languages." Rousseau continues that he knows the reason but does not want to give it, since, as he says, the reason does not pertain to his subject. In the *Contrat social* the reason does pertain to the subject and finds itself expressed in it: The spirit of Christianity has seized everything, has won everything, has infected everything.[134] Under these conditions, the articles of the "purely civil profession of faith" are first and foremost articles of defense.[135] But independent of the political success or failure of the legislative proposal, they are in addition a final confirmation of the diagnosis from which the *Contrat social* began and to which it has returned again and again: The chains cannot be removed from sociable man, they can at best be made legitimate. It is no accident that Rousseau calls the dogmas of civil religion views of sociability.

The final chapter of the treatise consists of a short paragraph comprising two sentences. Rousseau claims that he has set down "the true principles of political right." After he has sought to ground the State on its foundation, it would remain for him to "buttress the State by its external relations." That would require the discussion of international law, of commerce, of the law of war, of conquests. It would be of particular interest to explore the possibilities that the establishment of confederations would open up for small States to assert themselves against the great powers.[136] "But all this forms a new object too vast for my short sight; I should always have fixed it nearer to myself." After Rousseau has treated the right and limits of politics, he

---

134. *Émile* I, p. 250. IV, 8, 11 (462). The spirit of Christianity blocks the path back to the "religion of the citizen," to the institution of the well-ordered political community on a foundation other than that of the equality of the rights of its citizens, to the assertion of insight as a title to rule. See Pp. 148–50, 163, 175–76.

135. "Maintenant qu'il n'y a plus et qu'il ne peut plus y avoir de Religion nationale exclusive, on doit tolérer toutes celles qui tolerent les autres, autant que leurs dogmes n'ont rien de contraire aux devoirs du Citoyen. Mais quiconque ose dire, *hors de l'Eglise point de Salut*, doit être chassé de l'Etat" IV, 8, 35 (469).

136. Chapter III, 15, which is of particular importance for the final sentence of the "Conclusion," contains the announcement : "Je ferai voir ci-après comment on peut réunir la puissance extérieure d'un grand Peuple avec la police aisée et le bon ordre d'un petit Etat." Rousseau adds the footnote: "C'est ce que je m'étois proposé de faire dans la suite de cet ouvrage, lorsqu'en traitant des rélations externes j'en serois venu aux confédérations. Matiere toute neuve et où les principes sont encore à établir." III, 15, 12 and note (431); cf. III, 13, 6 (427).

reminds himself in the "Conclusion" of what always deserves his greatest attention. He refers to something of the greatest importance that stands outside the brackets within which the investigation of the *Contrat social* is conducted. Rousseau's reminder to himself comes to pass and is heeded in *Les rêveries du Promeneur Solitaire*.

APPENDIX

Leo Strauss, *Thoughts on Machiavelli*: The Headings

PRELIMINARY REMARK

Upon a visit with Professor Jenny Strauss Clay in Charlottesville in November 1994, she made available to me a number of manuscripts, notes, and other documents from the estate of her father. Among them was the manuscript of *Thoughts on Machiavelli*. When I saw the clean copy written by Leo Strauss with an ink pen, I noticed that the author had not only numbered all the paragraphs chapter by chapter, but also, deviating from his usual practice, furnished each of them with a heading. I later transcribed the headings and shared them with friends.

The transcript, which is being made public here for the first time, reproduces all the headings exactly as Leo Strauss noted them for himself before he wrote the paragraphs of the book. Supplements that he made in pencil are indicated. Abbreviations and shorthand expressions were not eliminated in order to leave entirely untouched the private character of the notations. For the headings were not meant for publication. I also include the dates of the manuscript by which Strauss, following a habit maintained over decades, recorded for himself the periods of time during which he worked on his texts.

The manuscript of *Thoughts on Machiavelli*, one of the great philosophic books of the twentieth century, has been archived in the Leo Strauss Papers, Department of Special Collections, University of Chicago Library since 1995. The transcript of the headings is published with the kind permission of Professor Nathan Tarcov, Literary Executor of the Estate of Leo Strauss.

Munich, September 20, 2015

H. M.

Thoughts on Machiavelli

Introduction and Chapter I: 2.3.1956–25.3.1956; 25.7.–16.8.1956

Introduction.

1 M. a wicked teacher of wickedness.

2 M. *the* wicked teacher of wickedness.

3 The simple minded view attacked by the sophisticated.

4 It is misleading to call M. a patriot or a scientist.

5 M. may have been a teacher of wickedness, although or rather because he was a patriot or a scientist.

6 [no heading, originally no separate paragraph]

7 = 6 The denial of his wickedness due to his influence.

8 = 7 It is necessary to understand M. from the front, not from the back.

9 = 8 M. a fallen angel—a theoretical man.

10 = 9 M. and the USA.

11 [no heading, originally no separate paragraph]

12 = 10 Our task: recovery of the permanent *problem*.

I The <dual> twofold character of M.' teaching.

1 Two books whose relation is obscure.

2 *Prince* : *Disc.* = principalities : republics.

3 Since republics are not timely, *De rep.* becomes *Disc.*

4 Objections.

5 Each of the two books contains everything M. knows—no difference of subject matter.

6 On the extent of M. knowledge.

7 [no heading, inserted by Strauss as paragraph 6a]

8 = 7 The 2 books distinguished by their addressees: actual princes ≠ potential princes.

9 = 8 *Prince*: brief, urgent, call to action—*Disc.*: the opposites.

10 = 9 *Prince* : master—*Disc.* : friends.

11 = 10 *Prince* less straightforward than *Disc.*

12 = 11 First appearance of *Prince* more traditional than that of *Disc.*

13 = 12 Reticences of the *Prince*.

14 = 13 The *Disc.* too are not altogether frank.

15 = 14 The *Prince* in some respects more frank than the *Disc.*

16 = 15 Is M.' perspective identical with that of *Prince, or* of *Disc.,* or different from both?

17 = 16 How to read M. [in pencil:]—as he read Livy.

18 = 17 According to M., Livy reveals his opinions (= his disagreement with common view) most clearly by silence.

19 = 18 M.' silences: silence about *this* world, *this* life, hell, devil and soul.

20 = 19 His allusion to eternity—creation and to human origin of Christianity.

21 = 20 His allusion in the beginning of the *Prince* to the problem of the Church.

22 = 21 Censorship → concealment.

23 = 22 - - -

24 = 23 Manifest blunders are intentional.

25 = 24 M., being a clever enemy, is intelligent but not moral.

26 = 25 Contradiction—here: he cannot introduce the new except by appealing primarily to ancient antiquity.

27 = 26 Difference between headings and bodies of chapters: M. does not indicate in headings that the Roman nobility used religion or deception in order to control the plebs.

28 = 27 M.' intention: quasi impossible combination of gravity and levity.

29 = 28 Alludes to difficulty of knowing his *enemy's* intention.

30 = 29 Parody of scholastic disputation—(3 impostors)—M. uses enemy of Christianity in order to say truth about Christianity.

31 = 30 Repetitions.

32 = 31 Digressions.

33 = 32 Ambiguous terms.

34 = 33 Numbers.

35 = 34 M.' blasphemy.

36 = 35 Numbers continued.

37 = 36 Conclusion.

II. M.' Intention: The *Prince*

22.8.56–6.10.56

1 A treatise.

2 —and a tract for the times.

3 The movement of the *Prince* is ascent followed by descent: the <descent> center is the peak.

4 Movement of first part: from the familiar, Here, Now, ordinary to the unfamiliar, ancient, rare, and thereafter descent. [Pencil note above *unfamiliar, ancient*: the highest theme.]

5 Movement of the 2nd part: quick ascent to the roots of traditional understanding of the greatest doers.

6 Movement in ch. 15–23: ascending to full truth about greatest doers which implies uprooting of Great Tradition, and then descent.

7 Movement in 4th part of *Prince*.

8 Tradition → timeless truth (≠ tract for the times) is related to time because it is new or revolutionary (≠ traditional)

9 "Treatise—tract" must be understood in the light of "traditional—revolutionary".

10 The specific difficulty caused by "tract" (= ch. 26): silence about the political conditions of liberation of Italy.

11 Political conditions of liberation of Italy presented surreptitiously in ch. 3–5.

12 Liberation of Italy requires complete revolution, especially re: morality.

13 Secularization of the Church—break with Christianity.

14 The theme of the *Prince*: prince, but especially new prince.

15 Ambiguity of "new prince".

16 Addressee of *Prince* is advised to become an imitator.

17 —an imitator of Moses → he will not conquer Italy.

18 The appeal to religion in ch. 26 is sufficient proof of the exoteric character of the particular council given in ch. 26.

19 M., the enemy of Fortuna, tries to become the adviser of Lorenzo, the favorite of Fortuna.

20 M. not only adviser of Lorenzo but teacher of an indefinite multitude.

21 M. the new Chiron, not a mere man (he replaces Christ).

22 The shockingly novel teaching concealed by ch. 26.

23 M.' patriotism.

24 His pedagogic policy: toughening up.

25 M. the new prince, the new Moses.

26 But M. is an unarmed prophet—is he not bound to fail?

III. M.' Intention: The *Discorsi*.

26.10.–23.12.; 26.3.–27.5.57

1 *Disc.* → republics = peoples → more frank: *Disc.* chief source of M.' rhetoric.

2 *Disc.*: new modes, orders = modes and orders of antiquity.

3 *Disc.*: proof that ancient rules and orders can and ought to be imitated by modern men.

4 *Disc.*: not to return to rules and practices of the ancients.

5 *Disc.*: Livy I–X—united Italy controlled by a hegemonial republic.

6 Intention of *Disc.* → the typical chapter—but a great variety re: character of chapters.

7 The typical chapter of *Disc.* (III 7) → *Disc.* deal with the horrors inherent in the ultimate causes, and: → general rules re human conduct derived from ancient, modern examples (≠ proof of superiority of ancients to moderns).

8 M. is compelled to argue dialectically: he appeals to a prejudice in favor of class. antiquity.

9 M. is compelled to establish the authority of ancient Rome or of Livy: ancient Rome the known πατριον → Livy M.' Bible.

10 On his way from ancient Egypt to ancient Rome M. by-passes the Bible.

11 M. : Rome, Livy = theological apologetics : Bible.

12 M.' purpose ≠ Livy's purpose → M.' subject is not Rome at all—it is at least as much Asiatic as it is Roman.

13 M.' Livy ≠ Livy's plan: the authority of the Livian order asserts itself when the light of M.' plan is dimmed.

14 Plan of *Disc.* II—M. impresses his form on Livian matter—*Disc.* II devoted to critique of Christianity.

15 Plan of *Disc.* III: private counsel about private benefit; and: why not "use of Livy", but "references to Livy".

16 Plan of *Disc.* III: founder-captain; multitude; M. himself.

17 M. another Fabius: the incredibility of his <enterprise> exploration of the Ciminian Forest secures him against detection.

18 First Latin Livy quote prepared by complete break with authority or with ἀγαθον = πάτριον.

19 First Latin Livy quotes re religion: need for Livian authority for attack on Christianity—M. changes Livian stories to facilitate <use> imitation of ancient religion by modern men.

20 Second Latin Livy quotes (density) in I 40: perfect neutrality re tyranny—freedom—connection between Christianity and tyranny.

21 First Livy references (I 7–8)—ancient Rome : modern Florence, ancient Tuscany = politics : religion = accusations : calumnies = aristocracy : democracy.

22 Criticism of Rome after contrast between moderate foundation of Roman republic and barbarian foundation of Moses' kingdom → not Rome, but Livy, a book, is *the* authority → entirely new modes and orders.

23 M.' "faith" in Rome's authority undergoes a radical change in the progress from *Disc.* I 6 to I 59.

24 Criticism of Rome in *Disc.* II: Rome criticized not only on political grounds but also as trailblazer for, and model of, the Church; the Romans themselves did not believe in authority.

25 Criticism of Rome in III → the Romans were religious—M. is an enemy of the Romans because he is irreligious—not religion but necessity produces the highest virtue.

26 Teaching of *Disc.* transmitted between the covers of *Disc.* and of Livy; Livy M.' theological authority: the authority as [regards] Fortuna.

27 Criticism of Livy in *Disc.* I 1–57: questionable character of histories; Livy's errors on virtue and on plebs.

28 Criticism of authority in general in *Disc.* I 1–57: connection between "belief" and "people".

29 M. attacks in I 58 all writers and authority as such: reason, youth, modernity stand up against authority, old age and antiquity.

30 M. attacks the whole tradition on democratic grounds; by this he intimates that the people (≠ ἐπιεικεῖς) are the depositories of morality and religion.

31 M.' democratism follows from ironical premise that morality is the highest, from his being a revolutionary = upstart, from the necessity always to appeal to some ἔνδοξον.

32 Prince : *Disc.* = founder : people (Bible)—*Disc.* closer to ἔνδοξα because it contains more detailed destructive analysis of ἔνδοξα.

33 M. makes the ancient Romans "better", i.e. less religious and moral, than they were.

34 *Disc.* II pr.—there is nothing wrong if a Christian becomes a Turk—higher rank of works of art, writings than of deeds.

35 *Disc.* II 1: M. disagrees with Livy and the Roman people re: fear of fortune, but distinguishes between Livy and his characters: Livy perhaps not only expositor but also critic of pagan theology.

36 Peculiarities of Livy treatment in *Disc.* II–III: Livy ≠ his characters; sermons on Livian texts; Livy fa fede and è testimone.

37 By using enemies of Rome as his characters, Livy succeeds in being not only the expositor of pagan theology but also its critic: his *History* contains both the Roman fraud and its detection.

38 M. uses Livy book as an instrument (quâ expositor of pagan theology) and as a model (quâ critic of it) for his criticism of Bible—Livy a character of M.

39 Since Biblical writers do not use enemies of Bible as their mouthpieces, one must use pagan literature to discover truth re Bible; pagan letters preserved by persecuting Biblical religion because the latter is "disarmed".

40 Particular incredibility of Bible due to miracles—hence special need for extra-Biblical elects.

41 The self-deception of Biblical writers → God : Biblical writers = Livy : characters of Livy.

42 Biblical writers "make" God say and do what a perfect being as they conceive of it, ought to say and do.

43 Livy consciously creates perfect captains (Biblical writers create their great captain unconsciously), hence Livy (≠ Bible) corrects his creation.

44 Function of treating Ought as Is: creating hope; perfect beings needed for mastering τυχη : perfect beings are causes of τυχηρα. Livy presents criticism of Roman religion by using characters of characters or by using Romans addressing different audiences. Patricians : plebs = clergy : laity.

45 "Fabius" disregards auspices, debunks a dictator's holy zeal and gets away with it.

46 M. abandons "Livy the teacher of Oughts" as soon as his own intention becomes the theme (i.e. in III 35–49).

47 M. wages a new war against a new enemy in new territory—for his purpose he must be a knower of sites in Livy.

48 The first two Livian sermons: Primacy of love or charity leads to pious cruelty.

49 The third sermon: the moderns trust Fortuna, the ancients tempted Fortuna.

50 "Authority—reason" in center of central book (II 10–24) → the greatest sin consists in lack of presumption.

51 Tacitus is treated as authority par excellence because he is the greatest historian who speaks about the origins of Judaism and Christianity.

52 M. is converted by his credere Tacitus from love to fear (to Moses) and from the preserver to the founder.

53 Christ is the synthesis of gentleness and severity—his pride.

54 M. attacks principle of authority by denying primacy of Love and asserting primacy of Terror → a modest and humane goal—no paradise but therefore no hell.

55 M. communicates the new modes and orders to all, but their ground (atheism) only to the young.

56 M. is less a conspirator than a corruptor of the coming generations.

57 The end of Christianity—can be hastened by M.' action.

58 M.' hope rests on split between ardent and lukewarm Christians = lovers of heavenly and earthly fatherland.

59 M. imitates Christ by propaganda (≠ sacrificial death).

IV. Machiavelli's teaching

IV 1–42: finished August 31, 1957

APPENDIX

1 Captatio benevolentiae for myself and for M.—esotericism and philosophy.

2 M. not a "pagan" but a savio del mondo, i.e. a faylasûf [written in Arabic].

3 M.' silence about Bible not due to ignorance or indifference.

4 First statement on essence of Christianity: Christianity has rendered the world weak without making it more God-fearing.

5 2nd statement on essence of Christianity → Christianity has not shown the truth—humility and the God who assumed humiliation.

6 Third statement: absurdity of do not resist evil.

7 Specimen of our argument: M. seemingly wrong but actually right.

8 Weakness of moderns: no modern empire and no strong modern republics.

9 Christianity stems from the servile East and a weak Eastern nation.

10 Christianity → rule of priests = most tyrannical rule.

11 Rational account of victory of Christianity.

12 Christian strength and good Christian soldiers: Love—consuming fire—hell—stake → pious cruelty and fanatical zeal.

13 Propria gloria (consciousness of excellence) vs. gloria Dei (consciousness of sin)—for: necessity to sin.

14 Humanity and goodness vs. humility and cruelty.

15 Conscience replaced by prudenza.

16 Providence: M. does not distinguish between the core and the periphery of Bible; he identifies providence with God being a just King.

17 Providence in *I. F.*: God saves the Florentines by threatening his Vicar with the Infidels.

18 God is a neutral.

19 Denial of providence and of immortality of the soul.

20 Denial of man's being the cause of evil and sin → denial of creation.

21 Need for recourse to "Averroism" in order to understand M.

22 No shred of evidence in favor of revelation.

23 Biblical phenomena matched by pagan phenomena.

24 In the light of Livy (reason) Christianity appears as an abortive populist movement.

25 Monotheism: present misery—hope for future—polytheism: present splendor and no hope.

26 Practically the whole criticism of revelation is Aristotelian—only the opposite of humility is not humanity but magnanimity.

27 *Disc.* silent about God's or gods' existence.

28 M. replaces God by Cielo or Cieli—by Fortuna.

29 M.' tentative theology: there exist compassionate intelligences in the air (≠ angry and cruel gods).

30 M. replaces "signs" by "accidents".

31 Fortuna an improved image of the Biblical God.

32 Fortuna = extrinsic accident [in pencil:]—not hopes, but regulate Fortuna.

33 Fortuna far from being heaven has a subordinate place within heaven; cannot be completely controlled by man → ἀταραξια (≠ conquest of chance).

34 The emergence of gods out of cooperation of τυχη and fraud.

35 Contradiction between omnipotence and freedom.

36 Break with Ar.—turn towards "Democritus".

37 M. prefers "Aristippus—Diogenes" to Ar.

38 Religion is essentially untrue belief.

39 Religion salutary—? It stems from weakness of mind and fosters such weakness.

40 Fear of God can be replaced by fear of prince—a prince cannot be religious.

41 Even in republics, function of religion can be discharged by other methods.

42 Religion *is* needed, especially for the multitude.

43 Incomprehension of M. (and his successors) due to our being under the spell of post French Revolution outlook.

44 M. more explicit re morality than re religion since morality is less grave an issue than religion.

45 M.' moral-pl. teaching (≠ teaching on religion) is radically new—taking one's bearing by how men live (≠ how they ought to live)—point of view of practitioner and therefore normative.

46 M. reproduces ἔνδοξα: goodness = moral virtue or = unselfishly benefitting others—is happiness (or way to happiness)—onesto ≠ onorevole

47 Conflict between ἔνδοξα (λογοι) and ἔργα → conflict between λογοι; difference between public and private λογοι.

48 Virtue as mean: equanimity has only one opposite vice which merely appears as two opposite defects.

49 Virtue as mean: liberality is not the good mean between prodigality and stinginess—stinginess is required by justice.

50 The right way (the life κατα φυσιν) is indeed a mean—yet a mean not between opposite vices but between virtue and vice.

51 M. rejects via del mezzo because it is connected with notion of summum bonum and ens perfectissimum, i.e. a good perfectly free from evil.

52 Virtue is voluntary: M. defends liberum arbitrium against Fortuna (God) [inserted in pencil:] Man can be the master of his fate [end of insertion]—but:

chance is based on nature and necessity → what is the relation of freedom and necessity?

53 [inserted as a new paragraph:] Virtue incompatible with necessity but also = submission to necessity [added in pencil:]—for: necessity to sin.

54 [originally: 53] Men are compelled by their natures to act in specific ways—extraordinary virtue is a gift of nature (not voluntary) compelling its holder—similarly stupidity.

55 [originally: 54] The necessity which causes men to operate well is fear of violent death to be avoided only by actions against men's natural inclination.

56 [originally: 55] The necessity which <makes> causes men to operate well (justly and industriously) is hunger (→ crucial importance of property).

57 The necessity which makes men good is compulsion exerted by laws, by government.

58 Yet, choice : necessity = founder : people = strong : weak → not necessity but wise choice makes men operate well.

59 Choice (ambition, glory) are themselves necessary; it makes men[,] superior men operate well; necessity to make man operate well must be known as such.

60 Operating well depends on chance; but malleability of matter; above all: man can be master of his fate only by *knowledge* of necessity.

61 M. attacks class. p. philosophy with a view to the fact that men are bad.

62 Virtue presupposes society → society cannot be based on morality but only on immorality.

63 The end of society is not virtue but the common good; republican virtue (≠ moral virtue) the means for the common good.

64 Republican virtue ≠ moral virtue.

65 End justifies means → moral = ordinary, immoral = extraordinary.

66 Common good demands even sacrifice of republican virtue.

67 A patriotic intermezzo.

68 Moral virtue = requirements of living together absolutized.

69 Case for principalities = questioning of the common good in the name of private good (freedom of opinion).

70 Case for principalities: humanity demands acceptance of corruption; prudent selfishness of prince sufficient for making him a good prince; virtue = prudent and strong selfishness.

71 Collective selfishness of ruling class in city; perfect republican virtue due to a specific temper, not to προαιρεσις.

72 The case for tyranny.

73 The case for tyranny—continued.

74 The selfish consideration.

75 Oppression coeval with society → only difference of degree between best republic and worst tyranny.

76 for: men are bad—i.e. selfish.

77 The principles of M.' statecraft: men's selfishness and the need for selfreliance (→ virtù).

78 M.' neutrality re "republics—tyrannies": the only simply common good is the truth.

79 Pol. common good supplemented on the same plane by strictly private good (love) → quest for truth = synthesis of gravity and levity.

80 Desire for glory → quest for truth quâ beneficial truth (≠ detachment) → bias in favor of republics.

81 Delusion of glory → *the* motive is desire for truth—gravity : levity = knowledge of truth : communication of knowledge.

82 M. breaks with the whole Socratic tradition—he forgets Socrates.

83 He forgets tragedy.

84 He sees only the social source of morality: he forgets the soul.

85 Obfuscation of philosophy and its status → *appearance* of radical novelty.

86 Philosophy → gulf between philosophers and δημος → punitive rhetoric; M. accepts τελη του δήμου, because popular—conquest of nature—lowering of standards.

87 The entering wedge of M.' criticism: encouragement of inventions re war— no periodic cataclysms—need for reformulation of "beneficence of nature".

Finis—Laus Deo.

December, 9, 1957.

INDEX OF NAMES

Aeschylus, 9n14
Alfarabi, Abu Nasr (Farabi), 10, 20, 45, 46, 48, 50, 60, 85, 105
Amyot, Jacques, 146n58
Anaxagoras, 10
Andilly, Arnauld d', 147n60, 150n65
Anytus, 6
Aristippus of Cyrene, 76, 195
Aristophanes, 3-6, 3n1, 4n4, 5n7, 6n8, 6n11, 10, 17, 21
Aristotle, 9, 9n12, 10, 19, 24, 56, 59n67, 68-70, 70n86, 75-76, 81, 83n108, 88-89, 93-95, 93n132, 106, 106-7nn157-58, 109, 112, 194, 195
Augustine, 110, 177
Averroes, 10, 105
Avicenna, 10

Bachofen, Blaise, 124n12
Bacon, Francis, 10, 58n64
Bayle, Pierre, 174
Beaulavon, Georges, 117n1, 150n65
Beaumont, Christophe de, 182n131
Benardete, Seth, 9n13, 11n16, 18n28, 77n101, 180n39
Bernardi, Bruno, 117n1, 124n12
Bion of Borysthenes, 76
Boccaccio, Giovanni, 46n39
Bossuet, Jacques Bénigne, 120n5, 125n13, 177
Bultmann, Rudolf, 16n25
Buttafoco, Matthieu, 136n33

Caligula, Gaius Caesar, 147, 147nn59-61, 148, 150, 150n65, 172n106, 183n132

Calvin, John, 13n21, 120n5, 140n44, 159, 160n85, 177, 182
Camillus, 112, 112n167
Cato, Marcus Porcius, Censorius, 96
Chiron, 82-83, 190
Cicero, Marcus Tullius, 10, 12n19, 59n67, 85, 169
Cropsey, Joseph, 108
Cunaeus, Petrus, 183n132

Derathé, Robert, 117n1
Descartes, René, 24
Diderot, Denis, 124-25n13, 131n25
Diogenes Laertius, 4n3, 76
Diogenes of Sinope, 76, 119
Dionysus, 83n108
Dreyfus-Brisac, Edmond, 117n1, 124n11
Du Peyrou, Pierre-Alexandre, 117n1

Fabius, 103, 191, 193
Ferdinand of Aragon, 57, 58n63
Frege, Gottlob, 17, 17n27
Frederick the Great, 77

Gildin, Hilail, 22n33, 159n83
Goethe, Johann Wolfgang von, 91n126
Grimsley, Ronald, 117n1
Grotius, Hugo, 147n61

Halbwachs, Maurice, 117n1, 150n65
Hegel, George Wilhelm Friedrich, 20, 107n158
Heidegger, Martin, 14n22, 16-17, 17n26, 28
Hobbes, Thomas, 10, 33n20, 49n45, 55, 59n67, 63n77, 92, 160n21, 174, 178

Homer, 172
Horace, 144, 165

Isaiah, 109

Jesus Christ, 13n21, 17n27, 39, 52, 83, 110,
    110n162, 140n44, 173, 190, 193
Josephus, Flavius, 147n60, 150, 183n132
Jouvenel, Bertrand de, 117n1
Jupiter, 112

Kant, Immanuel, 102, 102n151
Kojève, Alexandre, 85
Krüger, Gerhard, 83n108, 86n115

Leigh, Ralph A., 136n33
Livy, 35, 35n24, 38, 72, 74-75, 103, 112,
    149n63, 189, 191-94
Locke, John, 102
Löwith, Karl, 83n108
Lucretius, Titus Carus, 66n81
Luther, Martin, 53-54n54, 177
Lycurgus, 137, 140n44, 142n49

Machiavelli, Niccolò, vii-viii, 10, 19, 20, 25,
    25nn1-2, 26, 29, 30-113, 123, 135, 139,
    140n44, 149, 156, 159, 168, 188-97
Maimonides, Moses, 10, 20, 28, 85, 85n113
Marcus Aurelius, 76-77, 77n98, 96
Marlowe, Christopher, 88, 88n120
Marx, Karl, 102
Masters, Roger D., 160n100
Minos, 140
Mohammed, 174n111
Moses, 38, 54n55, 74-75, 172, 172n108,
    174n111, 176n115, 190, 191, 193
Moultou, Paul, 117n1

Napoleon Bonaparte, 63n77
Nerva, 76
Nietzsche, Friedrich, 6, 6nn9-10, 11n17, 14,
    14n23, 20, 24, 26, 55, 55n58, 73, 82-83,
    83n108
Numa, 140, 169n100

Olivo, Gilles, 124n12

Paoli, Pasquale, 145n54
Pascal, Blaise, 25
Paul, 13n21, 49, 120, 120n5, 121n7, 159, 177

Peter I, 142n49
Peterson, Erik, 13n21
Philo of Alexandria, 147, 147n60, 150n65
Plato, 4, 4n3, 5nn5-6, 6, 9-11, 11n18, 12n19,
    13, 13n20, 16, 17, 18, 18n28, 18n30,
    19-20, 21, 24, 45, 45n37, 46, 56, 80,
    84, 84n112, 85, 86n114, 100, 105n156,
    106, 119, 123, 131, 139n42, 141n46,
    146-47, 146n58, 147n59, 147n61,
    149
Plutarch, 112, 137, 146n58

Romulus, 169n100
Rousseau, Jean-Jacques, viii, ix, 11, 11n18,
    14-15, 20-22, 22n32, 55, 82-83, 83n108,
    115-85

Savonarola, Girolamo, 49, 66n80
Servet, Michel, 182
Socrates, vii-viii, 4-6, 6n11, 12, 13, 17, 18n28,
    19, 21, 26, 34n21, 41, 43, 47, 54n54, 76,
    80, 80n106, 84-86, 88, 96, 100n148, 102,
    109, 112-13, 112n168, 197
Solon, 140n44, 142n49
Sorel, Georges, 6, 6n11
Spinoza, Benedictus de, 10, 24, 55, 55n58,
    111, 183n132
Strauss, Leo, vii-viii, 4n2, 5n5, 5n7, 13n20,
    18n30, 21, 23-113, 136n34, 149n63, 187,
    188
Swift, Jonathan, 82, 83n108

Tacitus, P. Cornelius, 193
Theodorus the Atheist, 76
Theophrastus, 76
Tiberius, 173n110

Vaughan, C. E., 117n1, 178n124
Vettori, Francesco, 107n158
Vico, Giambattista, 183n132
Virgil, 169n100
Voltaire, François Marie Arouet, 142n49,
    179n125, 183n132

Warburton, William, 141, 141n47, 174
Wellhausen, Julius, 55
Wittgenstein, Ludwig, 17, 17n27

Xenophon, 4, 4n3, 10, 12n19, 17, 21, 21n31,
    27n5, 28, 45n37, 80, 112

www.ingramcontent.com/pod-product-compliance
Lightning Source LLC
Chambersburg PA
CBHW051357290426
44108CB00015B/2057